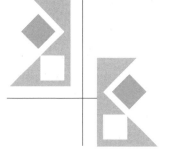

DEVELOPMENT EVALUATION IN TIMES OF TURBULENCE

DEVELOPMENT EVALUATION IN TIMES OF TURBULENCE

Dealing with Crises That Endanger Our Future

Ray C. Rist

Marie-Helene Boily

Frederic R. Martin

Editors

THE WORLD BANK
Washington, D.C.

ISBN (paper): 978-0-8213-9879-1
ISBN (electronic): 978-0-8213-9891-3
DOI: 10.1596/978-0-8213-9879-1

Cover design: Naylor Design, Washington, DC

Library of Congress Cataloging-in-Publication Data
Boily, Marie-Helene.
  Development evaluation in times of turbulence : dealing with crises that endanger our future / Marie-Helene Boily, Frederic R. Martin, and Ray C. Rist.
    pages cm
  ISBN 978-0-8213-9879-1 — ISBN 978-0-8213-9891-3 (eISBN)
  1. Economic development projects—Evaluation. 2. Economic assistance—Evaluation. 3. Economic policy. 4. Crises—Political aspects. 5. Crises—Economic aspects. I. Martin, Frederic R. II. Rist, Ray C. III. World Bank. IV. Title.
  HD75.9.B65 2013
  338.91—dc23
                                                                    2013009228

CONTENTS

Chapter 13. A Pilot Experience for Evaluating M&E Systems for Social Programs in Latin America   213

Juan Abreu, Marie-Helene Boily, Idania Fernández,
*   and Frederic R. Martin*

Chapter 14. Conclusion   229

Marie-Helene Boily and Frederic R. Martin

Index   235

Boxes

Figures

Tables

PREFACE

"The dogmas of the quiet past are inadequate to the stormy present."

—Abraham Lincoln, 1862

More than one hundred and fifty years later, Lincoln again has it exactly right. The stormy presence of turbulence in multiple areas of present-day societies—be it in food, fuel, or finances to name but three—means that long-held assumptions no longer hold, that the past is not prologue, and that the future is not clear.

Enter into this unstable present the discipline of evaluation—a discipline formed and shaped in the past 50 years of stability, little turbulence, and strong assumptions that everything will go according to plan. Conventional evaluation behavior and beliefs are ill suited for present times. The transformational nature of the "Arab Spring" is just one arena in which it is clear that a business-as-usual approach to evaluation is entirely inappropriate.

The chapters in this volume come from the 2011 Global Assembly of the International Development Evaluation Association—also known as IDEAS. This biannual assembly, held in Amman, Jordan, in April 2011, brought together about 350 development evaluators from 85 countries. The Arab Spring was very much on the minds of participants. Change was under way in Jordan where we were meeting, as well as in Tunisia, Libya, the Arab Republic of Egypt, Bahrain, and the Republic of Yemen—to name just six of the countries in the Middle East. The sense of turbulence was in the air. In fact, some persons who had planned to come to Amman backed out for fear for their personal safety.

The intent of this collection of papers is to systematically address changes during this time of turbulence and how these changes are impacting the craft of evaluation. This collection makes it clear that trying to hold to a set of assumptions about the status quo is no longer helpful and no longer true, that the past is truly the past (even the past of 36 months ago), and that the traditional paradigm that has defined and guided evaluation for these past many decades is outmoded and even passé. To reach back into history for a phrase to describe the present, consider this quote from Marx and Engels, "All that is solid melts into air."

The intention of the IDEAS assembly was to focus on turbulence in food, fuel, and finances. But the realities of the Arab Spring brought a new and pressing urgency to the gathering—nation states were falling, leaders were being deposed, the streets were filled with persons calling for fundamental changes in the structures of their societies, and blood was being shed for the sake of change. These events could not be ignored for the sake of adhering to a defined intellectual framework. Consequently, the focus of this book has broadened to reflect these new realities—we have chapters on evaluation reflecting turbulence in the three "F's," but we also have papers on the effects of the turbulence of the Arab Spring on evaluation. We trust readers will appreciate this real-time approach.

This book is divided into four parts. The Introduction has two chapters. First is a single brief paper by His Excellency Dr. Saif Ibrahim, Secretary General of the Economic and Social Council of Jordan. Dr. Saif explicitly addresses many of the forces and pressures evident in the Arab Spring and how these dynamics are impacting evaluation. Second is Jan-Eric Furubo's cogent case for augmenting the traditional paradigm focused on incremental change with elements to better address societal turbulence.

Part One has four chapters, including the two keynote speeches—one by Saraswathi Menon, who at the time was the head of the evaluation office for the United Nations Development Programme, and one by Robert D. van den Berg, director of evaluation for the Global Environment Fund. The other two chapters focus on the pressures and constraints of trying to establish viable monitoring and evaluation systems in the turbulence of Afghanistan and in India.

Part Two addresses the consequences of turbulence on the ground. Three chapters are in this cluster. The first examines the impacts of turbulence on the education system in Nepal through the collection of monitoring data—imperfect as they may be in turbulent times. The second examines one of the Arab Spring nations, Jordan, and describes how it was (barely) possible to set up and operationalize an impact assessment group and the constraints on doing such work. The third chapter turns to Brazil and evaluates an effort by the Brazilian government to increase productivity by offering loans to domestic firms to help bring the country out of the economic turbulence that had gripped it.

Finally, Part Three focuses on exercising the craft of evaluation in turbulent times. It has four chapters. The first focuses on the role of civil society organizations in helping build and strengthen monitoring and evaluation systems, especially in aid-dependent, developing countries. The second chapter again focuses on Jordan and how the government was able to build a monitoring and evaluation system in its Ministry of Social Development amid clearly unsettled times. The third chapter examines efforts in Botswana to build a national performance reporting system and describes how Botswana hopes to use this system to track and monitor performance to improve governance. The final chapter proposes a diagnostic tool to assess existing M&E systems against the standard of a fully developed results-based M&E system and describes a pilot of the tool in Latin America. The book closes with a concluding chapter by two of the editors.

The editors wish to thank the contributors to this book for their care and craft. The papers reflect the difficulties of trying to deploy monitoring and evaluation in times of turbulence—whether as a coherent system of data collection and analysis or as an effort at making sense in unsettled times. The editors also wish to thank the donors who helped sponsor this book by providing scholarships to authors to attend the assembly in Amman. Specifically, thanks are due to the United Nations Children's Fund (UNICEF); the U.K. Department for International Development (DFID); Norwegian Development Assistance; the Islamic Development Bank; the Ministry of Planning and International Cooperation, Jordan; and the Swiss Development Council. It is not trite to say that this book would not have been possible without their help and support. Thank you!

Marie-Helene Boily and Frederic R. Martin
Quebec City

Ray C. Rist
Washington, DC

ABOUT THE EDITORS

Ray C. Rist is in his second term as president of International Development Evaluation Association (IDEAS). He is also a cofounder and codirector of the International Program for Development Evaluation Training (IPDET). Retired from the Independent Evaluation Group of the World Bank, he continues to advise organizations and governments throughout the world on how to design and build results-based monitoring and evaluation systems. His career includes senior appointments in the U.S. government, academic institutions, and the World Bank. He is the author or editor of 31 books and more than 150 articles. He presently serves on the boards of nine professional journals.

Marie-Helene Boily is a senior economist and the training program coordinator at the IDEA International Institute in Quebec, Canada. She has more than a decade of experience supporting the implementation of monitoring and evaluation systems in public policies, programs, projects, and training initiatives. She has worked extensively in Africa, Asia, and Latin America. She is coeditor of *Influencing Change: Building Evaluation Capacity to Strengthen Governance*, copublished by IDEAS and the World Bank (2011).

Frederic R. Martin is cofounder, senior economist, and copresident of IDEA International. He is also in his second term of serving on the IDEAS board of directors. For 18 years, he taught at the University of Laval, Canada, where he served as professor and chair for international development. He has more than 30 years of experience conducting evaluations in countries of Africa, Asia, Europe, and Latin America. He is coeditor of *Influencing Change: Building Evaluation Capacity to Strengthen Governance*.

ABBREVIATIONS

AGCHO	Afghan Geodesy and Cartography Head Office
ANDS	Afghan National Development Strategy
ANP	Afghan National Police
AIMS-DAD	Aid Information Management System Development Assistance Database
RAIS	Annual Social Information Report (Relação Anual de Informações Sociais)
PIA	Annual Industrial Research (Pesquisa Industrial Annual)
ADB	Asian Development Bank
BNDES	Brazilian Development Bank (Banco Nacional de Desenvolvimento Economico e Social)
IBGE	Brazilian Institute of Geography and Statistics (Instituto Brasileiro de Geografia e Estatística)
CSO	Central Statistics Office
CSOs	civil society organizations
COIN	counterinsurgency theory
CSIS	Center for Strategic and International Studies
DOFE	Department for Foreign Employment, Nepal
DAC	Development Assistance Committee
DFID	U.K. Department for International Development
ECG	Evaluation Cooperation Group (ICG) [of the development banks]
FGD	focus group discussion
FDI	foreign direct investment
SECEX	Foreign Trade Secretary (Secretaria de Comércio Exterior)
FEC	free entry condition

GIS	geographic information system
IDEAS	International Development Evaluation Association
GEF	Global Environment Facility
GSPA	Global Partnership for Social Accountability
GDP	gross domestic product
GCC	Gulf Consultative Council
HOH	head of household
HMEP	Helmand Monitoring and Evaluation Programme
IDEA-AIM4R	Assessing and Improving M&E for Results
IDRC	International Development Research Centre
IDA	International Development Association
IMF	International Monetary Fund
IPDET	International Program in Development Evaluation Training
ISAF	International Security Assistance Force
KRA	key result area
NDP	10 Medium-Term National Development Plan, Botswana
NORAD	North American Aerospace Defense Command
MCA	Millennium Challenge Account
MoI	Ministry of Interior Affairs, Jordan
MoPIC	Ministry of Planning and International Cooperation, Jordan
MoSD	Ministry of Social Development, Jordan
M&E	monitoring and evaluation
OECD	Organisation for Economic Co-operation and Development
OECD/DAC	Organisation for Economic Co-operation and Development's Development Assistance Committee
ODI	Overseas Development Institute
PRSP	Poverty Reduction Strategy Paper
PATI	Programa de Atención Temporal al Ingreso, El Salvador
RdO	Programa Red de Oportunidades, Panama
PSM	propensity score matching
PRT	Provincial Reconstruction Team, Afghanistan
RAPID	Research and Policy in Development
RBM	results-based management
RIDA	Research Inputs and Development Action, Kathmandu
SISCA	Secretaria de la Integración Social Centroamericana

SMART	indicators (specific, measurable, achievable, relevant, and time-bound)
SADC	Southern African Development Community
TWG	technical working group
UNICEF	United Nations Children's Fund
UNDP	United Nations Development Programme
UNEP	United Nations Environment Programme
WFP	World Food Programme
ZCP	zero cut-off profit condition

CHAPTER 1

Linking Evaluation Work in Arab Countries to the Crises in the "3 F's"—Finances, Food, and Fuel

Saif Ibrahim

In the past five years, the global economic crisis has been shaped by the financial, food, and fuel crises. The economic crisis resulting from the "assets bubble" in the United States and the resulting weak connection between prices and the real value of assets has created a lack of confidence in financial assets. Investors have focused on commodities markets to hedge against uncertainty in financial assets. An associated increase in demand for food and fuels has aggravated the situation in many developing countries. The resulting increase in prices will likely continue, and poor countries are expected to face tough choices.

International development agencies continue to provide funding, financial support, and humanitarian aid to governments around the world in an effort to curb the effects of the crises of the "3F's." Despite relief efforts, challenges remain in coordinating donor efforts with local efforts and in the lack of proper evaluation mechanisms for policies and crises, especially in the Arab countries.

Evaluation of economic policies is key for understanding progress, but the question is should we continue viewing economic growth and progress in terms of sectoral gross domestic product (GDP) growth? Or, should we move toward measuring progress by monitoring and evaluating various indicators including education, health, governance, democracy, equity, human rights, and freedoms?

The aftermath of the recent social and political unrest in the Arab region and the growing "youth quake," suggest that "bread" is not the root cause of the protests. Reasons go beyond economic difficulties, stemming from inequality, lack of freedom, and tainted dignities. Such widespread protest movements call for revisiting and reevaluating economic and social policies adopted in the Arab region over the past two decades and drawing lessons for the future.

We should remind ourselves that the Arab region comprises a diverse range of countries with different assets and social and political conditions. Countries with oil revenues, such as Gulf Consultative Council (GCC) countries, have some financial cushioning from shocks, but nevertheless are experiencing a sharp downturn in revenue. In countries without considerable financial capacity, the drop in economic growth has been felt more intensely. Countries such as Lebanon, the Syrian Arab Republic, the Arab Republic of Egypt, Jordan, Morocco, West Bank and Gaza, and Tunisia, despite the differences in economic structures, are highly exposed to western European markets in terms of exports and remittances, are highly dependent on fuel consumption, and have little emphasis on agriculture. Pressure on these countries due to decreases in remittances and tourism, high unemployment and youth bulge, traditional budget deficits, and weak governance are affected by slow policy response. Countries such as Iraq, the Republic of Yemen, and Sudan, which are also coping with conflict, increased poverty, and social tension, suffer further from the economic crisis.

Despite differences in their social and economic structures, countries in the region do share commonalities, including a lack of proper and continuous evaluation mechanisms for economic and social policies that would allow policy makers to rethink some of their policies over time. Two reasons might explain the weak condition of evaluation in the region; one involves a lack of appreciation of the importance of monitoring. But even when appreciation exists, there may be a lack of institutional capacity and political will to undertake the task. The outcome has been a very poor record in evaluation and, as a result, adherence to policies that are not necessarily the most appropriate for the countries.

The Arab region, especially its poorest countries, faces the recent surge in food and oil prices within an increasingly fragile macroeconomic context.

For example, the undermining of the agricultural sector in developing countries and imports from staple-surplus countries geared the developing world into a dependency relationship with the developed world. High food prices may heighten inequality within countries; aggravate child malnutrition; diminish opportunities for education; and destabilize the social conditions for those living amidst conflict, instability, and drought. Poor countries are constrained in their fiscal capacity to respond to inflationary pressures. What policy choices are left to the developing countries? Can some countries revisit their policies and investment programs? In which direction can they redirect them? These are valid questions in this turbulent time. Although theses question are simple, they are unresolved since they go beyond the conventional way of pursuing economic policies.

The challenge of crafting appropriate policy responses in the Arab countries to the financial, food, and fuel crises is made harder in the context of rising oil prices. The World Bank's food price index increased by 15 percent between October 2010 and January 2011 and is only 3 percent below its 2008 peak. The past six months have seen a sharp increase in global prices of wheat, maize, sugar, and edible oils. According to the World Bank, rising food prices have pushed 44 million people into extreme poverty and hunger since June 2010 in low- and middle-income countries. Instability in the region will also lead to an increase in prices and will pose further challenges for economic growth, imposing a heavy fiscal burden on governments apart from creating social and political unrest. The region's recent widespread unrest is causing global economic fear and impacting global oil markets. The price of oil and grains jumped again amid fears that growing unrest in Libya and the significant disruption of its oil production could spill over into other oil-producing countries in the region.

Some Arab countries are more vulnerable to the oil price increase and their room for maneuvering on the macroeconomic front is limited. Many poor countries face the risk of impeding or reversing years of progress toward achieving social development and poverty alleviation. Governments in the region are currently scrambling to produce reform policies to address the challenges posed by the economic crisis and its impact on their citizens. Although the expansion of social protection programs, such as school-feeding and conditional-cash-transfer programs focused on the most vulnerable groups, can be coordinated through international development agencies, it is challenging to implement comprehensive policies within the timeframe requested by the people, since the impact of economic policies with limited budgets cannot be realized in such a short timeframe.

This brings us to the challenges of coordination between donor and local efforts and the lack of evaluation mechanisms for policies, especially in the

Arab countries. In the past, the links between international and domestic efforts were limited, and the mechanisms through which these efforts were evaluated were also limited. The criteria used to evaluate, and the indicators used to understand, the flow of goods were vague and inconsistent. The manner used by the International Monetary Fund (IMF) and World Bank to evaluate local budgets was usually critical toward the public spending flow, nature, and style. The true challenge lies in the lack of a proper evaluation mechanism of economic crises, their impact, and the policies of governments in addressing economic and financial crises. A clear understanding of the mechanisms of monitoring and evaluation should be established: How should these mechanisms grow? What benchmarks should be used? The Arab region should invest in building capacity toward creating economic policy evaluation systems that will aid and protect against future economic downturns. It should also realize the importance of evaluation. The need to assess, understand, and evaluate the effects and impacts of economic crises is crucial for the formulation of appropriate, timely, realistic, and implementable economic policies.

CHAPTER 2

When Incremental Change Isn't Enough

Jan-Eric Furubo

Introduction

This chapter advocates the need for an adaption of evaluation to a world that is very different than the world that existed in the formative years of evaluation. I will justify this assertion based on an interpretation of a central assumption about societal development, decision making, and politics that has been inherent in the form of evaluation that we see today as a feature of modern statecraft. I will also point out possible consequences for evaluation if the evaluation community will adapt to new challenges.

What Evaluation Was All About

We can safely say that evaluations have been conducted for thousands of years. After throwing a primitive spear, some of our ancestors certainly made observations in relation to criteria such as accuracy and power and used their observations to improve the spear. Even if we narrow to evaluation of an activity based on a scientific set of methods, we can certainly say that evaluations have been conducted for more than 100 years in the United States and Europe. An important idea developed about public administration in the United States during the end of the 19th century and the beginning of the next was that it was possible to scientifically judge the efficiency of different interventions in relation to their intended objectives.

In both Europe and the United States, we find discussions from more than 75 years ago about what we later labeled central problems in evaluation. For a 1934 Swedish government commission, Gunnar Myrdal, later a Nobel Prize laureate, discussed the importance of counterfactual comparisons in establishing the effects of economic regulations (Myrdal 1934). In 1936, Merton discussed unanticipated consequences of "purposive social action," but he also defined outcomes in counterfactual terms and addressed the problem (well known to evaluators today) of unclear goals: "Moreover, it is not assumed that in fact social action always involves clear-cut, explicit purpose. It may well be that such awareness of purpose is unusual, that the aim of action is more often than not nebulous and hazy" (Merton 1936, 896). About 10 years later, during World War II, Kurt Lewin carried out what he described as evaluation (Mark and others 2011, 5, 8ff). It also seems clear that the period after World War II saw an increased interest in how social sciences could be used in the construction of public interventions. Many of these efforts are associated with the development of policy analysis and names like Laswell. However, as we have already observed, the term *evaluation* was used many years earlier. In 1953, Henry W. Riecken wrote a memorandum to the Ford Foundation stating, "[E]valuation is always undertaken with reference to some intentional action designed to influence people or change a material situation. *Evaluation* is the measurement of desirable and undesirable consequences of an action intended to forward some goal that the actor values" (Riecken 1972, 86).

In 1967, Edward A. Suchman published *Evaluation Research: Principles and Practice in Public Service and Social Action Programs,* in which he noted, "We are currently in the midst of a 'War on Poverty' which has as its ultimate goal nothing less than the elimination of economic, educational, medical, and social deprivation." He continues to point out that "some attempt be made to determine the effectiveness of such public service and social action programs has become increasingly insistent.... The result has been a sudden awakening of interest in a long-neglected aspect of social research—the evaluation study." (Suchman 1967, 1f).

Suchman gives an overview of earlier definitions and his own definition of evaluation:

as the determination (whether based on opinions, research, subjective or objective data) of the results (whether desirable; transient or permanent; immediate or delayed) attained by some activity (whether a program, or part of a program, a drug or a therapy, an ongoing or one-shot approach) designed to accomplish some valued goal or objective (whether ultimate, intermediate, or immediate effort of performance, long or short range (Suchman 1967, 31 f).

Weiss, a few years later, is quite clear what evaluation "is all about": "Basically, evaluation research is concerned with finding out how well action programs work" (Weiss 1972, 5). She further notes that almost all authors, like Marvin C. Alkin and Egon G. Cuba, agree that the "purpose of evaluation research is to provide information for decision making about programs" (Weiss 1972, 14).[1]

More contemporary definitions of evaluation (for example, Vedung 1997, 3; Rossi and others 1999, 4ff) show the same consensus as Weiss noted 40 years ago. Evaluation is about making judgments about a specific intervention, a program, or, as Riecken expressed it 60 years ago, an intentional action. In the public sphere, it is about actions taken by governments, municipalities, international organizations, and other entities that decide about actions aimed to influence the behavior of individuals or organizations.

Evaluation took off in the 1960s. In the preface of *Evaluating Actions Programs*, published in 1972, Weiss discussed the increased emphasis on evaluation and a demand "not only (for) more evaluations, but more imaginative and skillful evaluation." She also noted the quantitative expansions of evaluation: "A recent review of only *federally* funded evaluations with budgets in excess of US$25,000 turned up approximately a thousand such studies in one year (1970)" (Weiss 1972, xif). In today's dollars, the equivalent would be federally funded evaluations with budgets exceeding US$140,000. In a study of the development of evaluation in the United States, Rist notes, "Evaluation, by all measures, developed quite remarkably in the twenty years from 1960 to 1980" (Rist 2002, 226).

It seems safe to state that even if evaluation existed earlier, it was in the 1960s that it became an integrated part of the thinking and the theories around political and administrative decision processes, budgeting, and program development. Thus, we can talk about the 1960s as the formative period of evaluation. The diffusion of evaluation around the globe in the following decades, encouraged by strong entrepreneurs like the Organisation for Economic Co-operation and Development (OECD) and the World Bank, was diffusion of a "package" that was developed in the United States in the 1960s. Evaluation has been further integrated into ideas about budgeting and public administration that have dominated since the 1960s. When evaluation became a mode in some European countries in the 1970s and 1980s, it did not build directly on the earlier European tradition of using social sciences in political decision making. Instead, Europe, and later other countries around the globe, imported an intellectual commodity from United States. However, a decisive factor for the interest in adopting this American "package" was the earlier relation between the social sciences and the political and administrative sphere in different countries (Furubo and Sandahl 2002).

The conclusion of this rough sketch of the historical development of evaluation is the following. When we are talking about evaluation in the context of government, governance, international development, and so on, it is not about evaluation as a generic term but about something associated with specific notions about politics, implementation, policy development, knowledge, psychological, and social mechanisms.[2] Many of these notions are more explicit in earlier writings than in the contemporary stream of books and journal articles. Understanding these notions is crucial when evaluation is acting in a world very much different from the world of 30, 50, or 70 years ago. This chapter will deal with such a notion, namely, evaluation as part of incremental decision making.

Incremental and Nonincremental Change

This sketchy historic overview demonstrates that evaluation was about incremental change: it was about helping to improve programs to make interventions better. Evaluation was constructed in a country, which, as Weiss noted, had become "increasingly aware of the social problems that plague special groups of the population and it has undertaken an array of programs to improve their lot" (Weiss 1972, 4). She points out that there comes a "time in the life of many programs, when it is important to ask: How are we doing? Are we accomplishing what we set out to do?" (Weiss 1972, 4). In these formative years of evaluation, it is not difficult to find similar formulations by other leading evaluation theorists. This central perspective also dominates more recent texts about evaluation, for example, *The Road to Results* (Morra Imas and Rist 2009).

The pursuit of improving programs is, of course, a good ambition. After creating programs, we cannot be satisfied with their existence and their good purposes—we want to know to what extent they reach their purposes, how efficient they are compared with other possible interventions, and which mechanisms lead or hinder intended change.

However, in many situations, we need forms of knowledge other than those produced by evaluation. We sometimes reach the point where we have to leave the incremental mode of decision making.

The assumption that stable periods in a society are replaced by more turbulent ones is certainly not new. Marx and Engels' manifesto of 1848 pointed out that historical development sometimes can be seen as a process in which all that is solid melts into air (Marx and Engels 1848). From a different camp, Lincoln expressed the same idea in his annual message to the Congress in 1862: "The dogmas of the quiet past are inadequate to the stormy present" (Lincoln 1862).

Both Marx and Engels and Lincoln expressed an awareness that societies can be seen as stable. During such stable periods, the fundamental institutions and policies continue and the adjustments are gradual and often based on the idea of "more (or less) of the same." However, politicians, bureaucrats, and researchers do not always acknowledge stable times. More often they emphasize that "what our party suggests" is radically different than what "the others want to do." It is an obvious tendency to describe marginal changes as great reforms. After all, it is more fun to do something important than something unimportant. It is much more satisfying for a leading politician to change history than to be one of the many who leave a soon-disappearing imprint.

Despite such rhetoric, we have adapted to a world in which changes are incremental and in which we can use our knowledge about existing actions and institutions to make decisions about future actions.

This incrementalism can be explained by an important observation made in contemporary research: Change is expensive! It often costs more to change a policy than to continue the present one. Any change creates new forms of uncertainty, brings other players into a situation, shifts the stakes and the relations among institutions, parties, individuals, and so on. Political parties and the electorate are familiar with politicians' descriptions and prioritizations. Policy shifts are expensive even if they have future potential. So, why change, especially as the probable effects of the change will not be seen for 10 to 15 years? The question was raised by a Swedish political scientist after a discussion about the price of change (Bergström 2006). Pierson quotes Hacker's discussion about path dependence as developmental trajectories, which are inherently difficult to reverse, and adds that "the *relative* benefits of the current activity compared with once-possible options increase over time. To put it a different way, the costs of switching to some previously plausible alternative rise" (Pierson 2004, 21).

Turning Points

The literature on decision making and policy learning points out that change processes sometimes reach a turning point at which it becomes evident that we cannot continue with marginal changes and small diversions from the stable course. Decision makers find that the earlier road is blocked, the earlier course of action is closed, and they must do something very different. In these situations, they must leave the stable course and the known terrain where they can rely on earlier experience. We can call such situations *unstable* or *turbulent.* They are the times when the chain of events takes a new direction, however unclear.

In the 1990s, in *Agendas and Instability in American Politics,* Baumgartner and Jones adopted Eldredge and Gould's theory about *punctuated* equilibrium as an explanation of biological evolution. They emphasized that policy generally changes only incrementally due to a set of conditions and that the accumulation of such incremental changes can be important. However, changes occur not only incrementally but also in *bursts,* and "when the bursts occur, old ways of doings things are swept aside, to be replaced by new organizational forms" (Baumgartner and Jones 1993, 235).

Baumgartner and Jones' book is a study of American politics; however, the same observation is made in many other political and historical contexts. In his study on the rise of the modern market economy, Polanyi expresses much the same idea when he writes about "critical periods" and "connecting stretches of time" (Polanyi 1944, 4). Capoccia and Kelemen point out that the "dualistic conception of political and institutional development, based on an alternation between moments of fluidity and rapid change and longer phases of relative stability and institutional reproduction, has a venerable pedigree in the social sciences and political history" (Capoccia and Kelemen 2007). Similar ideas are part of the theories of "formative moments" and "critical junctures." A *formative moment* is the moment in which a policy is shaped on a fundamental level. In his discussion of formative moments in Swedish politics, Rothstein emphasizes that:

> [P]olitical systems are usually so tightly structured that the prospects that actors may introduce significant changes are very small. The playing field, the rules of the game, the resources of the player—the institutional order, in other words—is at any point in time a given, and so the political actors' room for maneuver is extremely limited. Under normal conditions, therefore, the possibilities of fundamentally changing the structure of the political system are small to non-existent. Yet political systems nonetheless change, at times both rapidly and thoroughly. During certain special periods marked by mounting social and economic conflicts and crises, it appears that possibilities of changing the rules of the political game arise.
>
> ... What differentiates the notion for formative moments from the notion of critical junctures is the importance of action in the former, i.e. the *formative* in the formative moment (Rothstein 1992, 174).

So, the idea that we sometimes have to leave the "incremental mode" is not new. Even though change demands more than continuing the present course of actions, sometimes the balance point changes—after all, policies do change. Sometimes the price of continuing with "more of the same" is higher than the uncertainties connected with a change in direction.

Before going further, it is important to emphasize that stability and turbulence can exist on different scales. What is a very turbulent situation on one level can be part of an ongoing, hardly notable process, at a superior level. For example, what an agency head regards as an existential question for the agency can be merely a marginal question from the perspective of a president or prime minister. Different hierarchical levels have different scopes of possible actions. This point is expressed by Wildavsky when he states, "a department secretary might conceivably gain by learning that there are greater benefits in shifting resources from national parks to urban recreation. But the men who run the parks and forests cannot use this information; they need to know about allocation within the parks." (Wildavsky 1979, 217). They may regard a reallocation of resources within the parks as a fundamental reorientation within their scope of action. Thus, the discussion about stable and turbulent times can be carried out on different levels. In this book, our discussion is about turbulent times on a more aggregated societal level or within a policy field. Turbulent times are when earlier policies or interventions are questioned, when new ones are created, and when there is a fundamental change of goals and basic policy tools. Change in such times will be much less incremental.

Will Change Be Less Incremental in the Future?

Even if we accept the idea of "stable and turbulent" times, it is not clear that the situation today is more turbulent than the situation in the 1960s. Many will question such a description. It is obviously impossible to answer the question of whether we are living in a more turbulent world than we did in the 1960s or 1970s; while we are in the midst of *now*, the answer would be more about subjective perceptions than objective realities. It is probably not fruitful to argue that the world in some objective meaning has changed position on a stable–turbulent scale since 30 or 50 years ago.

Another question is more fruitful. How did the men and women who developed the fundaments of what we call evaluation *perceive* the world? A subjective interpretation is unavoidable, as the evaluation theorists from the formative years of evaluation assumed, and wished for, incremental societal betterment. Reading their texts several decades after they were written, it is not difficult to feel their deep conviction that an arsenal of different programs could gradually lead to social betterment and that society was on a road that could be seen as stable. Such an interpretation does not mean that the discussants of evaluation imagined that the course toward social betterment could not be blocked. After all, the formative period took place in the midst of the cold war and the political weight among different political forces within the United States at that time could change the fundamental policy direction. But assuming that these threats were warded off, the incremental journey could continue.

However, it can be argued that it is possible that objective circumstances have made the world more turbulent. These factors have to do with time and distance. Countries are much more interwoven than a few decades ago. What happens in financial markets in one part of the world more or less immediately influences the conditions for ordinary people on the other side of the globe. Turbulence is triggered not only by what happens in the local or national community or even among national neighbors. Each society is much more exposed to factors that can lead to turbulence. To this can be added the fact that the diffusion of new ideas, including questioning different societal structures, is much more rapid today than only 10 years ago.

Confronting Crises

It is not difficult to argue that we perceive our societies as more turbulent than they were decades ago. Today we are confronting crises (without defining the term) that can be seen as a demonstration of more fundamental, more permanent problems. We also lack the explanatory power through interpreting earlier efforts to interpret current societal developments. Events, whether they concern climate, financial instability, upheavals of violence, or breakdown of social order, can be transferred to a more fundamental notion of "unstable conditions," which can give policy makers the feeling that it is impossible to continue earlier policies. Unstable conditions can lead to an awareness that the earlier paradigm from which different explanations and solutions of societal problems were constructed is now insufficient and must be replaced.

Crises can spotlight imbalances and imperfections that may have been seen earlier. Individuals and groups (including evaluations) may have observed underlying problems in a policy. However, the picture has been uncertain or contradicted by other experts, or the effects of alternative strategies may have been disputed. In light of the cost of changing policies, it was natural—and perhaps rational—to continue the earlier policy. But a crisis reveals difficulties that were earlier seen unclearly or not at all. What was earlier regarded as latent or distant possibilities, or even the doomsday warnings of prophets, are now manifest in the daily news.

Turbulence Caused by Factors Other Than Crises

That crises sometimes create a break in the earlier order does not mean that a crisis is the only factor that can lead to a "punctuation" of equilibrium and a perception that times are so turbulent or unstable that searching for alternatives seems unavoidable. In other words, we can talk about *punctuations—* to use Baumgartner and Jones' term—even if we cannot point out dramatic episodes. An accumulation of "signs" of problems related to a societal development can demonstrate that it is impossible to continue "piecemeal engineering," to borrow Popper's phrase.

Before going further, a point made by Bennet and Howlett must be emphasized. They note that "[W]hy policies change, however, is not a well-understood phenomena" (Bennett and Howlett, 1992, 275). This statement is true even if empirical studies tell why old policies are replaced with new ones. In his study regarding economic policy reversals, Hood distinguishes four main explanations, or groups of explanations, for policy reversals. One group has to do with "climate changing ideas" caused by intellectual development and new economic theories. Hood notes two possibilities of how ideas can turn policy around. One "is that public policy follows the ideas of social science (particularly economics) and that theoretical breakthroughs and 'crucial experiments' can put it into reverse" (Hood 1994, 5). An alternative possibility is the role of *"packaging* rather than content in explaining how economic policy ideas become persuasive" (Hood 1994, 6). A second group of explanations puts " the dynamic of political interest into the center of the theoretical stage" (Hood 1994, 7). A third group has to do with changes in social structures, which form the "habitats" for corresponding types of public policies (Hood 1994, 11). Hood describes the fourth main group of explanations as policy self-destruction and refers to Wildavsky's claim that polices tend "to create unexpected and problematic side effects, which, in turn, create conditions for the introduction of new polices to correct or modify the effects of the earlier ones" (Hood 1994, 14).

Both crises and other forms of change have an impact on how *existing* policies are perceived in such a way that decision makers will search for new alternatives on a more fundamental level.

Examples of such changes include the following:

- Changes in what we regard as fundamental problems in society. Fifty years ago, global warming and the environment in general were not regarded as problems. Over time, we may use new information and data to fundamentally redefine the crucial challenges in society. Kingdon emphasizes that constructing "an indicator and getting others to agree to its worth become major preoccupations of those pressing for policy change" (Kingdon 2003).

- Changes regarding which problems we think should be handled by governmental policies, that is, which problems we regard as tasks for the political sphere to solve or to handle.
- Changes in our notions about the role of scientific knowledge in framing public policies. The notion that it is possible to build knowledge about the causal relations among phenomena and construct interventions to influence causal processes can underlie governmental interventions. However, some question the notion that it is possible to build such value-free knowledge (for example, Fischer 2003). Geyer and Rihani demonstrate that notions regarding the degree to which scientific knowledge can predict outcomes of public policies is embedded in our understanding of science in general (Geyer and Rihani 2010).
- Fundamental changes in previous explanations of societal mechanisms. If we apply Kuhn's idea of paradigms to social science, it is possible to see that new knowledge can create a reconstruction of our fundamental ideas about what constitutes certain developments in society. Such shifts make earlier policies and interventions, and also—at least partly—earlier studies and evaluations, invalid.
- Changes in the relations between parties and institutions and the development of new coalitions. These changes can also change expectations more generally in society both internationally and nationally. In the 1990s, we saw important changes in relations between nations that made it necessary to create new ideas about international relations. Very stable political conditions and electoral success over an extended period lead to significant changes, including shifts in the expectations of social actors. "At some point, these actors begin to recognize that there is a new status quo, and they adjust their policy preferences to accommodate the new environment. By doing so, they help to propel coordination around these new expectations, reinforcing the new regime" (Pierson 2004, 85).

Naturally, there are tradeoffs. An administration's lack of ability to handle its undertakings can lead to a search for explanations for its lack of success. Such a search can lead to a shift in what are regarded as valid explanations of different developments.

Several of these factors have an intrinsic relationship to values. As mentioned earlier, statistics about societal problems can influence what we regard as important and can have an impact on what knowledge we produce. The selection of which phenomena are important to describe and explain also has to do with values. For example, if we try to measure changes in the number of children living on the street, it is evident that we regard this issue as important because of our values. Some developments are measured in some countries and not measured in others.

All of these factors can be discussed in relation to a time perspective. A shift in what we conceive as the fundamental problems in society can take many years and even many decades. The transition from one dominant mode of explanation of certain phenomena in society to another can certainly take a very long time. However, the point about formative moments, punctuated equilibrium, windows of opportunity, and so on, is that at some points in time, one factor becomes so important, or several factors converge in such a way, that we can talk about a "burst" or a historical watershed.

The Role of Evaluation in Turbulent Times

The language and the literature in fields like public administration, policy learning, and so on indicate that we regard the policies and tasks of governments and other enterprises as ongoing. We see them as a sequential process, often described as a circle, whose elements can be foreseen and planned in advance. We easily recognize phases such as "identification of alternatives for future action," "analysis of costs and benefits of the alternatives," "choice of alternative," "implementation, monitoring," "evaluation," and "identification of possible changes."

When we move from phase to phase in this circle we are moving in a well-known terrain and we can use earlier experiences. In this ideal type of rationalistic decision making, it is easy to grasp the role of evaluation: it is part of an ongoing *incremental* process of improvements and adjustments of a policy or an activity. Different evaluation systems feed this ongoing process with information to gradually improve programs or governmental interventions. The procedures for monitoring and evaluating an intervention, therefore, often reflect the same assumptions that were implicit or explicit in developing the intervention (Leeuw and Furubo 2008).

One way to describe what happens when we are moving around this metaphorical circle is that we assume we know which information is relevant when we want to judge the success of different elements of the intervention. Even if the environment in which the intervention takes place changes, we know—or assume that we know—what changes are important to observe. We imagine how things might have developed without the intervention.

However, when we move outside our circle, we have growing, and more obvious, problems handling the counterfactual.

The incremental way of decision making has been seen as a realistic picture of political decision making, not least for budget decisions, although empirical studies point out that the characterization of budget processes in terms of incrementalistic decision making can be questioned (for example, Jordan 2003; Anderson and Harbridge 2010). However, the point is that we are so used to the idea that decision making in the political sphere is incrementalistic that we risk not understanding the fundamentally different situation we face in turbulent times.

In turbulent times, when earlier courses of action are closed or fundamentally questioned, we need a very different form of knowledge than in stable periods, when earlier courses of action are assumed to continue. In stable times, policy makers need knowledge about hundreds of questions related to the intervention itself and its interplay with other factors. Relevant questions are based on earlier interventions: how they worked, how they can be changed to work better, and so on. In turbulent times, new priorities and new actions are being discussed and the knowledge produced within earlier policy frameworks is less relevant. The uncertainties are deeper.

Thus, the role of evaluation is different in turbulent times, when we are moving outside the framework of existing policies and policy paradigms. The questions now asked by decisions makers are about *alternatives*. Turbulent times can shake the foundations of policy interests and structures. Institutions and structures are put under pressure.

Turbulent situations also create new arenas with new players and involve new stakeholders and interests, who ask different questions. The new players are more open and less oriented toward evaluation of earlier policy interventions. They want answers that can give them ideas about fundamental alternatives for the future, or, as Boswell puts it, "Policy makers are more likely to recognize gaps in research where they become aware of the emergences of new types of problems, such as climate change, the impact of new technologies, threats to public health or security, or the emergence of new forms of criminality or social pathology" (Boswell 2009, 243).

The perception that there is an ultimate need to change a policy, or the direction of a whole society, must be matched by an interpretation of the potential of alternative policies or directions. The object in earlier evaluations is knowledge produced by existing interventions, which is now obsolete. In the creation of new policies, new instruments and new institutions are constructed and new questions raised. The questions are ex-ante and evaluation is now about identifying the best possible knowledge that can be used in discussing alternative solutions.

Consequences for Evaluation

Even the reader who accepts the need for new forms of knowledge in turbulent times and agrees that we are confronting problems and issues that will make nonincremental change unavoidable will ask, What are the consequences for the practice of evaluation? I will point out two consequences. The first is a changing relationship between evaluation and the social sciences and the second is the need to rethink who is the audience of evaluation.

A New Relation to Social Sciences

Decision makers, and any group that formulates possible courses of action to decide on actions to meet fundamental challenges that cannot be met within earlier policy frameworks, are asking, "What works?" Their questions concern causalities in society. Evaluation of earlier interventions and programs can be relevant, but we must be aware that evaluation is only one source, and a limited one, of knowledge about what causes certain changes. To judge the possible impact of a certain intervention, we need knowledge about causalities that goes far beyond the purview of social sciences (for example, which factors explain variations in the halt of carbon dioxide? To what extent will smoking increase the risk for a certain type of cancer?). However, every governmental intervention will also be based on assumptions about how individuals and collective players will act. They ask questions such as: How will big companies react to a certain regulation? How will other nations react to a certain incentive or a threat? How will parents react to changes in the financing of education? How will certain actions influence terrorism?

Whether an intervention is about saving the banking system or counteracting terrorism, decision makers must decide which, or which combination of, policy options will create the best possibilities to reach their objective. They are searching for knowledge about causalities and need to examine intervention theories for different, often competing, possible interventions. And they usually have to find the best answers in a short time, sometimes a few days. The question will, therefore, be asked: "Where can we find the best possible supplier of answers?"

Obviously, the answers can be based on knowledge from many sources: controlled laboratory experiments, theoretical analyses, empirical studies of social phenomena (such as Durkeheim's study of suicide, Rosenthal and Jacobson's study of expectations of teachers), but also from evaluations. Even if the purpose of evaluation is to improve interventions, many forms of knowledge other than evaluation can be used to answer important questions in constructing future interventions. It is naïve to assume that evaluation can be more than one of many sources of knowledge in the construction of interventions. When policy options become broader, knowledge built on earlier interventions is less relevant.

Evaluators must accept that turbulent times will lead to a broader discussion about how social sciences can contribute to answering questions that are crucial for framing public policies. As expressed in a recent report by the National Research Council of the National Academies in the United States, "Scientists—when they are practicing science—do not tell policy makers what should interest them or what policy choices they should make. Scientists deal with accurate descriptions of conditions and explanations about the causes or consequences of those conditions." (Prewitt and others 2012, 9).

Conversely, evaluation has to be discussed in a much broader social sciences context. In *Mind the Gap: Perspective on Policy Evaluation and the Social Sciences* (2010), editors Jos Vaessen and Frans Leeuw argue that:

> From the 1970s onwards several developments took place which led to an emancipation of evaluation as a professional practice on its own, while the relationship with the social and behavioral sciences weakened. One of the reasons for the emerging gap between evaluative practice and the social sciences was the increasing importance and institutionalization of evaluative activities inside public administration and policy-making. While evaluation studies in the first half of the twentieth century were largely researcher-led studies shaped by the interests of scientists, in the second half, and especially from the 1970s and 1980s onwards, evaluation agendas were increasingly determined by policymakers and administrators of public interventions (Vaessen and Leeuw 2010, 5).

In *The Evaluation Society* (2011), Peter Dahler-Larsen raises fundamental questions about the role of evaluation in contemporary societies and how "the mysteries behind the evaluation wave" can be explained. In discussing definitions of evaluation as "part of the sociological story," he makes an important remark on Scriven's definition of evaluation.

> Scriven is one of the founding fathers of modern evaluation as a distinct field and one of the first to analytically distill what it means to do evaluation. His definition is interesting in many respects. The object of evaluation, the so-called evaluand, is described as 'something.' Perhaps it is the very generalization and abstraction of the evaluand, and its liberation from any specific and substantial human activity, that now makes it possible to conceive of evaluation as a distinct cognitive activity in and of itself. If you wanted to evaluate music, you might call a good musician. Now, if you want to evaluate something, there is a need for an evaluation specialist (Dahler-Larsen 2011, 5).

These examples can also be seen as an indication of a growing interest among evaluation scholars in the relationship between evaluation and social sciences. Owen's discussion of evaluation in relation to an "expanded definition of evaluative inquiry" (Owen 2007, 18) seems to be based on a broader use of science and not only on earlier evaluations.

Accepting that the relationship between evaluation and the social sciences has to change, we can discuss the audience of evaluation.

A New Audience for Evaluation

For several decades, the field of evaluation has been preoccupied with its relation to decision makers and different stakeholders. Even Weiss, who discusses the question in broad "knowledge-terms" rather than in "evaluation-terms," regards the relationship as between the evaluator (or the evaluations) and the decision maker. Boswell noted, "... the assumption remains that research is valued first and foremost as a means of influencing policy. Policy-relevant knowledge is produced and used in order to adjust policy output—even though it is acknowledged that its influence is somewhat less direct than the problem-solving account implies. In effect, then, such critiques modify the instrumentalist account but do not essentially break with it" (Boswell 2009, 5).

Boswell's comment is important. The idea underlying the debate about use of evaluations is based on an instrumental model, which starts with the evaluation that will be disseminated (through product or process) to decision makers, who will use it in their decision making, or to other groups in the policy framework.

This relationship between evaluators and policy makers is important in stable times characterized by incremental processes. However, in turbulent times, different questions demand a broader influx from the social sciences. Therefore, evaluators need to have a relationship to wider social science communities. Metaphorically speaking, evaluations are like deposits in "knowledge banks." Bank officials, to continue the metaphor, interpret the information from different studies, rearrange it, and relate it to earlier knowledge in the field.

The immediate users of evaluations are now not only decision makers, but also the officials of our metaphorical bank. The form of knowledge structures is usually compatible with social science disciplines. The extent to which the information gained from earlier governmental interventions will be channeled into the political and administrative system depends on how much it contributes to building more general knowledge. Some policy areas are part of strong, well-defined knowledge structures, such as a specific social science discipline or subdiscipline. When discussing the choice of financial regulations, it is not difficult to know which academic fields contain the relevant knowledge. If we are discussing which actions will limit the spread of a certain disease, the situation is similar. For other policy areas, such as crime prevention, it is more difficult to define the relevant knowledge structure.

A Final Remark

We have focused on the role of evaluation in helping decision makers and others judge different policy options when there is a need to change the earlier course of action. Although, times may shift between stability and turbulence, the incremental form of decision making will probably remain dominant in the future, even if the punctuations happen more often.

Evaluation will continue to have an important role in helping political and administrative decision makers and stakeholders understand how existing interventions can be improved. Evaluation can also be important from an accountability perspective.

Even these traditional roles demand that evaluation asks more critical questions. The debate about different systems for measuring the effects of programs through indicators, based on the same assumptions as the programs, is a memento. Evaluation can be conservative, showing problems and possible improvements in programs, but not questioning the fundamental assumptions behind the programs.

In the research about the utilization of evaluation many different forms of utilization have been discussed, and we can certainly talk about uses of evaluation in terms such as symbolic and legitimating. From a political science or anthropological perspective, such forms of utilization can be important to study. However, in discussing how evaluation can contribute to a better society, the main question is: To what extent can evaluation contribute knowledge that can help us to make tough choices about the future?

Notes

1. A terminological question is *evaluation* vs. *evaluation research*. This question will not be discussed here. However, the quotations can be interpreted in such a way that the meaning will be the same even if we use the word *evaluation* instead of *evaluation research*.
2. Thereby, it is also said that evaluation can be used in quite different, and more generic, ways than discussed here. It can mean, as Scriven strongly advocates: The process of determining (or the act of declaring) something about the merit, worth or significance of any entity" (Scriven 2013: 170).

References

Anderson, S. and L. Harbridge. 2010. "Incrementalism in Appropriations: Small Aggregation, Big Changes." *Public Administration Review* 70 (3): 464–74.

Baumgartner, F.R., and B.D. Jones. 1993. *Agendas and Instability in American Politics.* Chicago: University of Chicago Press.

Bennet, C.J., and M. Howlett. 1992. The Lessons of Learning: Reconciling Theories of Policy Learning and Policy Change." *Policy Sciences* 25 (3): 275–94.

Bergström, H. 2006. *Vem Leder Sverige Mot Framtiden?* Stockholm: SNS förlag.

Boswell, C. 2009. *The Political Uses of Expert Knowledge.* Cambridge: Cambridge University Press.

Capoccia, G., and R.D. Kelemen. 2007. "The Study of Critical Junctures: Theory, Narrative and Counterfactuals in Historical Institutionalism." *World Politics* 59: 341–69.

Dahler-Larsen, P. 2011. *The Evaluation Society.* Stanford, CA: Stanford University Press.

Fischer, F. 2003. *Reframing Public Policy.* Oxford: Oxford University Press.

Furubo, J.E., and R. Sandahl. 2002. "A Diffusion Perspective on Global Developments in Evaluation." In *International Atlas of Evaluation,* edited by J.E. Furubo, R.C. Rist, and R. Sandahl. New Brunswick, NJ: Transaction Publishers.

Furubo, J.E., and O. Karlsson Vestman. 2011. "Evaluation for Public Good or Professional Power." In *Evaluation: Seeking Truth or Power?* edited by P. Eliadis, J.E. Furubo, and S. Jacob, 1–35. New Brunswick, NJ: Transaction Publishers.

Geyer, R., and S. Rihani. 2010. *Complexity and Public Policy.* New York: Routledge.

Hood, C. 1994. *Explaining Economic Policy Reversals.* Buckingham: Open University Press.

Jordan, M.M. 2003. "Punctuations and Agendas: A New Look at Local Government Budget Expenditures." *Journal of Policy Analysis and Management* 22 (3): 345–60.

Kingdon, J.W. 2003. *Agendas, Alternatives and Public Policies.* Second Edition. New York: Longman.

Lincoln, A. 1862. Annual Message to Congress. http//quotationsbook.com/quote/44576 (accessed November 21, 2012).

Leeuw, F.L., and J.E. Furubo. 2008. "Evaluation Systems: What Are They and Why Study Them." *Evaluation* 14 (2): 157–69.

Mark, M.M., S.I. Donaldson, and B. Campbell. 2011. *Social Psychology and Evaluation.* New York: Guilford Press.

Marx, K., and F. Engels. 1848. *Communist Manifesto.* Wikipedia (accessed November 21, 2012).

Merton, R.K. 1936."The Unanticipated Consequences of Purposive Social Action." *American Sociological Review* 1 (6): 894–904.

Morra Imas, L.G., and R.C. Rist. 2009. *The Road to Results.* Washington, DC: World Bank.

Myrdal, G. 1934. Finanspolitikens ekonomiska verkningar. SOU (Statens offentliga utredningar/ Official reports of the Swedish Government) 1934:1.

Owen, J.M. 2007. *Program Evaluation: Forms and Approaches.* New York: The Guilford Press.

Pierson, P. 2004. *Politics in Time: History, Institutions, and Social Analysis.* Princeton: Princeton University Press.

Polanyi, K. 1944. *The Great Transformation: The Political and Economic Origins of Our Time.* Boston: Beacon Press.

Prewitt, K., T.A. Schwandt, and M.L. Straf. 2012. *Using Evidence in Public Policy.* Washington, DC: National Research Council of the National Academies.

Riecken, H.W. 1972. "Memorandum on Program Evaluation." In *Evaluating Actions Program: Readings in Social Science and Education,* edited by C.H. Weiss. Boston: Allyn and Bacon, Inc.

Rist, R.C. 2002. "The Rise and Fall (and Rise Again?) of the Evaluation Function in the U.S. Government." In *International Atlas of Evaluation,* edited by J.E. Furubo, R.C. Rist, and R. Sandahl. New Brunswick, NJ: Transaction Publishers.

Rossi, P.H., H.E. Freeman, and M.W. Lipsey. 1999. *Evaluation: A Systematic Approach.* Sixth Edition. Thousand Oaks, CA: Sage Publications.

Rothstein, B. 1992. "Explaining Swedish Corporatism: The Formative Moment." *Scandinavian Political Studies* 15 (3): 173–91.

Scriven, M. 2013. "Conceptual Revolutions in Evaluation: Past, Present and Future." In *Evaluation Roots: A Wider Perspecitve of Theorists' Views and Influences,* edited by M.C. Alkin. Los Angeles: Sage Publications.

Suchman, E.A. 1967. *Evaluation Research: Principles and Practice in Public Service and Social Action Programs.* New York: Russel Sage Foundation.

Vaessen, J., and F.L. Leeuw. 2010. *Mind the Gap: Perspective on Policy Evaluation and the Social Sciences.* New Brunswick, NJ: Transaction Publishers.

Vedung, E. 1997. *Public Policy and Program Evaluation.* New Brunswick, NJ: Transaction Publishers.

Weiss, C.H. 1972. *Evaluating Actions Programs: Readings in Social Science and Education.* Boston: Allyn and Bacon, Inc.

Wildavsky, A. 1979. *Speaking Truth to Power.* Boston: Little Brown & Company.

PART ONE: IMPLICATIONS OF TURBULENT TIMES FOR EVALUATION APPROACHES

CHAPTER 3

Evaluation and Turbulence: Reflections on Our Time

Saraswathi Menon

IDEAS' Early Vision

It is a great privilege to be at the global assembly of the International Development Evaluation Association (IDEAS) and I would like to thank IDEAS for this opportunity to share some thoughts with you. It is good to meet in Jordan, which has been the meeting point of many cultures and peoples and, therefore, an appropriate meeting place for evaluators from across the globe.

IDEAS is, after all, an institution that has its roots in a vision that development evaluation must represent and catalyze a broad spectrum of actors, countries, interests, and ways of thinking. The United Nations Development Programme (UNDP) Evaluation Office is proud to have been an early champion of IDEAS and to have played a lead role from the London Declaration in 2001 to the formal establishment of IDEAS in Beijing in 2002. The vision of that period, which combined three strands—to strengthen evaluation practice, to move beyond aid evaluation to development evaluation, and to contribute to governance for development—remains with us today. These strands are still on our website. IDEAS was intended to be a forum that was inclusive and responsive to new trends in evaluation and in development and, thereby, to explore the interstices between development and evaluation as a two-way, dialectical process.

It is significant that this global congress focuses on evaluation in a time of turbulence. I am assuming that we all see turbulence from the point of view of development. In fact, I would argue that people across the world, especially those who live in deprivation and exclusion, constantly live in a time of turbulence and of crises, including, but not just related to, food, fuel, and finance. What makes this economic crisis significant is that it affects the North and not just the South, that it affects governments and not just people prompting democratic movements to improve governance in many countries, and that it has worsened conditions for those who were not poor or who recently escaped poverty, not just for those who have been trapped in poverty for generations. It is for these reasons that turbulence, crisis, and fragility so readily come to our lips when we talk about development today. It is important that we unpack turbulence from the standpoint of people's lives if we are to understand it in development terms.

Linking Evaluation and Development

Let me begin by positing a broad link between evaluation and development.

What is the ultimate end of evaluation and how does it intersect with development? Simply put, I would say that it is to improve public action to contribute to people's well-being. Public action can be seen in its broadest sense as the agency of people combined with the actions of the state and its partners. Learning and accountability, which are so often seen as the purposes of evaluation, are only channels by which the process and results of evaluation temper and galvanize public action. Learning and accountability should not necessarily be seen as the end, but only as a means to development. Only by reinforcing public action and fostering change can evaluation contribute to development.

More concretely, let me explore the interplay between the three purposes of IDEAS and this larger objective of development evaluation: to catalyze public action.

Strengthening the Practice of Evaluation

First, with regard to strengthening the practice of evaluation, evaluation as a discipline has advanced considerably in the past few years. As a professional discipline standing on the shoulders of several social sciences from whom it gathers methodologies and analytical approaches, evaluation may be said to have come of age. Evaluation's visibility as a profession may be measured crudely by the number of universities offering courses in evaluation, dedicated evaluation units in governments and organizations, regional and country-level associations of evaluation professionals, conferences on evaluation where new methodologies are discussed, consulting companies that specialize in evaluation, and, not least, the plethora of evaluation reports published annually that seek to make a constructive contribution to change. There is no doubt that technical and methodological progress in evaluation is critical to making evaluation more robust and credible.

IDEAS has played an important role as facilitator of this progress. Successive global assemblies have provided forums to discuss new developments in methodologies and approaches and to hone the skills of evaluators. The strong bond that has been built with the International Program in Development Evaluation Training (IPDET) in recent years reflects the emphasis increasingly placed on evaluation methods and approaches and continued networking among those who have participated in common training programs. An important, although less pronounced, link with the regional evaluation associations reflects the important global span of IDEAS envisioned by its founders. The networking platform that IDEAS provides has the potential to catalyze professional interaction that goes well beyond IPDET and the regional associations. My sense is that this potential is not yet fully tapped because we are mainly evaluators talking to evaluators. I will return to this challenge later.

Moving beyond Aid Evaluation

Let us now examine the second purpose of IDEAS, which talks of moving beyond aid evaluation. As we in UNDP understand it, development effectiveness can be conceptualized only within a national context. At best, international or aid partners contribute to development effectiveness by effectively partnering with national efforts. The evaluation of this support can only be termed an assessment of aid effectiveness. I would argue that it is a travesty to talk about the development effectiveness of a bilateral or multilateral agency. It is more appropriate to talk of their contribution to development effectiveness. Development effectiveness is the result of public action, national policies, national capacity, and national engagement. Our focus in development evaluation, therefore, requires an understanding of change in a national context and demands of us methodologies and criteria that can assess the complexity of development as it is played out in a country in interaction with global trends and forces.

The criteria and approaches that have served development evaluation were born of the practice of aid that was intended to fill resource or capacity gaps in developing countries. The extremely useful criteria developed by UNDP's Development Assistance Committee (DAC) with the bilateral donors in the context of evaluating projects—relevance, effectiveness, efficiency, impact, and sustainability—have become core criteria for all types of evaluation and are embedded in professional evaluation capacity-development efforts. These criteria are a natural fit for the discrete universe of projects and programs through which development cooperation, and sometimes targeted spheres of government action, are delivered. Similarly, the pathbreaking work on impact evaluation begins, and too often ends, from the perspective of a single intervention and its results.

Evaluation criteria and questions must be expanded and fundamentally rethought if they are to yield meaningful information when looking at more complex phenomena such as outcomes, strategies, policies, and public goods. They yield only partial, and not necessarily the most crucial, information for influencing public action that spans the state, civil society, and the citizen. They do not capture the complexities and interactions among policies. If evaluation is to reorient public action, evaluation criteria and questions must answer what is important for the citizen and policy maker, not only what is important for the funder and manager of the initiative, whether national or international.

What issues concern citizens? Let us look at the questions being raised during this period of "turbulence." Citizens are raising questions regarding prioritization and choice of policies. They want to know how national policies affect equity or reinforce social and economic gaps. They want objective assessments that will capture the persistence of inequality and discrimination and point to ways to overcome them, ways that are sustainable in a broader sense and not just based on continuing the results of isolated interventions. Citizens are concerned about the quality of governance and growing corruption. Development evaluation has to respond to such challenges. It must be underpinned by the principles of human development and use different criteria and different approaches if it is to respond to the type of knowledge about development effectiveness demanded by citizens. This is a second challenge that we face and to which I will return.

Contributing to Governance

Let us now take a look at the closely related, very important third purpose of IDEAS—to contribute to governance for development. We evaluators pride ourselves on basing our judgments on evidence that has been rigorously collected and validated. And yet it is striking that in the recent past, judgments about the performance of governments have been shaped by evidence from a source very different from evaluation—Wikileaks. And indeed public action has been catalyzed by this "evidence": The recent mass movement against corruption in my own country, India, is a case in point. The publication and analysis of official documentation unleashed a public outcry for changes in legislation. What can we evaluators learn from Wikileaks? Wikileaks stays true to its sources and does not compromise or hedge its information. Importantly, it allows others to analyze its raw information.

Development evaluation, however, perhaps because of its origins in aid evaluation, has stayed programmatic and, as a result, has had limited relevance or impact on governance. Its purpose, by and large, has been to improve programs within the framework of defined or intended and unintended results and not to question the basis of public action.

My colleague, Alan Fox, was to have presented at this forum our experience in the UNDP Evaluation Office of conducting an evaluation in Tunisia and the Arab Republic of Egypt in recent months—a time of "turbulence." He was unable to come, not because of security concerns, but because he is revisiting and finalizing our evaluation in Egypt. If we had maintained the usual practice of evaluating against intended results and using the standard DAC criteria, the UNDP program in Egypt would have done rather well. But we are using other criteria. We evaluated against United Nations (UN) norms and values as well, and it is only by doing so that the traditional assessment begins to unravel and we begin, very partially I would be the first to admit, to address the kind of concerns that the youth of Egypt have been raising regarding development and governance and to look at the implications for development cooperation.

Development evaluation has also, I would argue, been rather ahistorical although development is historical. A little over a year ago, the UNDP Evaluation Office together with the Human Development Observatory of Morocco organized a meeting on national evaluation capacity. Please note it was not a meeting on capacity development. It was a forum to share national experiences so that South–South and trilateral cooperation in evaluation could take place. The themes discussed are familiar to all of us and are reflected in the content of this assembly: institutional setups for evaluating public policies and programs; the relationship between monitoring and evaluation; independence of evaluation; the important distinction between capacities to manage, conduct, and use evaluations; quality and use of evaluation; and technical capacity and the political economy of evaluation.

Because countries were sharing their own experiences, the historical analysis was important. The origins of interest in evaluation varied. For some, as in Ghana, it was an initial push from donors that was later internalized. For others, as in India, it grew out of a national planning system crafted immediately after independence from colonialism. And yet for others, as in South Africa, it was part of the public accountability of a new democracy that had to overcome years of discrimination in order to create a new free society.

But in all countries, the national project and demands of citizens shaped evaluation systems. In all, the value of evaluation was seen as the ability to question the basis of policies themselves and not just to assess their implementation. An important conclusion of the meeting was that although a lot of work was being done on how to conduct an evaluation, far less attention was being paid to the use and users of evaluation. For this reason, the theme of the use of evaluation will be central in a follow-up conference on national evaluation capacity that is being organized by the Government of South Africa and the UNDP Evaluation Office this September.

Three Challenges

Development evaluation has to emerge from a programmatic, ahistorical world view to a much more complex understanding of development reality driven by the demands of public accountability. I talked earlier of three challenges that must be met if the three central purposes of IDEAS are to be achieved.

- The first challenge is the need for broader platforms and networks going beyond evaluators. These broader platforms should engage users. Already in countries in Latin America, evaluation systems interact much more closely with civil society than elsewhere. There is much we can learn from their experience and IDEAS is the ideal forum.
- Second is the need for new evaluation criteria. Chinese evaluators already use criteria such as equity and innovation, which are more relevant for development evaluation. In the United Nations, we prioritize human rights and gender equality in evaluation and are developing

methodologies to do so not merely from a perspective of closing gaps but also of overcoming structural discrimination and vulnerability. In UNDP we evaluate on the basis of an understanding of the multidimensionality of poverty, not just income poverty.

- Third is the need to respond to the concerns of citizens. Evaluation systems and evaluation approaches must be responsive and nationally rooted. For too long we have talked of country-led evaluations and country-led evaluation systems. The term "country led" implies either that external partners had grabbed the leadership and we need a coup to restore ownership, or that nationals had abdicated their role in the past and now must be urged to take ownership. Moreover, national systems are not just government systems. They are a complex mixture of government systems, national capacity, citizens' voices, and public accountability.

The time of turbulence that we live in—a turbulence that also affects the North, governments, and the nonpoor—can be seen as a time of opportunity for evaluation. By unpacking the content of turbulence, we can analyze development more concretely from the point of view of people's lives. We will be forced to look at the interplay of policies and not just at individual programs, because turbulence is the result of this interplay. Even in the North, issues of policy coherence are coming to the fore and it is not enough to evaluate development cooperation separately. New institutional arrangements for evaluation in the United Kingdom and elsewhere reflect this trend. And in a situation where traditional economic and political theories are turned on their head because their consequences have been disastrous, we can look for greater innovation in evaluation methodology from a variety of sources and disciplines. It is 10 years since the London Declaration that led to the founding of IDEAS. Perhaps it is time for a new commitment to fostering development evaluation that will do intellectual justice to the complex issues that have to be addressed and to fostering the use of evaluation so that public accountability and governance can be better served and evaluation can contribute to public action.

CHAPTER 4

Evaluation in the Context of Global Public Goods

Rob D. van den Berg

Introduction: The Roots of Turbulent Times

The International Development Evaluation Association (IDEAS) conference in Amman in 2011 addressed challenging subjects: turbulent times and
crises that endanger our future: those of food, fuel, and finance. This chapter aims to weave these subjects and crises together into a third, overarching crisis, namely, the slowly encroaching crisis of rising global public costs
caused by the careless way in which humanity continues to deplete natural
resources and to treat our environment as an endless bounty for looting and
spoiling.

In March 2011, I attended a meeting in Manila on how the international
financial institutions had coped with the global credit crisis.[1] A common element from evaluations was that only a few experts had foreseen the crisis
and those who should have listened, did not. A common recommendation
was to listen better. During the second part of that meeting, I had a captive
audience when, as director of the Global Environment Facility (GEF) Evaluation Office, I presented evaluative findings of the GEF. I used this golden

opportunity to tell the audience that not just a few experts, but hundreds and thousands of them, foresee three other emerging major global crises that we need to confront.

The first crisis is known to all: climate change. The second is the mass extinction of species caused by human behavior. The third, and least known, is the unfolding drama of poisonous chemicals threatening environmental and human health. In Manila, I told the audience that they have been forewarned. Experts are convinced that these three global crises—climate change, mass extinction of biodiversity, and poisonous chemicals—are endangering a prosperous and equitable future. In economic terms, these three crises are leading to dramatically increasing global public costs. They undermine achievements in development and poverty alleviation in the long run.[2]

Yet international institutions and governments have spent billions to solve the global credit crunch without paying much attention to the three unfolding global environmental crises. Some even say that to spend money on solving environmental problems is a luxury we cannot afford at the moment. Instead money has gone to bailing out banks and ensuring funding is available for "business as usual." When the disastrous economic effects of the credit crisis became clear, many of us desperately hoped for "business as usual." However, my contention is that "business as usual" is *causing* the three global environmental crises.

Global gross domestic product (GDP) has risen substantially over the past 50 years, from just a few trillion U.S. dollars in 1970 to US$70 trillion in 2011, with a slight downturn in 2009 due to the credit crisis.[3] However, the growth of global GDP has been accompanied by a dramatic increase in global public costs. Using relatively scarce public resources to solve problems in the private financial sector means that hardly any resources are left to solve global public problems. The world is getting richer all the time and yet most, if not all, countries are facing a crucial shortage of funding for public issues.

The Role of Public Funding: Public Goods and Costs

The first part of this chapter will address the role of public funding in tackling public goods and costs. The discourse about global and national economies has for the past few decades focused on how to strengthen and extend the role of markets, and there has been a relative scarcity of discussions on public goods and funding. So let us go back to some fundamental principles and reestablish these issues. Public goods are defined in economic terms as "nonrival" and "nonexcludable." In other words, they are goods that are almost impossible to trade. The air you breathe is available to everybody, and the fact that you breathe does not make it impossible for anybody else to breathe. It is difficult to exclude anybody from breathing and put a price on it—although this situation changes if one were to go diving with an oxygen tank to breathe under water.

Public goods are strongly related to another economic concept: that of externalities, which point to costs and benefits that are created in markets that are additional and external to the product that was produced for and bought on the market. The benefits of externalities usually do not pose a problem—it is their costs that concern us. Many economists tend to speak of external costs in terms of "market failure." The most recent and famous example concerns climate change. When Nicholas Stern, a former chief economist of the World Bank, reported to the U.K. government on the costs of climate change, both on preventing it and adapting to its consequences, he noted that climate change is a result of "the greatest market failure the world has seen." His conclusion was that "those who damage others by emitting greenhouse gases generally do not pay."[4] There is controversy over whether Stern and his team correctly calculated the damages and the costs of preventing them, but the point he raised concerning market failure was not disputed.

In general, governments have three ways to tackle market failures and ensure public goods. First, they can criminalize the behavior that leads to the external costs. Second, they can change behavior through regulation to such an extent that the external costs no longer appear. Last, they can recover the costs through taxation that aims to bring the external costs back into the market, for example, through a tax on pollution, or emission of greenhouse gasses, or energy consumption. However, some would argue that general taxation should be sufficient to ensure public goods and meet public costs, which are the foundation of taxation and of public spending. This argument was first developed by the economist Paul Samuelson (1954) in a theory of public expenditure.

There was no general agreement on Samuelson's theory, although after World War II, an economic discourse took place on how "the public purpose" could be served by strengthening the role of government and public funding. Perhaps John Kenneth Galbraith's 1973 publication, *Economics and the Public Purpose,* can be highlighted as the culmination of this perspective. Over time, the neoclassical school of economics gained ascendancy and questioned the role of governments. Instead, it focused on improving the functioning of markets to solve problems in society. Both market regulation and taxation were deplored as distortions that prevent markets from becoming fully efficient.

To many economists, the global financial crisis demonstrated the dangers of market fundamentalism, showing the need for governments to regulate markets. However, this issue continues to be contested and market-oriented economists continue to claim that it was actually government interference with the markets that caused the subprime lending crisis. The debate is far from over.

Transboundary Issues: The Role of Global Public Goods

Much of the discourse on public goods, the role of governments, and the efficiency of markets considers what should happen in one country. However, many of the externalities of markets are of a transboundary nature. If a company emits greenhouse gasses, these gasses will not respect political boundaries and will influence the global climate, not just a local micro-climate. The globalization of the world, and especially its economy, is, of course, a thoroughly discussed phenomenon and opinions differ wildly on whether it is beneficial or a challenge. However, the transboundary costs of markets are a fact and many local actions now have global consequences.

At the same time, we need to recognize that there is no global government to ensure the global public purpose. There are many elements in the direction of global governance: the United Nations is a forum for nations to discuss what needs to be done; several international treaties define criminal acts between nations; likewise several international conventions aim to regulate transboundary issues. There are even some minor examples of international taxation, but they do not amount to much. If there is a global public purse, it is filled by donations and grants from rich nations; some of it is channeled through the United Nations, but most of it either goes directly from country to country or through the international financial institutions—the International Monetary Fund (IMF), the World Bank, and the many regional and subregional banks that have a role in development, reconstruction, or transformation—or, more recently, through so called "vertical funds," of which the Global Fund to Fight AIDS, Tuberculosis and Malaria is probably the best-known example.

The financial crisis has led to substantive increases in both capital and funding of many international financial institutions (Moss and others 2011). The Asian Development Bank increased its capital in March 2009 from about US$55 billion to about US$165 billion. The International Bank for

Reconstruction and Development, part of the World Bank Group, received a boost in capital of US$86.2 billion in April 2010. The European Bank for Reconstruction and Development achieved a 50 percent increase in its capital, from US$30 to US$45 billion in May 2010. The International Development Association, also a member of the World Bank Group, increased its funding for the poorest countries with a record inflow of about US$50 billion in December 2010 at its 16th replenishment.[5] This money does not all come from the public purse—most of it is borrowed on the capital markets. These amounts are available for public loans that must be repaid over time. But as argued before, most of this money is available for "business as usual."

At the same time bilateral funding for development and global issues is still lagging behind the internationally agreed upon target of 0.7 percent of GDP and although many countries pledged to reach this target over time, the Organisation for Economic Co-operation and Development (OECD) projects that this will not happen in the near future. The OECD notes that aid is expected to grow at 2 percent per year between 2011 and 2013, compared with the average 8 percent per year over the past three years. Aid to Africa is likely to rise by just 1 percent per year in real terms, compared with the average 13 percent over the past three years. The OECD concludes that at this rate, any additional aid to the African countries will be outpaced by population growth.[6] The question is whether the current level of global public funding is sufficient to stem the rising tide of global public costs.

The Rising Tide of Global Public Costs

The dilemma of tackling the costs of market failure was most aptly put by the Stern review. It calculates that these costs in the case of climate change would amount to 1 percent of global domestic product annually. This is an astounding amount—about US$600 billion—to prevent climate change from happening. In other words, it would cover the costs of converting our energy sources, our energy consumption, and so on to ensure that we shift to a "green economy" that does not emit greenhouse gases. I'm sure that the reader will not be surprised if I reveal that what is currently spent on these issues is woefully insufficient. The Stern review calculates that if climate change happens, costs will rise. Adaptation to climate change will cost anywhere between US$100 and US$200 billion annually, and the world will be confronted with a reduction of up to 5 percent in our future GDP—an astounding amount of more than US$3 trillion that the world will not be able to generate due to climate change. These calculations have been heavily criticized as "deeply flawed" and as "scare mongering." Stern has taken all criticism on board and very carefully recalculated the costs, and admitted that his calculations could be improved—they were too low. He raised them from 1 percent of global GDP to 2 percent of global GDP.[7]

Many have drawn two conclusions from this debate:

1. The public costs of climate change are beyond public funding;
2. The longer we wait to address them adequately, the higher the costs will be, either to solve the problems or to rearranging our lives to adapt to the new reality.

A hypothesis in this regard could be that the increase in public costs, if unmet (that is, if no action is taken to avoid the costs, or no funding is forthcoming to meet the costs) accelerates over time either leading to a complete breakdown of the system, or a systemic change. The first possibility could be illustrated with the ancient civilization of Easter Island. As Jared Diamond posed in his book *Collapse: How Societies Choose to Fail or Succeed* (2005), the people of Easter Island used up their natural resources and did not survive. Let us hope that we have the fortune to end up with a systemic change rather than a collapse. Systematic change is in fact what many climate change skeptics assume will happen. Systemic change is central to the idea of a "green economy," which is becoming more urgent over time, because the gap between what we need and what we can bring to solve the problem is huge and growing. Increasingly, economists are adding their voices to the debate on how to "manage nature for global prosperity," to quote Paul Collier's subtitle for his 2010 book, *The Plundered Planet*.

"Mind the Global Gap"

In addition to the climate change gap, we face two other gaps that continue to grow. The world is currently moving toward a mass extinction of species greater than has been seen for 65 million years. Over time, the world has seen five mass extinctions, which only 10–25 percent of living species survived. We now bring you the sixth mass extinction, this time without the aid of a meteor crashing into the Gulf of Mexico, but brought to you in Technicolor by market failure (Barnosky and others 2011)! Biodiversity continues to decline dramatically, because the existence of a species is not a marketable property and thus is not incorporated into the price of products that through their production processes or consumption destroy natural habitats. Neoclassical economists are confident that market forces will, over time, correct failures. However, at the moment and in the foreseeable future, we cannot recreate extinct species. Once they are gone they are gone forever. Although no Stern review has calculated the costs of mass extinction, conservative guesses of the costs of preserving biodiversity tend to dramatically surpass available funding from all sources. Even if a species does not disappear, but just faces a mass loss of population, the costs can be gigantic. For example, bats in North America are facing massive population losses due to white-nose syndrome, caused by a fungus that is an invasive species, as well as due to being killed in unprecedented numbers by wind turbines throughout the United States, an unforeseen consequence of greening the economy. Yet the economic value of bats to agriculture in the United States and Canada has been estimated at more than US$3.7 billion per year (Boyles and others 2011). The economic loss due to the decline in numbers of one species that is not yet threatened with extinction, already go into the billions and cannot be recovered on the market because they are public costs, in this case related to agriculture.

The third gap is that of toxic chemicals in our environment. For more than a century, industries have introduced new chemicals in their production processes after what seemed like thorough testing. Many of them are "persistent organic pollutants": organic, carbon-based compounds that, somewhat to our surprise, turned out to be fairly indestructible and have become pervasive in the environment. Once they are introduced into the environment, often as pesticides, they travel vast distances and enter the food chain and our bodies. They may cause death and illnesses including disruption of the reproductive, immune, and respiratory systems (Resource Futures International 2001). The "dirty dozen" of these pollutants, with fancy names like aldrin, heptachlor, mirex, and toxaphene, have been identified as dangerous for human and environmental health by the United Nations Environment Programme (UNEP) since 1995. In 2001, a new multilateral agreement, the Stockholm Convention on Persistent Organic Pollutants, was signed to eliminate or restrict the production and consumption of these chemicals. Scientists continue to explore the health risks of many other chemicals that were introduced by industry and, in 2009, another nine chemicals were added to the list (Stockholm Convention on Persistent Organic Pollutants 2009).[8] One can safely predict that the list will grow in the next decade.

The problem is one of side effects that remain invisible in ordinary testing because of the geographic or time scale involved, or because of unexpected behavior. Some chemicals were introduced to help package food products. It was assumed that they would not interact with the food, but they did, and they entered into our bodies. Some chemicals arrived in places nobody expected them to turn up. The most illustrious example is that of ozone-depleting substances. When the hole in the ozone layer was discovered in the late 1970s, it took some time to establish why it had formed and what could be done about it. When ozone-depleting substances such as chlorofluorocarbons used in refrigerators were identified as the guilty parties, international action—leading to the Montreal Protocol—was relatively quick and successful, given the essential role the ozone layer fulfills in protecting life on our planet from harmful cosmic radiation. Calculations show that if this action was not taken, there would be no ozone layer left in 2060, just 50 years in the future.[9] The Montreal Protocol has been successful in reducing production and consumption of ozone-depleting substances, with about 95 percent of these substances now safely stored, but the problem is far from over. In 2009, the GEF Evaluation Office conducted an impact evaluation on support to stop producing and consuming Ozone Depleting Substances in Eastern Europe and Central Asia. The GEF Council had considered ending its support, but the evaluation alerted it that it was too early to do so. Whereas ending production and consumption can be done relatively cheaply, the challenge remains to destroy the stockpiles of these substances, as they may escape into the atmosphere if their current storage facilities break down or leak because of earthquakes or simple lack of care (GEF Evaluation Office 2010b).

The cost of destroying persistent organic pollutants and ozone-depleting substances is high. Recovering these costs through market regulations is impossible. These chemicals were put on the market decades ago at a time when the disastrous effects were not yet known. It is impossible to regulate the past. The cost to address this emerging global crisis is truly public, and the money to tackle it is not identified. These global public costs emerge out of current business practices. For example, the food industry continues to explore possibilities to "improve" storage, taste, and durability of its products. To increase its efficiency and increase profits, it introduces new substances from time to time, always carefully testing them, but perhaps not over long periods of time or with unintended consequences in mind. An example is Bisphenol A, better known as BPA, an organic compound used in the fabrication of certain plastics. In the 1980s this compound was used in plastics for food storage because it seemed safe and was economically attractive. It was considered safe because BPA was not supposed to travel from the plastic package into the food or into your body. In 2008, research showed that 95 percent of American adults had BPA in their bodies. Effects may include cancer and effects on the reproductive system and the thyroid and lead to several neurological conditions.[10] Isn't it nice to know that "business as usual" is presenting us with this potentially deadly cocktail of chemicals and organic pollutants, and let us not forget the rare metals we are now introducing into our environment through used mobile phones, batteries, personal computer components, and so on.

Business as usual means that one generation introduces new products, ingredients, and components that are thought to be safe and enable cheaper production and higher profits. The next generation faces the costs of removing these substances from the environment. Business as usual means that our generation continues to emit amounts of greenhouse gases that will dramatically change climate and lead to huge costs in adaptation. Business as usual means that we continue to destroy and poison our ecosystems, so that species lose their natural habitats and die out. Going over to a "green economy" will solve some of these problems, but it is by no means certain that all of these issues are on the radar screen of those who decide where the billions of dollars from the multilateral banks will go. Some will argue that these billions are meant for poverty reduction, not for environmental problems. But the poor are often the first to be confronted with a loss of biodiversity, with climate changes that endanger their subsistence farming, and with chemicals and metals that are dumped on them, sometimes from very far away.

The three widening gaps of climate change, biodiversity loss, and chemical pollution highlight the global public nature of the unfolding crises of fuel, food, and finance. In the Global Environment Facility, we are confronted with these gaps all the time. The team in the GEF Evaluation Office sees these gaps whenever we evaluate. They are part of the geography of our evaluation landscape. This leads me to the second part of this chapter, in which I will formulate some ideas on how evaluators can deal with these crises and with the nature of global public goods.

Consequences for Evaluation

Why should we consider these issues in evaluation practices? First of all, I would like to relate these issues to an ongoing discussion in economics, which has often been termed the micro–macro paradox: How is it possible that we see achievements at the intervention level, but these achievements do not seem to translate at the national level? How can a country have a lot of interventions that score moderately to highly satisfactory on achievement of outcomes, and yet the country itself, in its national development indicators, does not reflect the same levels of achievement? This paradox was formulated by economists, focusing on interventions that aimed to achieve economic growth, increased income, or increased economic activity through investment projects or public lending. Where these investments were successful, they looked for similar changes in the macroeconomic data of the country, but often could not find them. This debate over whether aid could be proven to contribute to macroeconomic development received a new impulse with the 1998 World Bank publication of *Assessing Aid: What Works, What Doesn't and Why* (World Bank 1998). When the debate could not provide a definite answer, interest in macroeconomic solutions waned and more emphasis was placed on microeconomic work. The poverty lab approach of the Massachusetts Institute of Technology is almost completely focused on microlevel interventions and promotes methodologies that are very difficult to apply at the national level. It is only recently that macro-economists have offered a response to this shift and tried to regain some of the lost ground (see for example Heckman and Urza 2009). The discussion is still lopsided, and many economists seem to have given up on the macro picture. Their approach is to concentrate on what works on the ground and to tests that would identify causal linkages.

I do not believe that this approach is sufficient. It may help decide which innovative programs should be scaled up and which interventions show promise for affecting human behavior. But these approaches do not address the micro–macro gap. And we see the evidence of this in the Global Environment Facility. The GEF has a pretty complete picture of the level of success of its interventions. Each project above a certain size needs to be evaluated on completion. We have "end-of-projects" evaluations from more than 400 projects and we review newly arrived evaluations annually to assess the performance of the GEF. Most of these projects have been implemented by three agencies: UNDP, UNEP, and the World Bank. Their evaluation offices have also looked at these projects. We agree on the evaluation criteria, and we agree on the level of achievements of these projects. Our joint conclusion is that the performance of these projects has been good. More than 80 percent of GEF projects are rated moderately satisfactory or above, up to highly satisfactory, in achievement of outcomes. An internationally agreed upon standard in the international financial institutions is that 75 percent of projects should perform moderately satisfactory or higher. So the GEF has a solid performance and good achievements, confirmed not just by the GEF Evaluation Office, but also by the evaluation offices of United Nations Development Programme (UNDP), UNEP, and the World Bank (see GEF Evaluation Office 2010a, 30).

When the office started to look into the impact of GEF activities, it also found evidence of short-term impact, and sometimes of longer-term impact.[11] Twenty years ago the expectation was that the white rhinoceros in Africa would be extinct within two decades. Now there is a thriving community of white rhinoceros in Kenya, thanks to an initial grant of the GEF. Local communities in Samoa in the Pacific now fish in a sustainable way, rather than through destroying coral reefs. China is making the shift from incandescent to fluorescent light bulbs through a GEF-funded introduction project. The Philippines has become one of the world leaders in geothermal power stations with technical support from the GEF. There are, of course, also failures— the GEF is not fail proof. But the main message is that there is much good news coming from GEF projects.

But is there? Let me turn to another stream of evaluations: country portfolio evaluations, where the focus is on how GEF interventions are supporting the country to tackle global environmental issues.[12] One such global issue is deforestation. GEF support has been used by countries to reduce, stop, or even reverse deforestation. The country portfolio evaluation in the Philippines in 2007 concluded that areas in which GEF support was provided had successfully stopped deforestation. The report also noted that the rate of deforestation in the Philippines overall had not changed and was still going strong in the wrong direction. There we have an environmental version of the economic micro–macro paradox. GEF support saves a species here or there, promotes integrated natural resource management at the community level here or there, initiates market change to reduce greenhouse gas emissions here or there while, in general, the world seems to continue to slide toward the abyss.

In the GEF's fourth overall performance study, an effort was made to identify why there is not more progress at the macro level. The conclusion was that the amount of public funding available for governments and public institutions to play their proper role to meet global public costs simply was dramatically insufficient (GEF Evaluation Office 2010a, 15–16). The gap between interventions and what is actually needed is widening. This is the crisis behind the fuel, food, and finance turbulence that we are currently facing: it is a crisis of rising public costs that cannot be incorporated into markets and a simultaneous reduction of availability of public funding. It is accompanied by a crisis in confidence in public governance. Taxpayers are unwilling to give more money, because they do not trust governments to do the right thing, whereas many governments increasingly need money to do the right thing, and without money the slide continues downward.

This conclusion is not just a conclusion of the GEF Evaluation Office. Since the GEF operates through both the United Nations and the multilateral banks, the GEF Evaluation Office is a member of both groups of evaluation offices, the United Nations Evaluation Group (UNEG) and the Evaluation Cooperation Group (ECG) of the development banks. The latter group took the initiative to provide a briefing on biodiversity-related findings to the international biodiversity conference in Nagoya in October 2010. A briefing note states the case for global public goods and for the lack of priority attention and funding (Evaluation Cooperation Group 2010). Let me quote two paragraphs:

> Much of the downward spiral of biodiversity loss is due to market failure: the failure of markets to price the potential loss of a species, or to price the dangers and opportunities of climate change, but also market forces that increase the possibility of extinction, such as over-fishing in the world's oceans, which in economic terms has been identified as a new example of the tragedy of the commons. These market failures lead to over-exploitation of the environment, because the negative externalities are not incorporated in pricing mechanisms, and they lead to inaction to improve this situation, because positive externalities that would emerge from improvements are to the benefit of everyone and cannot easily be captured by market forces. Where markets have been regulated or prohibited, illegal trade has become a danger, as has recently been highlighted when discussing the future of tigers in Asia.

> There is evaluative evidence that efforts and interventions to sustain biodiversity are working and do have positive impacts on ecosystems, genetic resources and species. Yet the downward spiral continues, because the interventions do not reach the scale which would change the overall trend. The main lesson from many evaluations is that neither the International Financial Institutions nor the UN agencies have woken up to the urgency of the situation, and they have not integrated biodiversity and environmental issues into their strategies and implementation. This situation must be turned around quickly through scaling up of positive examples of biodiversity conservation and mainstreaming conservation and sustainable use of ecosystems, genetic resources and species.

The generic idea behind statements like these is that international organizations and national governments do some good with a part of their portfolio on certain issues, but that the main body of the portfolio continues "business as usual," and if the usual practices are detrimental to the issue you want to change, the success of the portfolio will not bring about the aimed-for sustainable change. This idea is, of course, familiar in the discourse on development effectiveness: what one policy gives with one hand, another policy may take away with another hand. For example, agricultural development in the South has been supported by Northern donors, while, at the same time, Northern countries refused Southern agricultural products access to their markets, or distorted market prices through subsidies to Northern farmers. The question I am raising is whether evaluations pay attention to these issues. I raise the issue of the widening gap between global public costs and global public funding to argue that the evaluation community should report on such gaps. There are two ways we can do this. One is to fine tune the way we interpret the relevance criterion in evaluations. The second is the way we interpret and report on impact.

Fine-Tuning "Relevance"

Relevance is defined in the OECD/Development Assistance Committee (DAC) glossary of evaluation terms as: "The extent to which the objectives of a development intervention are consistent with beneficiaries' requirements, country needs, global priorities, and partners' and donors' policies." (OECD/DAC 2002, 6) This definition is clearly a retrospective *ex-ante* assessment. I have argued in the past that this is especially important in cases where, as evaluator, you want to check whether the decisions to fund or approve interventions were in line with the intentions of the donors or funders. This is especially important if a fund delegates the authority to approve projects, to a special committee or the CEO of the organization, for example, and later wants to review whether funding decisions were made according to its instructions. This follows from a strict interpretation of the definition.

Actual practice in development evaluation tends to look at relevance issues throughout the lifetime of the project, checking whether objectives continue to be in line with national policies and priorities, for example. We also sometimes see questions raised as to whether a project is "still relevant" given changed circumstances. This *ex-post* assessment of relevance is mentioned in a footnote of the OECD/DAC glossary definition.

I prefer a third practice that is not covered well in the glossary, which is to relate relevance to the question of whether the intervention made a difference, whether it actually contributed toward solving the problem it was meant to address. Efficiency and effectiveness are criteria that express relationships: the relationship between inputs and outputs in the case of efficiency; the relationship between outputs and outcomes in the case of effectiveness. Many evaluators use relevance as the third relationship: namely, between outcomes and impact. The accompanying question is: What difference did it make? (See figure 4.1.)

I know several evaluation offices that use relevance in this way and report on whether the intervention actually made a difference to the problem it was meant to solve. I would urge evaluators to adopt this practice. And when they do, they need to report on it—even if it would present a bleak picture. Evaluation reports should not spend a hundred pages on relevance, but they should have a few well-researched paragraphs, based on authoritative data available from other sources, on the relevance of the intervention or program to the ultimate impact to which it was meant to contribute.

Using the relevance judgment in this way ensures that we enable ourselves, as evaluators, to judge whether the intervention has contributed toward changing trends in society, the economy, and the environment. The question therefore becomes strongly related to the longer-term impact of

Figure 4.1   Evaluation Criteria

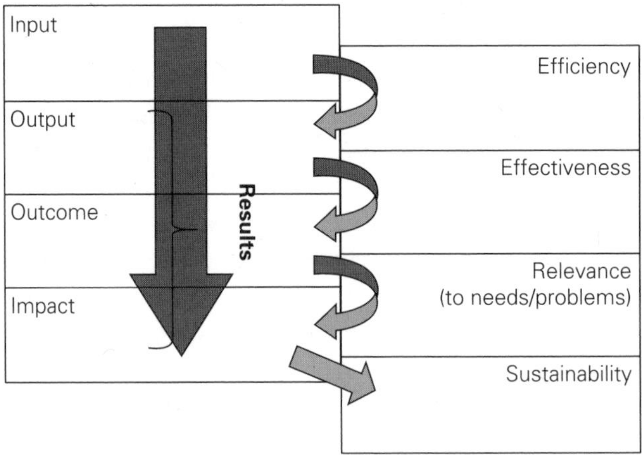

interventions and policies—which leads me to a short discussion of the term "impact" and how it is used nowadays.

Fine-Tuning "Impact"

The OECD/DAC glossary defines impacts as, "positive and negative, primary and secondary long-term effects produced by a development intervention, directly or indirectly, intended or unintended." (OECD/DAC 2002) Notice that it is not defined as a relationship, but as a final state, or a snapshot, of effects a long time after the termination of the intervention.

However, impact is now often used to denote something else: the causal relationship between actions in the intervention and changes in behavior. This relationship is evaluated in "impact evaluations," which seek to assess the changes brought about by an intervention (the impact) by comparing the observed result with a "counterfactual" (the result likely to have been observed without the intervention). If the counterfactual is carefully specified and empirically grounded, then the difference between results observed and the counterfactual can reasonably be attributed to the intervention itself, and not to extraneous factors. Ideally, this counterfactual should be built into the design of the project and observed during its implementation. We could refer to this kind of evaluation and what it studies as "direct impact."

The evaluation community has a history of undertaking ex-post "impact evaluations," which have a different nature. Rather than focusing on one or two of the causal mechanisms embedded in the intervention, these evaluations have focused on broad processes of change in which the intervention was one of many factors. These evaluations tend to focus on contribution analysis rather than counterfactual analysis and are ideally undertaken several years after the intervention has stopped to assess whether the processes of change that the intervention started have replicated, scaled up, or catalyzed trends in society, the economy, or the situation of the poor. If the contribution of the intervention can be demonstrated, these evaluations tend to provide crucial information on the relevance of the interventions (that is, did they really lead to longer-term processes of change or trends that are solving the problems). The focus of these evaluations could be referred to as "final or ultimate impact."

My proposal is to start making a clear distinction between "direct" and "final" impacts. Both practices bring us benefits, but the relevance of interventions for solving problems in society, the economy, and the environment needs to be found at the final or ultimate impact level. We need to be able to refer to "impact" at the highest level in our results chain because this conforms to ordinary usage of the term, for example, in public debates about whether "aid had any impact on Africa."

Following the Example of Cato the Elder

The role of evaluation should be to ensure accountability not only on what is achieved, but also on what these achievements mean in the long run. Long-term impact may be outside the scope of the organization we work for or the program or intervention we are evaluating, so we should be careful not to blame the organization or program. The Global Environment Facility has a solid level of achievements in its interventions. Nevertheless, in its *Fourth Overall Performance Study,* the GEF Evaluation Office reports that global environmental trends continue to go in the wrong direction (GEF Evaluation Office 2010a). This trend direction is not due to the GEF's achievements or lack of achievements—it is due to a lack of attention to environmental issues in many other sectors and to a lack of policy coherence. What is gained through environmental policies is not sufficient to compensate for the losses in other policies, like energy. But even more important, the GEF, a public institution, using public money, cannot address the level of market failure and global public costs associated with the way our economies function. These issues cannot be solved by governments and international institutions alone. Many influential thinkers, scientists, and concerned citizens speak out on these issues, but evaluators need to add their voice, based on evaluative evidence. By providing this evidence, we enable our institutions to raise these issues in the appropriate fora.

We know that the world will not change just because our evaluations point to the rise of global public costs. We may find ourselves in the position of the Roman Senator Cato the Elder, who became famous for ending each public statement with the phrase, "Furthermore, I think Carthage must be destroyed." His sentiment is not something we share; it is no longer civilized behavior between states to adopt an objective like that. But the intention of continuing to raise an issue because it has not yet been solved is something that evaluators and development practitioners should have the courage to follow.

Notes

1. Evaluation Cooperation Group, Special Session 1, "Crisis Response by MOBs: Preparedness and Response." March 16, 2011, Manila, the Philippines.
2. Evaluation Cooperation Group, Special Session 2, "GHG Implications of MOB Energy Assistance." March 16, 2011, Manila, the Philippines.
3. World Bank, World Development Indicators, http:ljdata.worldbank.org/ indicator/NY.GDP.MKTP.CD/countries?display=graph (accessed October 20, 2012).
4. Interview with Nicholas Stern in the *Guardian*, November 29, 2007. http:// guardian.co.uk.
5. International Development Association, "IDA Replenishments." World Bank website. http://www.worldbank.org/ida/ida-replenishments.html (accessed October 20, 2012).
6. OECD News Release "Development Aid Increases, but with Worrying Trends." April 6. 2011. http://www.oecd.org/document/29/0,3746, en_21571361_44315115_47519517_1_1_1_1,00.html.
7. For an overview of the discussion, see: http://en.wikipedia.org/wiki/ Stern_Review.
8. See "Persistent Organic Pollutants." Wikipedia. http://en.wikipedia.org/wiki/ Persistent_organic_pollutant and related articles.
9. See http:ljearthobservatory.nasa.gov/IOTD/view.php?id=38685 (accessed October 20, 2012).
10. For an overview of the many studies and conflicting claims on health effects, see http://en.wikipedia.org/wiki/Bisphenol (accessed October 20, 2012).
11. For an overview of impact reports and documents, see https://www.thegef.org/ gef/node/1560.
12. For an overview of country portfolio evaluation reports, see http://www.thegef .org/gef/node/787.

References

Barnosky, Anthony D. and others 2011. "Has the Earth's Sixth Mass Extinction already Arrived?" *Nature* 471: 51–57

Boyles, Justin G., and others. 2011. "Economic Importance of Bats in Agriculture." *Science* 332.

Collier, Paul. 2010. *The Plundered Planet: Why We Must—and How We Can—Manage Nature for Global Prosperity.* New York: Oxford University Press.

Diamond, Jared. 2005. *Collapse: How Societies Choose to Fail or Succeed.* New York: Penguin.

Evaluation Cooperation Group. 2010. "Ensuring Biodiversity in a Sustainable Future: Lessons from Evaluations." Presented to the Biodiversity Conference of the Parties in Nagoya, Japan, October 13, as briefing note UNEP/CBD/COP/10/INF/39. http://www.ecgnet.org/documents/biodiversity.

Galbraith, John Kenneth. 1973. *Economics and the Public Purpose.* Harmondsworth U.K.: Penguin edition 1975.

GEF Evaluation Office. 2010a. *The Fourth Overall Performance Study of the GEF.* Executive Version. Washington, DC: GEF Evaluation Office.

———.2010b. *GEF Impact Evaluation of the Phaseout of Ozone-Depleting Substances in Countries with Economies in Transition. Volume 1: Theory of Change.* Evaluation Report 56. Washington DC: GEF Evaluation Office.

Heckman, James J., and Sergio Urzua. 2009. "Comparing IV with Structural Models: What Simple IV Can and Cannot Identify." National Bureau of Economic Research Working Paper 14706, NBER, Cambridge, MA.

Moss, Todd, Sarah Jane Staats, and Julie Barmeier. 2011. "The ABCs of the General Capital Increase." Center for Global Development Brief. http://www.cgdev.org/files/1425485_file_IFI_Briefs_GCI_FINAL.pdf.

OECD/DAC (Organisation of Economic Co-operation and Development/Development Assistance Committee). 2002. *Glossary of Key Terms in Evaluation and Results Based Management.* Evaluation and Aid Effectiveness Series 6. Paris: OECD

Resource Futures International. 2001. *Persistent Organic Pollutants and the Stockholm Convention: A Resource Guide.* Prepared for the World Bank and CIDA. http://go.worldbank.org/KOJIG6N290 (accessed October 20, 2012).

Samuelson, Paul A. 1954. "The Pure Theory of Public Expenditure." *Review of Economics and Statistics* 36: 4,387–4,389

Stockholm Convention on Persistent Organic Pollutants. 2009. *Report of the Conference of the Parties of the Stockholm Convention on Persistent Organic Pollutants on the Work of Its Fourth Meeting.* May 8. UNEP/POPS/COP.4/38.

World Bank. 1998. *Assessing Aid: What Works, What Doesn't and Why.* New York: Oxford University Press.

CHAPTER 5

Innovative Approach to Evaluating Interventions in Fragile and Conflict-Affected States: The Case of Helmand Province

Samy Ahmar and Christine Kolbe

Introduction

"I can well understand those who feel less generous today given the state of our economy... but we will not balance the books on the backs of the poorest people on the planet."

It was in those terms that Andrew Mitchell, the U.K. Secretary of State for International Development, addressed the audience at last year's Conservative Party Conference to justify the pledge made by Prime Minister David Cameron during the general election campaign to preserve the budget for overseas aid in spite of Britain's abysmal deficit and the brutal cuts undergone by most other government departments. This decision, a politically difficult one in the current economic and social context, will enable the United Kingdom, by 2013, to join the handful of industrialized countries that meet their United Nations' obligation to spend a minimum of 0.7 percent of gross domestic product (GDP) on aid for development.

What this also implied, however, was that the Department for International Development (DFID), spared by the 2010 and 2011 budget cuts, would come under an increased level of scrutiny to demonstrate results and justify each pound of taxpayers' money spent overseas. It is for that very purpose, for instance, that a group of conservative, labor, and liberal-democrat members of Parliament set up the Independent Commission for Aid Impact, a watchdog organization dedicated to maximizing the effectiveness and impact of U.K. aid to developing countries, with a particular focus on value for money. This push toward results-based decision making had already been emphasized by DFID in a 2009 white paper, which stated that it would, "work to ensure every pound of U.K. aid is spent well" (DFID 2009). Recent developments indicate a reinforcement of this trend for the foreseeable future.

Although it has long been advocated that results-based monitoring and evaluation (M&E)—the most commonly used method for assessing the success of public policies in industrialized countries—should become the rule rather than the exception in the field of international development, it has proven difficult for donors to carry out or commission systematic and robust M&E programs. Alongside the lack of political will, to which the current economic conditions have contributed, the intrinsic challenges associated with setting up meaningful M&E systems in poor and unstable environments and the prohibitive cost of doing so have contributed to poor uptake and chronic lack of robustness in outcome and impact measurement.

This situation is rapidly changing. A combination of economic pressure and a flow of technical M&E expertise into the field of international development have made the prospect of setting up comprehensive, robust, and innovative M&E systems attractive for many donors and groups of donors wanting to show that they are making a difference to a skeptical and increasingly aware audience of taxpayers and auditors. This change is particularly true in conflict-affected environments, where entire economies and governance mechanisms need to be built from next to nothing, and where success in achieving economic, social, and institutional development is a prerequisite for stabilization and, ultimately, the departure of foreign troops.

Arguably, nowhere is pressure for results-based M&E as strong as it is in Afghanistan. Conversely, there are few environments where the challenge is greater.

Helmand province, Afghanistan, crystallizes this tension and exemplifies the value in establishing a robust monitoring and evaluation system. As the focal point of the United Kingdom's diplomatic, defense, and development efforts in Afghanistan, practitioners in Helmand are under ever-growing pressure to justify British presence and activity.

Scrutiny of progress in Helmand spans the general public and the media and extends up to Members of Parliament who expect to receive quarterly updates on progress there. Increasingly, the requirement is not just to report progress, but to demonstrate outcomes and effects. Doing so requires the implementation of an integrated evaluation system with established baselines and objectively verifiable indicators that can go further than counting outputs to provide an assessment of impact.

The establishment of such a system, particularly when linked to solid knowledge-management tools, enables practitioners to communicate information to multiple audiences quickly and effectively. For international donors engaged in Helmand, this system enables better management of reputational, political, and fiduciary risks, and supports the government's commitment to demonstrate value for money, impact, and facilitation of transparency.

In addition to the external value of M&E in Helmand, the more fundamental impact is arguably for practitioners. Development and stabilization efforts in Helmand are borne out of classic counterinsurgency doctrine in terms of the rationale for and nature of the interventions pursued, for example, the notion that improved service delivery by the government of Afghanistan will confer legitimacy on the government and lead the populace to reject the insurgency. Counterinsurgency doctrine is, to a large extent, based on assumptions about the impact of development on security. By interrogating assumptions inherent within programming, M&E enables those engaged in programmatic development at the grassroots level to better understand their contribution and impact on wider goals and to effect midcourse corrections to programming where necessary. In an environment where successful development initiatives are bound to national and international security, impact evaluation becomes inextricably linked to the protection of our national interest.

Challenges to Evaluation in the Helmand Context

Although results-based programming is fundamental to internal and external stakeholders in Helmand, it is also fraught with challenges. In Helmand, challenges are political, relating predominantly to the complexity of the international community's operating environment; logistical, associated with the challenges to evaluation in an insecure environment; and cultural, reflecting the difficulties in applying rigorous research methods in a traditional, Islamic society.

Institutional and Political Challenges

In Helmand, the weakness, nonexistence, or fractured nature of government systems present serious challenges to data collection and M&E. Data systems required for baselines have been weakened, destroyed, or discredited by association with the deposed regime leaving a dearth of baselines or time-series data and unclear responsibility for data collection spread across disparate agencies. The government of Afghanistan's statistical capacity has begun to recover, but there remains an all-round skills shortage.

Problems presented by the government's institutional weakness are compounded by the institutional complexity of the operating environment in Helmand. Because the international community is represented by a range of nations, agencies, and actors, there is a risk of operational activity being guided by multiple plans, differing timescales, and reporting up mutually exclusive chains of command. Without careful attention to coordinated planning, the coalition effort can result in a lack of synchronicity in the objectives and agendas of actors engaged in Helmand, which makes the establishment of a holistic and useful M&E program problematic.

The preeminence of political and military considerations means that contradictions can also exist within the programming of individual organizations. For example, stabilization interventions supporting counterinsurgency in Helmand—which have a shortened timeframe and more immediate objectives—are arguably designed around a different "endgame" than programs designed to realize the Millennium Development Goals of more traditional development projects. An example is the health and education initiatives in Helmand, which are not specifically designed around the actualization of Millennium Development Goals 2, 4, 5, and 6, but rather aimed at ensuring that the government has the capacity independently to control, employ, and maintain state institutions to provide governance to the population of Helmand.

Similarly, stabilization efforts in Helmand may not always be intended to have universal benefit. Rather, they may be focused on a particular group, for example, specific tribal leaders, or a small area, such as the Upper Sangin Valley, with this focus seeking to achieve a political end. There is a consequent need for spatial and target-group precision in evaluation efforts.

Finally, the scrutiny under which development activities take place in Helmand is one of the principal factors underscoring the need for a robust monitoring and evaluation framework. Conversely, this is also one of the factors that makes establishment of M&E more challenging. Afghanistan's profile as a British, U.S., and Danish foreign policy priority creates an inordinate pressure to deliver "good news stories." A robust, impartial, and objective M&E system is essential to ensure that assessment is nonpartisan and that an accurate and transparent portrayal of progress is made.

Logistical Challenges

Further challenges are presented to the implementation of an integrated evaluation process through the actualities of the operating environment and the constraints imposed by the security situation. The tensions between what it would be desirable to measure and what is achievable expose the delicate balance between adhering to best practices and accepting realities on the ground.

The reality in fragile states is that data is almost always patchy and of poor quality. This situation is extreme in a context like Helmand where a regime has been removed and 30 years of warfare has stunted governmental development. In such environments, there is likely to be a dearth of baseline data from which to begin measuring progress and a requirement to start from scratch, which poses additional pressures for the system.

The difficulty of embedding an M&E system in an environment considered to be naturally at odds to it is compounded by the wide range of staff expertise that is symptomatic of a multiagency mission. Helmund's Provincial Reconstruction Team, for example, represents military and civilian organizations that bring a range of skills to the campaign effort but that approach M&E with varying methodological perspectives.

Once the system has been designed, challenges are presented in delivery. Conventional evaluation techniques like household surveys designed to reach a representative sample of the population become fraught with challenges in Helmand where freedom of movement is significantly curtailed and association with the International Security Assistance Force (ISAF) puts enumerators' lives at risk.

The scale of the challenge and the perception that the populace is largely inaccessible to the international community can lead to a negativity about the feasibility of conducting research in Helmand, an associated skepticism regarding the reliability of results, and a subsequent reticence toward embracing a measurable approach. Given this backdrop, it is crucial to produce robust data that stands up to scrutiny. But again, the challenge is profound: the utility of the M&E system hinges on the credibility of the data it produces, yet the verification process is complex. Security constraints make it impossible to directly oversee field research while mistrust and fear among respondents mean they are often unwilling to provide contact details.

Once the system is embedded, attention must be given to its continuation. In fragile states, postings for international development workers are naturally shorter and the inevitable staff rotation creates difficulties in establishing institutional memory. In Helmand, civilian deployments are approximately 18 months and military tours are sometimes even shorter and can be unsynchronized with civilian associates. It becomes imperative that an evaluation system is linked to a robust knowledge management tool that can act as the institutional memory in the midst of considerable flux and that attention is given to the transfer of knowledge and capacity to local counterparts.

Events in capitals and shifting priorities challenge the continuation of monitoring systems in fragile states. By design, evaluation frameworks in fragile states must be adaptive, flexible, and capable of responding to the often-shifting strategic priorities that epitomize the environment.

Cultural Challenges

The third challenge to evaluation in Helmand is presented by the cultural differences between the host population and the international community. Afghanistan is a conservative Islamic society. Social interactions in Helmand are pervaded by the society's traditional mores, which have a profound impact on research. Although social desirability bias can be present in any opinion poll anywhere in the world, in societies such as Helmand, where individual rights can be constrained by culture and tradition and dominated by social hierarchies, social desirability bias is more likely to color opinions on contentious political, social, and security issues. Thus, questions on contentious issues can produce an abnormally high number of positive responses from some respondents, which raises concern about the use of statistics emanating from contentious questions.

The difficulties in reaching women in a conservative society pose a challenge to undertaking research in Helmand, as women's views may differ significantly from those of men, particularly with regards to themes such as the role of the Taliban as justice providers, the accessibility of public health centers, or education. The risk of collecting intrinsically skewed data is high, and finding ways to gather women's views becomes of critical importance for the establishment of a credible M&E system.

HMEP: A Cutting-Edge M&E Solution

The Helmand Monitoring and Evaluation Programme (HMEP), a project commissioned by DFID and the Provincial Reconstruction Team (PRT), designed in late 2009, seek to address these institutional, logistical, and cultural challenges through an innovative approach to M&E in fragile states.

Project Background and Overview

Since the British government entered Helmand in mid-2006, the tempo of activity has been such that it has been difficult to develop a comprehensive M&E framework. The nature of the environment prevented the establishment of the rigorous, best-practice approaches that the British government would employ in a more stable environment. One consequence is that while the United Kingdom could account for its spending in terms of inputs and had been able to measure outputs to some extent, there was little readily available evidence of the wider impact of its projects and programs in terms of outcomes and attitudes toward the insurgency. Hence the need for more rigorous monitoring of the effectiveness and impact of stabilization and development work in Helmand to improve the responsiveness of all stabilization and development actors to local needs, and to increase the visibility and influence of benefits.

The goal of HMEP is to improve the delivery and effectiveness of the contributions of Helmand's stabilization and development programs to the Afghan National Development Strategy (ANDS) and the Helmand Plan. This goal is achieved through supporting the PRT to make more effective use of M&E tools. HMEP has four key outputs:

- Baselines for the PRT program strands and DFID programs in Helmand against which to monitor effectiveness and impact, focused on indicators chosen by the PRT and DFID
- An operational, up-to-date, user-friendly database and geographic information system (GIS) database covering DFID, the PRT, and Task Force Helmand, Task Force Leatherneck, and other donor activities in Helmand
- New knowledge and recommendations from quarterly monitoring and up to four ad hoc reactive reports per year aligned with the PRT and DFID reporting requirements
- Improved programming capacity in the PRT that standardizes approaches and affords consistency in reporting across the PRT.

Data Collection

Political, logistical, cultural, and financial challenges associated with collecting data in conflict-affected environments have historically constituted the main challenge in setting up comprehensive, cross-cutting M&E systems where they are most needed. After an extensive phase of desk research, which examined the secondary information and data available in Helmand, it became apparent that discrete primary data collection would be required to build on existing measures and support the PRT to more comprehensively measure its effect.

Taking the Helmand Plan as the strategic starting point, the HMEP team worked with the PRT to design individual logical frameworks that established the conceptual journey from the intervention's rationale to the programs' outcomes and impacts. As part of this process, a series of indicators were developed to measure progress in each of the thematic strands (governance, rule of law, infrastructure, agriculture, counternarcotics, health, education, growth and livelihoods, and population engagement) at the outcome and impact levels. Recognizing that reporting was largely subjective and anecdotal at the output level, attention was given to developing quantitative, SMART indicators (specific, measurable, achievable, relevant, and time-bound) to measure impact. Given the considerable data collection constraints, particular weighting was given to attainability.

The dearth of readily available secondary data as well as the absence of existing baselines made primary data collection and analysis necessary as a means to populate indicators. A combination of statistically robust, Afghan-led, quantitative, and informative qualitative data collection was carried out, complemented by primary and secondary data collected from third-party sources. This section of the chapter focuses on the first and the second research methods.

Primary data collection efforts in Afghanistan have suffered from numerous, well-documented problems.[1] HMEP's data collection methodology takes into account the lessons learned from existing primary research[2] so as to address the limitations of primary research in Helmand and to avoid duplication of effort. The HMEP approach to data collection is characterized by a carefully designed sampling strategy implemented by an Afghan research partner that involved robust sample sizes at provincial and district levels, a longitudinal approach, and a combined quantitative and qualitative method.

A Carefully Designed Sampling Strategy

HMEP took the 2004 census data and the Central Statistics Organization's (CSO) raw data on settlements (as per the 2004 administrative district boundaries) as its sampling universe. These data presented several difficulties for HMEP, as is common to environments where the reach of formal government is limited and data-collection systems are weak.

First, as administrative reorganization emanating from the Afghan Ministry of Interior occurred, district boundaries changed over time. These changes necessitated an update to the assignment of settlements to districts using the latest Afghan Geodesy and Cartography Head Office (AGCHO) boundary dataset. Second, the location of CSO settlements contained spatial coordinate errors. HMEP was able to correct these errors by mapping coordinates to village locations taken from spatial imagery. Finally, the population per settlement in the CSO data did not always reflect what could be seen on the ground through spatial imagery of Helmand Province. HMEP addressed this difficulty with a thorough spatial analysis and according adjustment to the number of inhabitants per settlement.

For reasons that were both statistical (for example, the views of people living under a same roof risk being similar as a consequence of one person's influence in the household) and cultural (for example, barriers to engagement with women), the decision was made to target only male heads of households (HOHs) through the household survey. To estimate the number of households in each district, a multiplier of 10 people per household was assumed in the sampling framework's design. This assumption held true as per the data gleaned during the first quarterly survey, which enabled HMEP to validate this assumption for the following waves. The unavailability of the CSO's household listing and the lack of other statistically robust datasets for Helmand province meant that the sample's statistical representativeness could not be tested using demographic, cultural, social, and economic characteristics. Therefore, profiling results from different waves of the same HOH survey were compared with one another to refine HMEP's understanding of the profile of Helmand's HOH. Once a series of quarterly surveys has been carried out, a regional profile of the HOH will be established, and results of the following surveys weighted by a number of key profiling variables (for example, age, tribe, income, occupation) to maximize the statistical representativeness of the HMEP survey. A multi-staged random probability sampling process[3] was used with a random route for selecting households in each sampling point.

The HOH survey is being implemented by an Afghan survey partner, which enables extensive reach within Helmand. Enumerators rely on local networks and facilitators to establish access to remote areas in Helmand and to provide insights into population groups that are inaccessible to the PRT. Although security constraints do impact the sample and the feasibility of implementing standard verification techniques, a research method implemented by local partners provides reach into Taliban-controlled areas and ensures a more representative sample is surveyed.

Robust Sample Sizes at Provincial and District Levels

To give a high level of confidence at the district level of disaggregation, over 4,000 HOHs are interviewed regularly across 11 Helmand districts, achieving a +/–5 confidence interval at the district level and a +/–1.5 confidence interval at the overall Helmand province level, each at the 95 percent confidence level (two-tailed) (table 5.1). The former is the industry standard and the latter constitutes a particularly rare level of statistical robustness in any field, including election polls in Europe or North America.

The HMEP HOH survey immediately became the largest survey ever carried out in Helmand, with nearly 4 percent of all HOHs living in Helmand interviewed every quarter. This unique magnitude at the provincial level, as well as the large number of profiling questions exploring household economy, access to facilities, and demographics, led the HMEP HOH survey to be widely considered as one of the primary statistical data sources in the Afghan international community. The HMEP HOH survey improves on the robustness and accuracy of other Helmand surveys and generates data to complement the national census as a tool to inform decision making in

Table 5.1   Sampling Framework Summary

District	Estimated number of residents	Percentage of province population	Estimated number of households per district	Target number of interviews	Confidence interval at the 95% confidence level
Lashkar Gah	87,062	7	8,706	368	+/– 5
Nahri Saraj Musa Qala	176,851	15	17,685	376	+/– 5
	129,427	11	12,943	373	+/– 5
NawZad	87 012	7	8 701	368	+/– 5
NadAii	103,082	9	10,308	373	+/– 5
Nawa-1-Barak Zavi	85,440	7	8,544	368	+/– 5
Garmser	99,172	8	9,917	370	+/– 5
SanQin	60,324	5	6,032	361	+/– 5
ReQ (Khanshin)	16,175	1	1,618	311	+/– 5
Nad Ali (Marjah)	108,662	9	10,866	371	+/– 5
Kajaki	113,228	9	11,323	372	+/– 5
TOTAL	1,066,610	88	106,661	4,011	+/– 1.5

Source: Coffey International Development report to DFID.

Development Evaluation in Times of Turbulence

Helmand. The national CSOs are also trying to identify how they can update the population estimates in lieu of a census this year.

Longitudinal Approach Provides Confidence in Time-Series Analysis

To enable HMEP to monitor dozens of outcome and impact indicators and hundreds of variables and combinations of variables over time, it was essential to ensure a consistent sampling-point selection method and continuity in the questionnaire rolled out each quarter. Building a panel proved impossible in Helmand because of the security issues associated with keeping interviewees' contact details and physical addresses, and because of the potential respondent fatigue that a quarterly survey could create. However, a range of statistical techniques, such as repeated cross-sections, enabled the development of pseudo panels to partially address this gap. Lanjouw and others (2011) explored the potential of using repeated cross-sections to investigate movements in and out of poverty. Potentially, a similar method could be employed in Helmand to consider movements in and out of satisfaction with the Afghan government, the police, or statutory justice mechanisms. Such methods will be explored as a way to overcome the impossibility of developing a genuine panel to carry out time-series modeling.

Combined Quantitative and Qualitative Research

The quantitative research revealed a number of interesting trends, some of which seemed counterintuitive or lacked geographical consistency, and warranted further analysis to investigate the causalities at play. Qualitative research was designed and carried out to complement the quantitative findings and to enable the program to fully unpack the observed trends in perceptions. It proved to be a crucial tool in assessing the broader picture of progress made against the Helmand Plan.

Because the quantitative HOH survey in Helmand excluded women, qualitative research was designed to capture their perceptions. The views of Helmandi women on quality of service provision as well as on the effectiveness of different governance structures and justice mechanisms are likely to differ significantly from those of men. In a traditional culture with strictly defined gender roles, females' perceptions and needs are likely to be gendered and research methods must be adapted to ensure they are captured.

Qualitative research also helped to unpack interesting trends resulting from the quantitative research, for example, exploring why only a fraction of respondents would consider going to Afghan National Police (ANP) if they were the victim of a crime despite the fact that the vast majority expressed trust in the ANP as an institution capable of resolving disputes fairly and efficiently. Qualitative research identified that, for example, a preference for family-based dispute resolution and perceptions of ANP approachability helped explain why ANP might be considered effective and yet underused.

Qualitative research was carried out specifically to better understand the data, that is, to reach those who could not be reached by a quantitative survey, as well as to provide a more in-depth understanding of the "story" and causal factors behind some of the less straightforward trends in perceptions observed through the quantitative survey. The survey results had to be appropriately analyzed before planning the qualitative research process and tools.

Qualitative research was designed to concentrate on perceptions of change in attitudes about the various aspects of "government," such as behavior and services, and to provide a means of exploring exactly what HOHs think is wrong, what should be done differently, and whether they have noticed changes in the recent past. The research took the form of a combination of semistructured, in-depth interviews and focus groups or kin group interviews with randomly selected HOHs and women. Twenty interviewing sessions were carried out in each district of interest, bringing the total interviewees to several hundred. Although not statistically representative, the qualitative research proved a crucial complement to the larger HOH survey in testing the theory of change and understanding some observed geographical differences.

Analytical Thinking and Theory of Change

The logical framework, which maps the conceptual journey of a specific stabilization and development intervention from its rationale through its inputs, activities, outputs, outcomes, and impacts, is the basic analytical tool through which an intervention is evaluated and against which its progress is measured over the project's lifetime. However, as explained earlier, this approach was complicated by the multiplicity of donors. Although committed to one plan, donor effort tends to be split by thematic area, which can reduce the visibility of cross-functional effects. For example, if donor A builds a school, but donor B builds the road leading to that school while donor C ensures security along the road, the success of A's program directly depends on the effectiveness and timeliness of B and C in running their respective projects. In the past, each donor reporting system has tended to be inward looking with little overarching analysis or reporting across interventions. In environments where progress in security, governance, and international development are mutually dependent, reporting within silos inevitably restricts ability to assess the relative effectiveness of programs at the outcome and impact levels.

The Helmand Plan's overarching objective was for the population of Helmand to progressively reject the Taliban as an alternative system of governance. The plan's underlying theory is that enduring security and stability will be possible in Helmand only if the state is able to demonstrate an adequate level of responsiveness to the needs of its citizens, fundamental to establishing its legitimacy, and thereby providing a more attractive alternative to either the insurgency or ongoing instability. This theory is inspired by and reflective of a widely accepted model of counterinsurgency.

Recognizing the complexity of people's perceptions of their government's legitimacy in a context of fractured government systems and the long-term absence of a formal state, HMEP's research approach was designed to provide details on the numerous factors influencing perceptions and how these causal factors were related to one another. Figure 5.1 shows a simplified example of the causal logic used as a basis for conceptualizing the journey from a range of infrastructure interventions in Helmand to improved

Figure 5.1 Example of Theory of Change Analytical Framework: Infrastructure

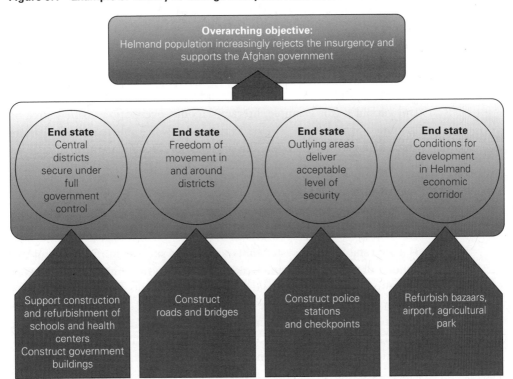

Source: Coffey International Development report to DFID.

perceptions of the Afghan government in the province. In addition to the conventional, vertical flow from inputs to impact, a horizontal dimension was introduced: this dimension reflects the basic principle according to which if X (for example, freedom of movements) and Y (for example, security along the roads) are both positively correlated with Z (for example, government legitimacy), then they should also be positively correlated to one another. A failing link between freedom of movement in and around districts and security along the roads could seriously undermine the plan's capacity to foster improved legitimacy of the Afghan government.

Diverse statistical techniques were used to measure progress indicators and to test the HMEP theory of change. They included simple bivariate cross-tabulations, multivariate cross-tabulations, and bivariate correlation analysis, as well as multivariate probit regression modeling. The latter was used to examine further some of the key relationships among legitimacy and state capability, accountability, and responsiveness that emerged from the early-stage, cross-tabulation analysis.

All variables were transformed into dummy (binary) variables, taking either the value 1 or 0. For instance, those who agreed that the district government had improved education services were given the value 1; the others were given the value 0. From then on, the team ran a series of linear, probit regressions, taking one key perception variable (for example, satisfaction with the Afghan government's education services) as the dependent variable, one or two key explanatory variables (for example, the availability of primary and secondary schools), and a range of control variables (for example, literacy, income, occupation, main source of income, assets owned). The resulting models were able to isolate relationships between, for example, the presence of a secondary school for boys nearby, and the likelihood of satisfaction with Afghan government education services, other things being equal.

Presentational Features

Having established a system able to test the success of the plan and the validity of counterinsurgency theory (COIN) assumptions, attention was given to the presentation and dissemination of this information. Recognizing that regardless of the richness of the data, M&E is only valuable if it is used, the HMEP team designed a website and database to store and display information. The website contains a range of innovative presentational features, including links to a GIS database supporting the visualization of progress of information. This tool effectively facilitates transparency regarding the PRT's effectiveness in making progress against the Helmand Plan.

Online Database

The HMEP Database schema design is based on the logical framework approach. Like the Aid Information Management System Development Assistance Database (AIMS-DAD), which was developed in cooperation with the United Nations Development Programme (UNDP) as a means to promote the transparency and accountability of overseas aid in a range of developing countries, the HMEP Database is an information repository displaying extractable graphics, GIS maps, reports, and documents relevant to stabilization and development in Helmand. The website is linked to an interrogable Oracle database and interactive geospatial database, which enables users to build their own GIS products.

Whereas AIMS-DAD focuses on the "input" aspect of overseas aid by collating financial and program information exclusively, the HMEP Database schema design is based on the logical framework approach. It is a repository of existing baseline data and updated quarterly data on selected outcome and impact indicators for thematic strands combined with collated contextual data. The website contains a library of relevant literature, as well as the quarterly, annual, and analytical HMEP reports.

A functional web interface allows users to extract and visualize the logical framework and associated indicator data. Graphs are generated in real time and display a timeline, showing whether indicators are progressing in the desired direction.

GIS Mapping

The HMEP database also serves as a repository of spatial data used in GIS analysis and map production. The HMEP website displays products generated by the team and links to an interactive geospatial database that enables users to develop custom-made GIS products.

The development of GIS products also attempts to resolve some of the problems created by the siloed working habits described earlier. GIS mapping enables users to visualize geographically the linkages and correlations among variables and illustrates in an accessible, user-friendly fashion the mutual dependence of the different strands of reconstruction, stabilization, and capacity-building efforts. For instance, by overlaying areas of intense poppy cultivation with recorded security incidents and the presence of schools and hospitals, stakeholders are able to instantaneously visualize to what extent these variables overlap with each other, and how their work is potentially impacted by, or impacting upon, the work of others.

Intelligent Use of Information

In a diverse and strategically complex organization like the Helmand PRT, HMEP supports more intelligent use of information in assessments, planning, and daily operations.

The HMEP evidence base is used to look back on a quarterly and annual basis on progress toward strategic goals. The HMEP team provides materials and leads quarterly workshops, which provide a forum to consider results and discuss policy implications. HMEP tools are also used to look forward in terms of planning and future strategic direction. For example, HMEP is supporting the development of the current Helmand Plan by developing a GIS map that uses various datasets to build a geospatial picture of the extent of the Afghan government's influence in Helmand. This product aims to provide an estimate of current reach, juxtaposed with a projection of future influence, thus providing PRT with a visual representation of its objectives. Finally, HMEP supports PRT's daily operations through improved information management in the collation and centralization of relevant data and its storage in a centralized and accessible information management system.

Conclusions: Future Prospects for M&E in Fragile States

HMEP's specificity lies in its holistic approach to implementing an M&E system in a part of the world where it is crucially needed but difficult to achieve. In demonstrating that stabilization, peace-building, and economic development efforts made by donors in Helmand are more than a sum of individual projects, HMEP overcomes a critical barrier to meaningful M&E in fragile states. Its focus on statistical robustness and comparable time series on a wide range of indicators and variables also makes HMEP unique in a conflict-affected environment.

Before assessing the replicability of the HMEP model, it is essential to understand what made it possible in the first place. The breadth of skills and areas of subject-matter expertise (for example, M&E, governance, peace-building, statistical modeling, database development, GIS mapping) as well as a sound contextual and cultural understanding of Helmand province and of the different forces at work in the province and the wider region, were a prerequisite for setting up a credible and sustainable M&E system.

Arguably the most important factor of success is the very presence of a PRT, which brings together all institutional donors and creates a single mission through which funds are delivered and invested, thereby creating a common sense of purpose. Such a structure facilitated the establishment of a comprehensive, cross-thematic M&E system. Afghanistan's 27 PRTs combine some of the world's leading defense, diplomacy, and development experts. As development and reconstruction efforts in conflict-affected states are mutually dependent, a holistic approach to M&E is crucial. It is particularly valuable in environments with substantial donor spending where entire systems of formal governance need to be built from next to nothing, and increasingly feasible where institutions like the PRTs are capable of pooling donors' resources to ensure progress against a joint plan.

It is important to recognize that each province, region, and country contains its own, specific set of contextual issues and challenges that must be reflected in the evaluation approach. Although HMEP does not purport to offer a magic formula, it does provide a model for the development of future M&E systems in conflict-affected states and, perhaps most significantly, it has demonstrated that implementing robust, meaningful, and sustainable M&E systems is possible even in the most difficult environments.

As we look to the future for Helmand and the increasing focus on building Afghan capacity for successful transition, the next challenge for HMEP will be to establish local ownership of a monitoring and evaluation system. As HMEP supports the measurement of the PRT's effectiveness in working to build capacity across thematic areas, so HMEP must work with local counterparts and in conjunction with national programs to transfer knowledge and ensure the sustainability of this fundamental approach.

Notes

1. Examples of documented problems include: Downes-Martin 2010; Cordesman 2010; Baker and others 2010.
2. See The Asia Foundation 2010; ABC News 2010; and U,S. Agency for International Development Office of Military Affairs, "The Tactical Conflict Assessment Framework (TCAF)." http://usacac.army.mil/cac2/call/docs/11-02/ch_2.asp, by way of example.

3. Probability sampling is where a sample has been selected using random selection so that each unit in the population has a known chance of being selected. It is generally assumed that a representative sample is more likely to be the outcome when this method is employed. The aim of probability sampling is to keep sampling error to a minimum. Sampling error is the difference between a sample and the population from which it is selected.

References

ABC News, "Afghanistan Poll: Where Things Stand 2010." http://abcnews.go.com/Politics/Afghanistan/afghanistan-poll-things-stand-2010/story?id=12277743.

Baker, T., R. Orlina, S. Pagano, M. Salwen, and R. Williams. 2010. "Methodological Considerations and the Use of Data from Afghanistan: A Review of the Utility of SIGACTS, TCAF, KLE and Polling Data for Population-Centric Assessment." Coffey International Development, Washington, DC.

Cordesman, A. H. 2010. *The Afghan War: Metrics, Narratives, and Winning the War.* Washington, DC: Center for Strategic and International Studies.

DFID (Department for International Development). 2009. *Eliminating World Poverty: Building Our Common Future.* London: DFID.

Downes-Martin, S. 2010. "Assessments Process for RC (SW)." May 24, 2010, technical report draft, Center for Irregular Warfare and Armed Groups, U.S. Naval War College, Newport, RI.

Lanjouw, Peter, Jill Luoto, and David McKenzie. 2011. "Using Repeated Cross-Sections to Explore Movements in and Out of Poverty." World Bank Policy Research Working Paper, World Bank, Washington, DC.

The Asia Foundation. 2010. *Afghanistan in 2010: A Survey of the Afghan People.* http://asiafoundation.org/country/afghanistan/2010-poll.php.

CHAPTER 6

Resource Crunch, Evaluations, and Mindset

Case Studies

Rashmi Agrawal

The Value of Existing Data

Two types of existing data can be used for evaluation purposes: socioeconomic and other documented data collected independently from the project under evaluation and data collected as a part of the project, including data on various parameters used for monitoring, inspection, and other periodic reports, past evaluations, and so on.

This chapter elaborates on the importance of devising an appropriate monitoring system with focus on evaluation at a later date and on the greater use of existing data to devise evaluations that are less costly but meet their goals. It offers cases from India showing examples of how the proper use of existing data and better monitoring can lead to optimum cost-effective evaluation results.

Turbulence and Evaluations

The world is passing through extremely turbulent times caused by economic and financial factors in the developed West and their impact around the globe, by social and political happenings unfolding in Middle Eastern and Northern African countries, and by natural calamities such as the recent tsunami in Japan. The threat of nuclear disaster, always a threat to the very existence of humanity, has again showed its ugly face in the wake of the tsumami. Above all, the impending disastrous impact of climate change, particularly on food security, looms over the world. Unfortunately, such turbulence is not a one-off phenomenon but rather confronts humanity with sickening regularity. What makes development evaluation in such turbulent times different from the normal evaluation process is a natural concern for the community of evaluators and is the main theme of the 2011 International Development Evaluation Association (IDEAS) global assembly.

A turbulent situation impacts evaluation in various ways. Such situations force governments to initiate desperate measures to tackle the immediate crisis, diverting substantial resources from the normal development process. Whereas a resource crunch is persistent in developing countries, the developed world has now witnessed the impact of an economic downturn in terms of recession and large-scale job losses. A difficult situation in the developed world may squeeze the flows of aid to developing countries. Thus, evaluation of development interventions must be more stringent so that each unit of money can be spent carefully. Short-term measures to deal with difficult situations must be judged regarding their efficacy. Therefore, a turbulent situation makes purposeful evaluations more necessary than in normal times as the resources available for development programs become scarce and what is available will have to be used in the most optimum manner. It is also true that in such a situation, evaluation results find greater acceptance because any means to improve program performance and reduce costs are welcome to program planners and implementers. As observed by Morra Imas (2009), "If there was ever a time when decision makers would gladly embrace evaluation, it would seem to be in the turbulent aftermath of the Global Economic Crisis of 2008. Even as we stand well in 2010, the effects stretch on."

Impact on Evaluation Practice

A judicious choice of practical evaluations can optimize the resources available. The body of theoretical knowledge accumulated and practiced over the years and the methods of evaluation available are not affected by turbulent events, but it is necessary to review the need for elaborate evaluations and choose a practical methodology that passes muster in a situation with severe resource constraints. The question arises as to how to reconcile the increased demand for evaluations of developmental interventions with the resource crunch. Resources are often a constraint in evaluations and it is not always possible for the evaluator to have unlimited access to them to design a technically perfect evaluation. This constraint seriously limits the freedom of the evaluator in designing evaluations.

A major component of evaluation costs relates to collection of quantitative and qualitative data. Evaluators across the world and especially in developing countries tend to conduct evaluations on the basis of data collected through a primary survey. This method may be justified on some occasions because baseline data is not available or is inadequate. It is also possible that the evaluators are unaware of the availability of baseline data or do not have access to it. Sometimes, they feel that available data is not reliable or is outdated and it would be more appropriate to go for a special survey. In countries where a large area has to be covered by field surveys, the cost is very high in terms of time, money, and human resources. Because of low literacy in most developing countries, survey data must be collected in person rather than by mail, which accelerates the cost of data collection manyfold. Various scholars have offered practical methods to reduce data-collection costs under resource constraints. For instance, Bamberger and others (2006) advocates simplifying evaluation designs, reducing sample sizes, adopting economical data collection methods, and so on.

This chapter argues that to optimize resource use in evaluations, the evaluator should squeeze the maximum value out of information about project performance already available in various forms and from various sources before embarking on primary data collection. It discusses the strengths and weaknesses of existing data, presents case studies where use of available data was beneficial, and recommends a strong monitoring system that could be helpful for later evaluations.

Types of Available Data

Available data, also called secondary data, is data that has not been collected by the evaluator for a particular evaluation but is available from various other sources. Available data of use to evaluators can be classified into two major categories: socioeconomic data and project-monitoring data.

Socioeconomic Data

National socioeconomic data are collected independently of any specific project under evaluation. They include data collected through regular or ad-hoc censuses, large-scale sample surveys conducted from time to time, and other data generated as a by-product of administrative operations of various wings of government. Most countries have these sources of data, which are accessible from national and international information networks. Evaluators would do well to scan such data and cull the relevant information for a specific intervention evaluation. Comparisons of the situations before and after a development intervention can provide some clue to what is happening or has happened. This sort of macro-information will be particularly useful in evaluating policies, though there could be problems of separating the influence of factors other than the intervention being evaluated.

Project-Monitoring Data

Every program or project collects data relating to itself as a part of project formulation and implementation. These data include program management documents, such as project proposals, terms of reference, project implementation guidelines, periodic progress reports, and data on parameters such as input and output indicators. Project management personnel who undertake missions to the project sites to review progress and identify problems, indicate findings in their reports, which can be useful for evaluation purposes at a later date. Ongoing national-scale development interventions often have built-in provisions for concurrent or periodic evaluations. Sometimes several micro-evaluations are carried out by different agencies independently in different parts of the country or covering certain aspects of the program before an overarching national-level evaluation is commissioned. The past reports and data from these evaluations can be useful.

Quality of Available Data

Availability of bits of data is one thing, but their suitability for use in the evaluation purposes is quite another. It can be challenging for the evaluator to cull out the data that can be useful for his or her evaluation. The existing information itself needs to be evaluated for quality as well as relevancy.

In general, available data may be scrutinized on three basic parameters: its reliability, its collection methodology, and the objectives for its collection. *Reliability* refers to the trustworthiness of the data source, the timeliness

Table 6.1   Three Parameters by Which to Scrutinize Data

Reliability	Methodology	Objectives
• trustworthiness	• sampling	• content
• credibility	• response rate	• source: original
• time lag	• quality	• comparability
• accuracy	• replicability	• generalization

of the data, and the extent of sampling and nonsampling errors involved. Data collected through "statistical returns" on various projects may not be reliable in terms of accuracy or trustworthiness. It has been observed that such statistical data at times are manipulated. *Methodology* refers to aspects such as the sampling method, the concepts and definitions used, and the process of data collection. For example, in examining past evaluations of a program, it is necessary to analyze the appropriateness of the methodology, the representativeness of the sample, the response rate, and whether any generalizations are possible. The *objectives for the data collection* need to be compatible with the evaluator's purpose. For example, if the original objective of the data collection was to find out the number of beneficiaries of a program intervention in a small village, the data may not be sufficient for comparability or generalization in a larger context (table 6.1).

Case Studies

In India, development interventions are made by governments as well as by other organizations such as industries and nongovernmental organizations. Generally, monitoring is a part of all such interventions and is restricted to input and output activities. Lately, emphasis is being given to evaluation of every project and its impact, but budget allocations for the purpose are usually limited. In spite of resource constraints, evaluators tend to collect primary data without first examining the usefulness of existing data. Such data are considered only at the time of preparation of the final report. The following case studies indicate how use of the existing data may or may not lead to significant benefits.

Case 1. Skill Gap Analysis (Ex-Ante Evaluation)

A study (IAMR 2006a) was undertaken in economically and socially backward areas of the country to analyze the gaps in skills among employable youth in relation to local demand in order to initiate development interventions. The study also assessed the status of training institutions in terms of courses offered, demand for those courses, facilities available, and placements. The study was sponsored by a central government ministry. Because of a paucity of time and funds, the approach adopted for the study was to organize focus group discussions involving all stakeholders including establishments, experts, training institutions, villagers, employers, students, and unemployed youth, to assess the situation. Focus groups were conducted in 50 districts of the country. Three days in each district was available for field work. Besides organizing focus groups, the evaluators collected district-specific available data related to the number of training institutions, employers, types of training available, details of the trained youth, and data on other demographic indicators. Reports were prepared for each district separately.

However, the officials who initially approved the terms of reference for the evaluation were transferred and the new incumbents did not accept the final reports because they did not include information collected through structured questionnaires and field surveys. They said no action was possible based on the conclusions and recommendations made on the basis of focus groups and secondary data.

Case 2. Employment Generation Program (Impact Evaluation)

The Government of India has long been implementing a program to provide financial and technical assistance to educated unemployed youth from low-income families to start a microenterprise. The scheme was implemented across the country. It was evaluated three times by the same organization. (IAMR 2000, 2002, 2006b). The evaluations were intended to assess the impact of the program in terms of the number of microenterprises created, their survival rates, the increase in incomes of the beneficiaries, employment generation, and the impact of the program on quality of life. In each evaluation, large-scale surveys had to be organized because existing information was either not relevant or inadequate.

Even though some information on the overall extent of self-employment among educated youth at different points of time can be gleaned from socio-economic surveys by the National Sample Survey Organization, any changes in the patterns over time cannot be attributed only to the program in question. The scale of the program is too small to have any discernible impact at the national level. Although detailed implementation guidelines indicated which records were to be maintained, the requirements were so onerous that implementers were not able to follow them. Although a monitoring system was proposed in the program, it was limited to obtaining information on the amount of loans disbursed by financial institutions and the number of unemployed youth who received the loans. Even this data was not maintained uniformly by each implementing unit. Thus, a proper monitoring system was not in place and even the baseline data was unavailable. A number of agencies and organizations were involved in the implementation of the program without adequate networking and synergies.

In the light of the lack of monitoring data, primary data had to be collected from all stakeholders and even the baseline data was prepared. All the surveys were conducted in person using structured questionnaires, which took more than a year with a substantial budget and human resources.

Case 3. Teacher Recruitment (Concurrent Evaluation)

An evaluation of a program to recruit teachers was done in one state (IAMR 2009). Its objectives were to assess whether the implementers of the program clearly and consistently understood the guidelines for the procedures to be adopted for recruitment, to assess the efficacy of the training provided to the implementers, to evaluate the effectiveness of the teacher recruitment process, and to assess the extent to which the guidelines issued were followed. The evaluation was in the nature of a concurrent evaluation. The approach was to examine the guidelines to evaluate the recruitment process for its transparency, effectiveness, and outcomes.

The methodology consisted of studying the data from official records, discussions with focus groups, and observations by the survey teams. The teams also assessed the guidelines and the maintenance of records at various stages. Whenever the study team reported any lacunae or other problems, the authorities took immediate remedial action. For example, when it was reported that training on the guidelines for recruitment was not effective, immediate arrangements were made for retraining wherever needed. The study team took up a few cases for a sample study to verify the available information. Thus, the evaluation was conducted using secondary data and was completed in just three months, which was cost effective in terms of money and human resources.

Discussion and Lessons Learned

In general, every evaluation uses some secondary data at some point. It could be at the stage of project formulation and evaluation design, or at the time of data collection and analysis, or at the stage of report preparation. However, the extent of utilization of such data varies. The utility of secondary data also depends on the type of evaluation as well as on the evaluation managers' knowledge of evaluation methods, techniques, and strategies.

In the first case, ex-ante evaluation, the original commissioners of the evaluation were aware of the design modifications and agreed on a strategy involving focus groups and secondary data because time was short. However, their replacements, who had a mindset that all evaluations need primary surveys through structured schedules, rejected the evaluations. This case points out the need for capacity building and knowledge dissemination among stakeholders in general and among commissioners and managers of evaluations in particular.

The second case study indicates the need for a comprehensive and effective monitoring system so that the project data can be used for evaluation purposes. The study also shows the importance of implementable guidelines that are properly understood by all.

The third study is an example of the adequate use of secondary data that could be possible with proper guidelines, maintenance of records, and an appropriate monitoring system.

Ex-ante and concurrent evaluations can be made more cost effective by using secondary data in situations where good baseline data are available and a comprehensive monitoring system is in place. In other types of evaluations, especially those measuring the impact of a program, there is a need for primary data collection. Even in those cases, the expenditure on such studies can be reduced if secondary data are analyzed as a first step before a primary survey is conducted. Further, the monitoring system of a project, which usually includes only input and output indicators, should also have outcome and impact indicators. In such a scenario, secondary data from the monitoring system would be an extremely useful tool in the hands of evaluators. It is also important to change the mindsets of evaluation commissioners and managers, as well as professional evaluators themselves, to appreciate that collecting primary data is not the only means for all evaluations.

Summing Up

To reduce the amount of time and resources spent on a project evaluation, consider the following recommendations that make appropriate use of available data:

• Review the large body of data already available from various sources on various parameters relevant to the development intervention to identify relevant and usable data. Identify gaps for follow up.
• Decide how the available data can be used for evaluation purposes.

- Develop skills and capacity to cull out relevant, reliable, and usable information.
- Organize sample studies only to verify the quality of the existing data and to fill gaps.
- Disseminate knowledge to stakeholders about various procedures and techniques for evaluations.
- Help change mindsets about the usefulness of primary and secondary data for evaluations.
- Develop a comprehensive monitoring system, which includes not only input and output indicators, but also outcome and impact indicators. Information from such a system would enable quick evaluation at a future time.

References

Bamberger, M., J. Rugh, L. Mabry. 2006. *Real World Evaluations: Working under Budget, Time, Data and Political Constraints*. New Delhi: Sage Publications.

IAMR (Institute of Applied Manpower Research). 2000. "Report on Evaluation of Prime Minister's Rozgar Yojana (PMRY) 1994–95." IAMR, New Delhi.

———. 2002. "Prime Minister's Rozgar Yojana (PMRY): An Evaluation (Second Round)." IAMR, New Delhi.

———. 2006a. "Reports on Skill Gaps in Backward Districts of India." 50 separate reports, IAMR, New Delhi.

———. 2006b. "Report on Evaluation of Prime Minister's Rozgar Yojana (PMRY): Third Round." IAMR, New Delhi.

———. 2009. "Report on Recruitment of Teachers in Bihar (Second Phase, 2008) Evaluation." IAMR, New Delhi.

Morra Imas, L. 2009. "Embracing Evaluation in Tough Economic Times." Keynote Speech to the Ontario Chapter of the Canadian Evaluation Society, Toronto, October 1, 2009.

PART TWO: TURBULENT TIMES, PRODUCTIVITY, AND RISKS

CHAPTER 7

The Impact of the Food, Fuel, and Financial Crisis on Children's Education

Findings from a Monitoring System in Nepal

Jeevan Raj Lohani, Purnima Gurung, and Laxman Bashyal

Background

All countries in South Asia have been adversely affected by the 3F (food, fuel, and financial) crisis. The recent crises in food prices, fuel prices, and the global slowdown precipitated by the international financial crisis affects households in Nepal through a multitude of channels. Nepal is especially vulnerable to this crisis because it is emerging from a decade of conflict and low growth; it is a low-income, food- and fuel-deficient country, and it is highly dependent on imports.

The United Nations Children's Fund's (UNICEF's) Nepal Country Office, Research Inputs and Development Action (RIDA) of Kathmandu, and the Government of Nepal's Department of Education have been monitoring the impact of the 3F crisis on children's education since June 2009. The monitoring system enables them to determine whether and how the crisis is affecting children's education by looking at indicators such as school enrollment, attendance, dropout rates, learning achievement, and child labor. It also highlights groups of children who are especially vulnerable in terms of geographic and socioeconomic characteristics.

The monitoring system consists of three components: (1) household-level monitoring, (2) school-level monitoring, and (3) community-level monitoring. Household-level monitoring was based on a quarterly vulnerability assessment and monitoring (VAM) survey of 800–1,200 households carried out by the World Food Programme (WFP). The school-level monitoring was carried out in 22 schools in 11 districts[1] that are likely to suffer from food insecurity, loss of migration opportunities, and a drop in exports—thus likely to be most affected by the 3F crisis. They were selected from all three ecological belts and five development regions. Out of the 11 districts, six schools from three districts were monitored intensively. Community-level monitoring comprised focus group discussions (FGDs) with three groups: mothers, teachers, and children (members of child clubs). In one quarter, FGDs were conducted with six groups from two schools.

The monitoring mechanism was operated during April 2009 to December 2011. However, this chapter is based on findings from seven quarters between April 2009 and December 2010, including three quarters in 2009 and four quarters in 2010.

Overall Scenario of the Crisis

The 3F crisis began with an increase in the price of crude oil, which rose to its highest level in 20 years and triggered increases in the price of staple foods by 150 percent in just four months from January to May 2008 (ESCAP 2009). Food prices often depend on the price of agricultural inputs and transportation. Food prices have dropped since their peak in mid-2008, but they are expected to remain firm over the medium term (ESCAP 2009). As crude oil prices dropped, triggering a decrease in food prices to an extent, the financial crisis, initially limited to Western countries, developed into a global crisis. Almost all developed and developing countries are now suffering from the global economic crisis (World Bank 2009). This section reviews the food crisis in terms of food shortages and rises in food prices, and their impact on hunger because these characteristics are similar at the global and national levels.

Nepal has experienced food, fuel, and financial crises in various forms for many years, but the current global 3F crisis could exacerbate the already difficult situation in many parts of the country. Nepal can be considered vulnerable to all three crises in view of several factors, including the following:

- Increasing dependency on imported fuel
- High dependency on agriculture (32.4 percent of national gross domestic product [GDP] is from agriculture)
- Decreasing agricultural productivity and worsening hunger status in some districts[2]
- High dependency on remittances (17 percent of national GDP is from remittances) and the decreasing availability of foreign employment[3]
- Weak fiscal capacity and structural constraints (World Bank 2009).

According to an economic report by the Nepal Rastra Bank (NRB 2009a), inflation remained high in 2011. When the market forced consumers to bear a 13 percent rise in food prices in 2007–08, prices of nonfood items had risen by only 9 percent. A year later, food prices jumped at an even higher rate of 19 percent. Food price inflation remained high at 11.3 percent in mid-June 2010, whereas nonfood inflation stood at 7.3 percent during the same period.[4]

The WFP regularly conducts studies on the food status of Nepal. Recent surveys show a remarkable increase in food prices. Market Watch Nepal (WFP 2009) mentions that the price of masuro (lentils) increased by 50 percent, soybean oil by 32 percent, and rice by 25 percent over the 18 months ending in May 2009. The greatest monthly price increase was observed for potatoes (up 28 percent). Thus, the 80–85 percent of households in Nepal that are net consumers of these agricultural products have been experiencing rapid food price increases.

According to a UNICEF study (2009a), there were 6.7 million hungry people[5] in 1970, 7.7 million in 1990, 4.1 million in 2001–03, and 4.2 million in 2004–06. Levels of hunger have intensified significantly since the beginning of the 3F crisis. The number of hungry people increased to 8.5 million in 2007–08 (figure 7.1). The total number of people at risk of hunger rose by 50 percent (from 6 million to over 9 million) in just six months in 2008. The out-migration trend to Middle Eastern countries is decreasing and the hunger trend is steeper than that of South Asia. Fuel prices, which were decreasing until the middle of 2009, have again begun to increase.

The growth rate of the world economy, which was 5.2 percent in 2007, dropped to 3.2 percent in 2008 and was expected to turn negative by 1.3 percent in 2009 (MOF 2009). Nepal's GDP growth rate is likely to register 3.8 percent at basic prices and 4.7 percent at producer prices in

Figure 7.1 Hunger and Out-Migration Trend

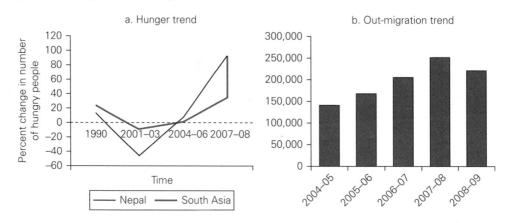

a. Hunger trend

b. Out-migration trend

the current fiscal year, based on revised estimates. This number is well below GDP growth of 5.2 percent in 2008 calculated at producer prices, and is reduced despite the reported increase in internal revenue. The GDP growth rate has declined because of various factors such as the energy crisis, unfavorable weather, a decline in capital expenditures, a disturbed industrial sector, the absence of elected local representatives, and the global economic crisis (MOF 2009). It is noteworthy that education received 17 percent of government expenditures during fiscal year (FY) 2010–11.

The number of people leaving Nepal for foreign employment is decreasing. Nepal is highly dependent on remittances: approximately 17 percent of its GDP is from remittances. Because the global financial crisis has diminished the demand for labor in many major markets, the number of Nepalese workers going overseas dropped by 12.8 percent during 2008–09 compared with a year earlier.[6] According to the Department for Foreign Employment (DOFE), the number of workers going to Malaysia and the United Arab Emirates decreased by 30.62 percent and 30.11 percent, respectively, compared with the previous year. Qatar, occupying 35 percent of total foreign labor, also observed a decline of 10.84 percent in Nepalese arrivals.[7] The growth rate in the number of people migrating to foreign countries for employment has decreased from +21.80 percent to –12.80 percent. According to the Nepal Association of Foreign Employment Agencies, overseas employers have reduced new labor demand in response to existing manpower requirements.[8]

The fuel crisis has contributed to a rise in price indices for food and nonfood items because of increased transportation expenses. Fluctuations

Development Evaluation in Times of Turbulence

Figure 7.2 Trends in Fuel Prices, 2003–10

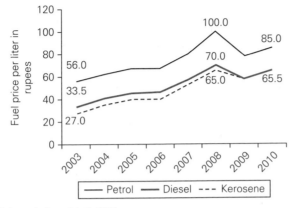

Source: The Kathmandu Post, July 7, 2010.

in the international petroleum price have affected the Nepalese price situation (MOF 2009). Increases in transportation costs have been linked largely to rapid fuel price increases in the first half of 2008. Transportation expenses were a major cost driver of food prices throughout the year (WFP 2008a). Although fuel prices have come down slowly, transporters have not reduced the cost of transport fares in line with fuel price decreases because of the syndicate system used by transport associations (WFP 2008a). In December 2008, the price of petroleum products was about 10 percent higher (NPR 80.5 per liter for petrol and NPR 59 per liter for diesel) than for the same period in 2007, while international oil prices had fallen by 125 percent over the same period (WFP 2008a). The price of petroleum products increased continuously over the years (figure 7.2). The annual growth rate in the price of kerosene (13 percent) was the highest, with the price of kerosene increasing to NPR 65.50 per liter in 2010 from NPR 27 per liter in 2003. The price of petrol increased by 6 percent (NPR 56 per liter in 2003 to NPR 85 per liter in 2010) and the price of diesel increased by 10 percent (NPR 65.50 in 2010 from NPR 33.50 in 2003).[9]

Key Study Findings

After seven quarters of monitoring, the impact of the food, fuel, and financial crisis was clearly observed on students' attendance, their involvement in child labor, the educational expenses of households, and ultimately on student learning. The crisis has affected children's education through the

Figure 7.3 Pathways for Coping with the 3F Crisis Lead to Lower School Attendance

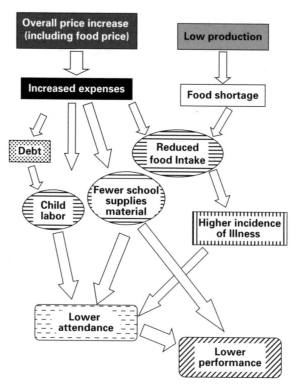

coping mechanisms that households took to deal with the crisis. Parents have allowed their children to attend school irregularly, involved them in paid work, reduced the amount spent on education, shifted children to cheaper schools, and even taken them out of school to work full time.

Figure 7.3 shows some of the pathways through which increased household costs caused by the 3F crisis have led to lower student attendance at school. This chapter explores these pathways, or coping mechanisms, and their impact on student performance.

Impact on Student Attendance

The monitoring of attendance and learning achievement of children over the past 17 months found that student attendance (65 percent on average) and the average examination scores (33 percent on average) are below standards. These conditions are due to various factors, mainly the inability of parents to purchase such items as notebooks, pencils, pens, and clothing; hunger; household workload; student involvement in paid work; and household dependence on expensive fuels such as kerosene. Children in about 15 percent of the households attended school irregularly, and children in about 2 percent of the households were removed from school to cope with the crisis.

After four quarters of monitoring, there were clear indications that the crisis (especially the increases in the prices of food and fuel) affected student attendance through: (1) an increase in child labor, (2) an increasing household work burden for children, (3) hunger, (4) a decrease in money spent on educational expenses (especially purchasing notebooks, pencils, and school clothing), and (5) migration outside the home for earnings.

Student attendance fluctuates by quarters and seasons. The average student attendance for the academic year 2009–10 was 67 percent with a huge standard deviation of 36 units. The average attendance rate increased from 65 percent in the second quarter of 2009 to 68 percent in the third quarter of 2009, then decreased to 66 percent in the fourth quarter of 2009 and rose to 69 percent in the first quarter of 2010 (see figure 7.4). Student attendance is lower in planting season (second quarter) and harvesting season (fourth quarter) because a large number of households in Nepal depend on subsistence agriculture.[10]

In the second and fourth quarters of 2009, a majority (29 percent and 30 percent respectively) of student absences were due to household work. The number of students absent due to hunger increased from 1 percent in the second quarter of 2009 to 4.4 percent in first quarter of 2010 (table 7.1).

Figure 7.4   Trends in Student Attendance Rate by Quarters

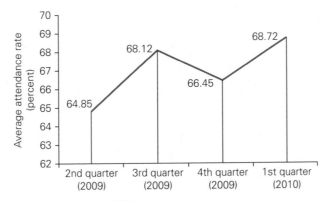

Source: School-level monitoring data, 2010.

The Impact of the Food, Fuel, and Financial Crisis on Children's Education

Table 7.1 Reasons for Student Absences by Quarters, 2009–10

	Reason for absence (percent of absent students)				
Quarter	Sick	Household work	Paid work	Hunger	No school supplies
Second quarter 2009	26.2	29.2	3.9	1.0	10.7
Third quarter 2009	21.0	25.6	8.7	1.6	13.2
Fourth quarter 2009	25.8	29.7	9.7	3.6	9.6
First quarter 2010	29.4	23.3	6.0	4.4	7.2

Source: School-level monitoring data, 2009 and 2010.

Community-level monitoring showed similar data. The months with higher school attendance were Falgun (February–March) and Chaitra (March–April), whereas lower attendance was reported in Baishakh, Jestha, and Mangisir (June, July, and December, respectively).[11] School-level monitoring found that the attendance rate was highest (78 percent) for Chaitra (March–April) and lowest (59 percent) for Ashwin (September–October).

The levels of attendance as well as barriers to attendance differ by districts, geographic regions, the caste of students, the gender of students, and whether schools are urban or rural. A summary of average student attendance by different categories is shown in figure 7.5.

Average attendance for girls was higher than that for boys. Three major reasons for boys to be absent throughout the year were sickness (26 percent), household work; (25 percent) and not being able to bring along school supplies (10 percent), whereas for girls the reasons were household work (27 percent), sickness (25 percent), and not being able to bring along school supplies (10 percent). Girls are kept from school more often than boys for household work and sickness of family members.

Students Work at Home and for Pay
The 3F crisis has affected school attendance through two routes. In districts like Dadeldhura, Panchthar, Saptari, Achham, and Tanahun, which have paid work opportunities, parents are increasing their work load, which has led to an increased need to keep children home from school to do household work. In the low plains adjacent to India, known as the Terai region, parents send their children to do paid work; thus, they attend school irregularly.[12]

In almost all districts, household work (50 percent in Kapilvastu), sickness (44 percent in Panchthar), inability to bring along school supplies

Development Evaluation in Times of Turbulence

Figure 7.5 Student Attendance Rate

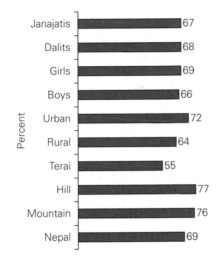

Source: School-level monitoring data.

Note: Janajatis represents certain ethnic groups of Nepal.

(19 percent in Jumla), and paid work (20 percent in Saptari) have been the four major reasons for student absences. Community-level monitoring in Humla and Kapilvastu found that hunger was one of the key reasons for students to attend school irregularly.[13]

Some Cannot Afford School Supplies

A major reason behind the absences was that some students were not able to afford school supplies (up to 21 percent in the third quarter of 2009). Parents reported that the increase in food prices made it difficult for them to purchase the necessary supplies including notebooks, pencils, and school attire. Scholarships are not usually used to purchase school supplies. Moreover, the scholarship amount (about US$5 per year per student) is inadequate compared with the opportunity cost of attending school (children in the 10–14 age group get about US$2–3 per day for paid work).

Hunger Keeps Some Students Away

Hunger was reported to be one of the major reasons for absences, accounting for 13 percent of the absences in the third quarter of 2009. The importance of food for children in rural Nepal can also be observed in the fact that, on average, 15 percent of parents sent their children to school to benefit from meals offered there. The government has been implementing school feeding programs in selected food-deficient districts, but its implementation differs by districts and schools. In the Humla district, schools provided children with money to buy food on their own. In the Jumla district, schools used the money to buy different types of food for different days, which resulted in differences in student attendance. In many districts, the rationale behind selection of specific schools was not clear—schools in great need of such programs are not getting them. In the Rolpa district, a school feeding program was implemented in primary schools but not in secondary schools, which included children from relatively poor economic backgrounds.

Impact of Irregular Attendance on Learning

The data indicate increasing incidences of irregular school attendance, child labor, and dropout rates. Reduced student attendance, increased child labor, and reduced funds available for educational expenses were found to have an impact on student learning.

Average student learning achievement (average marks) based on school reporting was 33 percent, almost equal for boys and girls; a grade of 32 percent is required to pass. However, the learning achievement differed according to several categories (see table 7.2). The learning achievement for Dalits (26.18 percent) was well below that of other castes such as Brahmins, Chhetris, Muslims, and Newars (36.14 percent).[14]

Table 7.2   Average Learning Achievements

Category	Learning achievement (percent)
Gender	
Boys	32.89
Girls	32.71
Caste	
Dalits	26.18
Other (Brahmin, Chhtetri, Newar, Muslims, etc.)	36.14
Janajatis[a]	34.16
Location	
Urban	35
Rural	31
Total average	33

Source: School-level monitoring data, April 2009–June 2010.

Note: a. Janajatis represents certain ethnic groups of Nepal.

The crisis is affecting student's learning through reduced attendance. School-level monitoring found that student learning is directly affected by student attendance. When student attendance decreased by 10 percent, the learning achievement (average marks) decreased by about 11 percent.[15]

As expected, the main reason for student failure observed in school-level monitoring was student attendance (45 percent) followed by inability to purchase necessary learning materials (18 percent) and other reasons (27 percent), like limited time to study at home, lack of interest, lack of parental support, and dropping out before examinations. Other minor reasons included more involvement in household work, involvement in paid work, and sickness.

The reasons for students failing their examinations differed by caste and region. Fifteen percent of Dalits failed because of not having sufficient learning materials, whereas only 2 percent of other castes failed for this reason. The average grades of Janajatis were also affected by their higher involvement in paid work. Of Dalit students, 7.5 percent failed examinations because of their involvement in paid work, whereas 2 percent of Janajatis and none of the other households failed for this reason. The major reasons noted during focus groups with teachers and students were similar to the school-level monitoring results.

The main barriers noted in all the community-level monitoring in 20 schools conducted in the past five quarters were irregular attendance, limited time for study, and unavailability of necessary learning materials (such as notebooks, pencils, and reference books). Other reasons included limited time spent on lessons in preparation for examinations,[16] household environment,[17] ineffective examination system,[18] lack of nutritious food,[19] heavy household workload, poor teaching methods, low parental awareness, and lack of student interest in school work.[20] Learning was also reported to have been affected by language barriers (difference in students' mother tongue and the teaching language).[21] In districts with paid work opportunities, parents were increasing their workloads to manage household expenses in the context of increasing prices. In the process, the household work burden for children, such as responsibilities for looking after cattle or siblings, increased and they were able to give less time to their studies.[22] Because of household work, some students did not manage to complete their homework.[23]

Over the last quarters of monitoring, the impact on students' learning due to reduction in education expenses was also reported. Mothers in the Humla district have started to reduce the number of notebooks they provide to their children. Teachers in the Jumla district reported that three brothers from the same family had started to share a single set of notebooks.[24]

A systematic mechanism to monitor the learning achievement level of children and the reasons behind their weak performance was lacking in almost all schools visited for community-level monitoring. Parents are mostly unaware of their children's learning levels.[25] A few schools have realized the need to enhance student learning levels and have made efforts such as monthly tests,[26] and child-friendly classrooms.[27]

Incidences of Child Labor

A comparatively mild but detrimental coping mechanism is the increasing involvement of children in household work. Where there is the opportunity, parents are increasing their paid workload to increase household income. Thus, the household work level of children has been increased, resulting in reduced school attendance and decreased learning hours at home. Where increased prices are putting pressure on families, involvement in child labor has become one of the preferred coping strategies for poor households. Incidences of child labor (paid as well as nonpaid) were observed in all the communities visited during the monitoring period. Various pathways led to involvement of children in child labor due to the impact of the 3F crisis under the overall context of household poverty.

Mothers in all communities included in community-level monitoring reported that they involve their children in household work. Household chores performed by children include cleaning dishes, fetching water, collecting fodder for cattle, and so on. The incidences of children's involvement in paid as well as nonpaid labor were also found in household-level monitoring. During the third quarter of 2010, of the households with students who attended school irregularly, 63 percent (69 percent in the third quarter of 2009) involved their children in nonpaid household work while 29 percent (22 percent in the third quarter of 2009) sent their children to do paid work.

Payment for Child Labor
All school-aged children perform chores to support their parents in household and agricultural activities. The average age at which children start being involved in paid work is 9–10 years old.[28]

Children get around NPR 100–NPR 250 per day. The payment differs by gender and age: girls get less (NPR 100 per day) than boys (NPR 150 per day).[29] Children of 15–16 years of age are intensively involved in paid work, and receive payment almost equal to adults. Most children involved in paid work do part-time work such as working during school holidays, missing school for one or two days, or working in the mornings or evenings.

However, there are also incidences of children being involved in full-time labor to help their households meet basic expenses. Some children from the outskirt villages of Birgunj are employed full time in local markets and earn about NPR 2,000-2,500 per month.[30]

Where do students spend the money they earn? In many cases, children give their earnings to their parents to meet household expenses, which include food and other daily consumables.[31] However, some children use the money to buy school supplies like notebooks, pencils, and school attire, and to meet other personal and recreational needs. There are different findings on the use of earnings from paid child labor. Mothers in Parsa mentioned that children use their money for personal consumption.

Factors That Determine Child Labor

A logit regression model based on household-level monitoring indicates that households using kerosene, households facing food shortages, poor households, households with a head who has a low education level, and larger households are likely to send their children to paid work and reduce their attendance at school.[32] The incidence of household work was reported to be higher in households with many children and in households depending on foreign employment.[33] In households with more family members, children have no option other than involving themselves in paid work to earn money for school supplies and other consumables that their parents cannot afford.[34]

Children involve themselves in paid work if their family is in great need of financial assistance or if they cannot otherwise afford school supplies.[35] There are increasing incidences of children's involvement in paid work due to increasing availability of work opportunities in urban areas.[36] Paid work is available even in agricultural areas since there is a shortage of agricultural labor due to out-migration. During the agricultural season, a few students take part in agricultural paid work and do not attend school.[37] The tendency to send children for paid work depends on the education level of the parents.[38] In communities with increased parental awareness and higher attention to school attendance, the incidences of child labor during school hours has decreased.[39]

Impact of Child Labor

Child labor has a direct impact on student absences, and ultimately on dropout rates.[40] Children who are intensively involved in paid work to feed their family have higher chances of dropping out of school if they get steady work.[41] The increased involvement of children in household work has also influenced student's attendance and learning to a large extent.

Student Dropout Rate

Taking children out of school is the most detrimental household coping measure. Initial coping practices, such as reduced student attendance, decreased learning achievement, and involvement in child labor are suspected to lead to students dropping out of school.

Few incidences of dropout were observed in the districts and schools monitored in 2009 and 2010. Quarterly household-level monitoring recorded that school dropout implicated only 1–3 percent of households throughout the monitored quarters: only about 52 dropout incidences were observed in six schools from three districts during this time.

Reasons for Dropping Out
Causes for student dropout can be categorized as immediate, primary, and secondary, because some factors have a direct impact whereas others gradually erode children's education. Figure 7.6 shows that immediate causes for dropout include failing examinations, out-migration for income, especially to India,[42] not being able to pay fees and purchase school supplies, the psychological pressure of becoming an overage student,[43] and involvement in full-time paid labor for a long period.[44] These immediate causes force students to abandon school quickly: teachers claim that lower attendance and examination failures forced 6 to 10 students to drop out of school in the four schools monitored in Dolakha and Parsa.[45]

Key primary causes for student dropout include the student being overage, having irregular attendance due to the reasons discussed previously, and decreased learning, possibly due to reduced study time. These primary causes can lead to the immediate causes for dropping out described above. Child labor can also act as a primary cause for dropout if working children began to attend school irregularly and fail examinations.[46] These primary causes are cyclical: irregular attendance can lead to failure in examinations, repetition of classes, and becoming an overage student. Learning ability, which is possibly linked to nutritional factors in households[47] and other personal factors, can also limit interest in studies and lead to examination failure: the school-level monitoring found that about 91 percent of students who dropped out had lower or mediocre learning abilities.

Community-level monitoring data indicates that various secondary causes lead to primary and immediate causes for dropout. Secondary causes include substantial household work, inadequate scholarship provision (relative to opportunity costs), low household income, and income deprivation. Children are also dropping out because households are unable to meet educational costs.[48] The socioeconomic condition of households

Figure 7.6   Incidences of Student Dropout

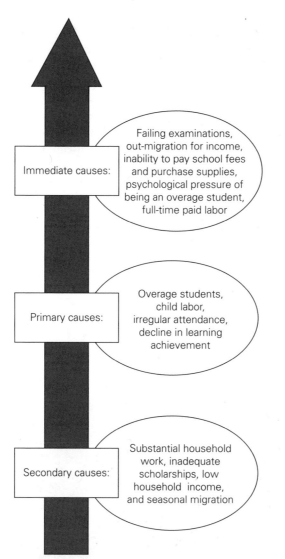

Immediate causes:
Failing examinations, out-migration for income, inability to pay school fees and purchase supplies, psychological pressure of being an overage student, full-time paid labor

Primary causes:
Overage students, child labor, irregular attendance, decline in learning achievement

Secondary causes:
Substantial household work, inadequate scholarships, low household income, and seasonal migration

was identified as a secondary cause: some dropout cases resulted from the decreasing ability of households to cope with rising school costs along with escalating food prices.[49] Children drop out of school to earn money to feed their family, look after siblings, or work in other homes.[50] Many children have also left school to migrate to the Middle East. Teachers in Bogatigaun,

Achham district, reported a dropout case triggered by aggregated economic hardship. A top eighth-grade student dropped out of school to search for work in India because his grandmother could no longer afford to cover living expenses and his education.

One of the key reasons for student dropout in Mugu and Bajura district schools is seasonal migration: students migrate with their parents from one place to another throughout an academic year, according to the change in seasons. This seasonal migration causes long absences, examination failures, and eventually, dropout.[51] Similarly, the migration of children and their families to India during the academic terms has led to student dropout.[52] The school-level monitoring data confirms community-level monitoring findings. School data revealed that children's involvement in paid work is a major reason for dropout, followed by scarce family income, household work, and out-migration (see figure 7.7). Teachers in Shiva Panchayan School, Damauli, reported that the incidences of dropout had increased in recent years due to children's increasing involvement in paid work. Parents require this involvement to support their families.[53]

Figure 7.7 Reasons for Student Dropout

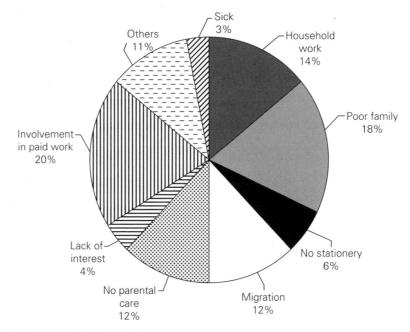

Source: School-level monitoring data.

Boys and girls drop out for different reasons. Boys are more likely to leave school to cope with the increasing economic pressure of households,[54] whereas girls are more likely to drop out of school to marry early.[55]

Factors Linked to Dropout

Detailed analysis points to three clusters of factors that drive students out of school: individual, school-related, and household-related factors. The combination of these three factors forces children into a critical zone where they are most likely to forsake school (figure 7.8). These three factors operate within a broader socioeconomic environment influenced by external factors such as rising food prices, loss of employment, availability of paid-work opportunities, and so on.

Individual factors include age, gender, position in the family, learning ability, circle of friends, opportunity costs, and involvement in paid work. Household-related factors include family size, number of siblings, economic conditions, source of household income, dependence on a particular family member's wages, food sufficiency, family reliance on children to undertake household work, and education and food expenses. School-related factors include service delivery aspects (which are linked to the country's overall education system), availability and accessibility of schools, teaching-learning processes, children's motivation to attend school, physical facilities, teacher regularity, provision of

Figure 7.8   Critical Zone of Dropout

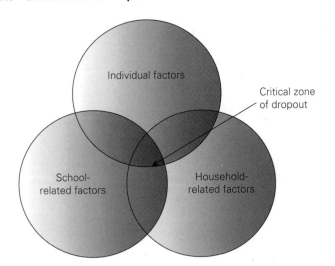

scholarships and school supplies, and homework and class workload. The unavailability of secondary schools and the inability of many to meet secondary education costs (living costs, school supplies, and so on) have forced dropouts in the Himalayan region. All of the eighth-grade students consulted during the community-level monitoring in Murma-gaun, Mugu district, reported that they will not be able to enroll in ninth grade next year if the class is not held in their current school.[56] Girls are even less likely to migrate to the district headquarters for second-ary education because of concerns for their security, early marriage, and socioeconomic barriers.[57] Small children also drop out of school due to their parents' inability to finance their education.[58]

Government scholarships are expected to support parents, but they are very small and do not cover the opportunity cost of having a student forego paid work to stay in school. A child's average daily income ranges from NPR 100 to NPR 200, whereas annual government scholarships normally range from NPR 350 to NPR 500.[59] Scholarships are provided on an ad-hoc basis to Dalits[60] and girls, regardless of family income, which results in some students who are not poor obtaining scholarships.

Characteristics of Dropout Cases
Children with poor learning abilities are dropping out of school. For instance, most of the children who dropped out this year had weak academic achievement according to teachers in various schools. Dalit children were more likely to drop out than children from other castes: more than half (51 percent) of the dropout cases reported were Dalit children. Moreover, over three quarters (76 percent) of the cases involved overage children. The proportion of boys dropping out (53 percent) was slightly higher than for girls (47 percent). It is interesting to note that all the households in which children abandoned school during the last quarter of 2010 were in the poorest category.

Overall Impact

The monitoring mechanism has produced five quarterly reports. In all quarters, the impact of the food, fuel, and financial crisis can be observed on student attendance, their involvement in child labor, the increased burden of educational expenses on households, and, ultimately, on student learning. The overall impact of the crisis on school attendance has remained stable compared with last year. Figure 7.9 shows changes in four coping mechanisms between the third quarters of 2009 and 2010. It shows

Development Evaluation in Times of Turbulence

Figure 7.9   Trends in Education-Related Coping Mechanisms, 2009–10

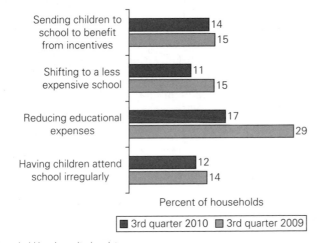

Source: Household-level monitoring data.

that in 2010 about the same proportion of families were sending their children to school to take advantage of incentives such as feeding programs, fewer families were shifting students to less expensive schools, fewer were reducing the amount of money spent on education, and slightly fewer were making their children attend school irregularly. The findings indicate that the overall impact of the crisis has remained more or less stable in 2009 and 2010.

The impacts were found dispersed throughout the country. Districts in the midsection of the country and the far west, along with a few districts in eastern region, were found to engage in a higher degree of education-related coping mechanisms compared with districts in the central and western regions.[61]

The studies found that not all households are affected by the crisis. Households that were more likely to use coping mechanisms included: poor households; large households (large family size, more children below age 12); households from districts in the Karnali region,[62] households using kerosene as a source of light; households depending on daily wages; Dalit households; and households with an illiterate household head. The vulnerability of these groups also matched their likely poor socioeconomic conditions. Their vulnerability has been worsened by the fact that there is insufficient targeting of scholarship programs: children from poor households are not getting scholarships while relatively richer ones are getting them.

Findings and Suggested Responses

Some of the findings reflect the challenging situation for the education sector and require adequate response from the government. These findings have been discussed in a steering committee formed in Nepal's Department of Education, involving senior government officials, researchers, and UNICEF officials for planning and implementation. The Department of Education can try to reduce the impact of the 3F crisis on children's education by suitable responses. The findings and proposed responses are presented below.

Finding 1. Many students lack necessary school supplies. There is a need for clear provision to distribute school supplies to children from disadvantaged communities through the schools.

Suggested Responses: Because parents clearly mentioned that the provision of textbooks has helped their children to continue their studies, there is a need for a learning materials package. The package needs to be brought under government financing by making detailed cost calculations. Education stakeholders must also understand that parents' inability to purchase learning materials is a key problem.

Finding 2. The percentage of children missing school because of hunger increased over the study period.

Suggested Responses: Advocacy and awareness is needed about school feeding programs at the district and school levels to implement the programs in line with their original objectives. There is a need for uniformity maintained through clear guidelines. Government needs to consider school-based midday meal programs more seriously and try to expand or institutionalize them. Resource pooling at local and community levels, depending on local context, can also be an option. This requires awareness activities targeting School Management Committees, Parent-Teacher Associations, teachers, and parents. Various nutrition-related programs implemented through government and donor channels need to be linked with schools at the local level. The government can synchronize the child nutrition programs through intergovernmental and donor sharing. Providing one meal a day to primary-level students could reduce the impact of the food crisis on children's education.

Finding 3. Government school scholarships do not cover the full cost of attending school, nor the opportunity costs of missing school for paid work.

Suggested Responses: The government should improve the targeting of scholarships and incentive programs to make sure they benefit the neediest students. Targeting Dalit households seem fair. However, there is still a need to strengthen the targeting mechanism to benefit needy children. The Education Management Information System (EMIS) can be revised to collect the statistics based on disaggregation suggested by the vulnerability profile.

Finding 4. Irregular attendance at school can lead to student performance failure and dropping out of school.

Suggested Responses: (1) Increase scholarship amounts to cover a substantial proportion of the opportunity cost for students to attend school. (2) Raise awareness among parents and students about long-term benefits of education. Awareness activities at the school level will also be useful. In a school of Sanfebagar, Achham district, counseling students on the advantages of remaining in school helped reduce irregular attendance. (3) Raise child protection on the advocacy agenda and make forceful child labor a punishable offense. (4) Establish a system to track student performance, promotion status, and dropout status.

Finding 5. Collection of reliable data helps identify problems and form responsible solutions.

Suggested Responses: The government should continue to play a key role in the monitoring process and analysis through the monitoring section at the Department of Education and District Education Offices (DEO) involved in data collection, and by providing educational data through the EMIS. The involvement of the government is expected to facilitate the institutionalization of the monitoring system and increase its sustainability and governmental acceptance of recommendations drawn from the system's findings.

Notes

1. The 11 districts are Humla, Tanahun, Achham, Mugu, Bajura, Jumla, Dadeldhura, Kapilvastu, Parsa, Saptari, and Panchthar.
2. The number of hungry people in Nepal reached 8.5 million in 2007–08 from 4.1 million in 2001–03, according to UNICEF (2009).
3. A decrease of 12.8 percent in 2008 compared with 2007, according to *Republica National Daily*, July 22, 2009.
4. *Republica National Daily*, July 29, 2010.
5. *Hunger* refers to those consuming less than the minimum recommended energy intake. In South Asia, this minimum averages 2,100 calories per day per person.
6. *Republica National Daily*, July 22, 2009. *The Kathmandu Post*, June 17, 2009, compiled by the Department of Foreign Employment, reported that the number of Nepalese migrant workers leaving for foreign destinations during the first 11 months of the current fiscal year decreased by 10.07 percent.

7. *Republica National Daily*, July 22, 2009.

8. *Republica National Daily*, July 22, 2009.

9. *The Kathmandu Post*, July 7, 2010.

10. Also reported by mothers in Bargadawa, Kapilvastu district.

11. Also reported by teachers in Taulihawa, mothers in Sante, and teachers in Bogatigaun, Achham.

12. As reported by mothers in Rupnagar, Saptari and Bargadawa, Kapilvastu.

13. As reported by mothers in Rupnagar, Saptari and Bargadawa, Kapilvastu.

14. Other castes like Brahmin, Chhetri, and Newar are the elite castes having higher income levels, educational attainment, and social status.

15. Derived through simple regression considering student learning as an outcome of student attendance based on school level monitoring data, which provide attendance rates and examination scores for each student.

16. Reported by teachers of Bhasa SS, Kagate, Dhankuta district.

17. Reported by teachers of SalMandir PS, Liwang, Rolpa district.

18. Reported by teachers of Baijanath SS, Dadeldhura district (third quarter of 2009).

19. Acccording to teachers in Bhagwandas LSS, Kapilvastu district (first quarter of 2010).

20. Teachers in Gadhi LSS, Panchthar (third quarter of 2010) reported that overage children are losing their interest in education due to higher opportunity costs, a bad circle of friends, etc.

21. Reported by teachers and students in Balmandir PS, Liwang, Rolpa district; Panchamrit PS, Pauwabhanjyang, Panchthar district; and Buddheswor PS, Saptari district.

22. This phenomenon was observed in Tanahun district (second quarter of 2009), Panchthar and Dadeldhura district, Saptari district (fourth quarter of 2009), and Dhankuta district (second quarter of 2010).

23. Reported by teachers in Bhasa HSS, Kagate, Dhankuta district.

24. According to mothers in Bhimsen PS, Simkot, Humla district (second quarter of 2009) and teachers in Kartikswami PS, Gairigaun, Jumla district (fourth quarter of 2009).

25. According to mothers and teachers in Bogatigaun, Achham district.

26. As reported by teachers in Panchamrit PS, Panchthar district (third quarter of 2009).

27. As reported by teachers in Balmandir PS, Liwang, Rolpa district.

28. Mothers in Charikot and Tikhatal, Dolakha district and Visuwa, Parsa district.

29. Reported by mothers in Chhapkaiya, Parsa district and mothers in Charikot, Dolakha district.

30. Reported by mothers in Chhapkaiya, Parsa district.

31. Reported in three out of four focus groups with mothers conducted in this quarter.

32. A logit regression was run on household-level data produced by WFP (third quarter of 2010) considering involvement of children in child labor as the

dependent variable, and socioeconomic and other characteristics of household as independent variables.

33. Reported by mothers in Tikhatal and Charikot, Dolakha district.

34. Reported by mothers in Tikhatal, Dolakha district and Visuwa, Parsa district.

35. Reported by mothers in Tikhatal, Dolakha district,

36. Reported by mothers in Dadeldhura district; Phidim, Panchthar district; Damauli, Tanahun district; and Charikot, Dolakha district.

37. Reported by mothers and teachers in Tikhatal, Dolakha district.

38. As reported by mothers in Tikhatal, Dolakha district and also supplemented by analysis of VAM data.

39. Reported by mothers in Tikhatal, Dolakha district, and Chhapkaiya, Parsa district.

40. Reported by mothers in Tikhatal, Dolakha district.

41. Reported by mothers in Tikhatal, Dolakha district.

42. More relevant in far west and midwestern districts including Mugu and Bajura districts.

43. Reported by children in Bogatigaun, Achham district; Sanfebagar, Achham district; and Bargadawa, Kapilvastu district.

44. Reported by teachers in Murmagaun, Mugu district and Damauli, Tanahun district.

45. Reported by teachers in four schools from two districts.

46. Reported by teachers in Balmandir PS, Liwang, Rolpa district.

47. Reported by teachers in Choyakot SS, Rajali, Bajura district.

48. Reported by mothers in Harirawa, Saptari district.

49. Reported by mothers in Guranse, Dhankuta district and Mijhingandliwang, Rolpa district.

50. Reported by teachers and mothers in Balmandir PS, Liwang, Rolpa district.

51. Reported by teachers in Bahalikot PS, Basali, Bajura district.

52. Reported by teachers in Murmagaun, Mugu district.

53. Reported by teachers in Shiva Panchayan PS, Tanahun district.

54. Reported by children in Bogatigaun, Achham district.

55. Reported by teachers in Bogatigaun, Achham district.

56. The students from Murmagaun have to go to Gamgadhi district headquarters to get secondary level education since secondary schools are not available nearby.

57. Reported by children and teachers in Murma, Mugu district.

58. As reported by mothers in Mijhing, Rolpa district.

59. As reported by children and mothers in Mijhing, Rolpa district. Note: the annual scholarship for a few students in the mountain region also reaches up to Rs 10,000 per year for secondary level.

60. Dalits are the low caste/untouchable groups under caste hierarchy.

61. Household-level monitoring data. The coping intensity was assessed by developing a composite score of education-related coping mechanisms and computing them by districts based on household-level monitoring of WFP.

62. The Karnali region is regarded as a region facing acute food shortage.

References

ESCAP (Economic and Social Commission for Asia and the Pacific). 2009b. *The Food-Fuel-Financial Crisis and Climate Change: Addressing Threats to Development*. Bangkok: ESCAP.

Gujarati, D. N. 2004. *Basic Econometrics*. Fourth Edition. New Delhi: McGraw-Hill.

MOF (Ministry of Finance). 2009. "Economic Survey for Fiscal Year 2008–09." MOF, Kathmandu.

NRB (Nepal Rastra Bank). 2009a. *Economic Report 2007–08*. Kathmandu.

———. 2009b. "Consumers Continue to Face Rising Prices." Nepal Rastra Bank. http://www.nepalnews.com.

UNICEF (United Nations Children's Fund). 2009. "A Matter of Magnitude: The Impact of the Economic Crisis on Women and Children in South Asia." UNICEF ROSA, Kathmandu.

WFP (World Food Programme). 2008a. "2008 Nepal Staple Food Market Review and Outlook for 2009." WFP, Kathmandu.

———. 2009. "Market Watch Nepal." No. 14. WFP, Kathmandu.

World Bank. 2009. *The Global Economic Crisis: Assessing Vulnerability with a Poverty Lens*. Washington, DC: World Bank.

CHAPTER 8

Institutional Impact Assessment: The Jordan Experience

Lamia Al-Zoubi

Introduction

Jordan's Ministry of Planning and International Cooperation (MoPIC) is a pioneering governmental institution that makes a significant contribution toward achieving sustainable socioeconomic development. Its mission is to coordinate and direct development efforts through planning, execution, monitoring, and evaluation of social and economic development plans in coordination with the public and private sectors and civil society organizations, as well as to enhance economic, financial, and technical cooperation with various countries and international organizations to achieve sustainable socioeconomic development and a better standard of living for all Jordanians.

For most of Jordan's development programs and organizations, impact assessment is still a one-off, donor-driven activity that is conducted halfway through a program or as part of post-program evaluation. This is also the case in government institutions, most of which hold the conventional view that impact assessment and market research studies are expensive and should be left in the care of donors and external consultants. This view is partly due to limited access to information on these tools, but also to lack of understanding about how these tools can be integrated effectively into operational activities.

At MoPIC, internal demand for impact information resulted in the establishment of an internal Impact Assessment Unit (IAU) in October 2010 to establish local ownership of impact assessment and cultivate trust among stakeholders. Hence, the unit sought to avoid reliance on external expertise at the expense of its internal capacities. Its first activity was an orientation briefing on the impact assessment program for MoPIC management and staff, which consists of a director, senior evaluators, researchers, and statistician specialists.

MoPIC's IAU's main objectives are as follows:

- Maximizing the benefits of implemented developmental projects to improve the economic and social developmental environment
- Institutionalizing the evaluation and impact assessment process
- Fostering institutional and community partnerships to achieve the developmental goals of government programs.

The IAU is a tool to help the government of Jordan assess the impacts of development programs and projects. It supports the process of policy making by contributing valuable empirical data to policy decisions, and by establishing a rational decision framework to examine the implications of capital investment options. This tool is an important factor in responding to the impact on modern economies of open international markets and budgetary constraints, and the consequences of competing policy demands.

The IAU at MoPIC makes evaluation and impact assessment an integral part of the implementation process of government development projects and promotes the importance of evaluation and assessment to other government institutions. The IAU process targets all concerned parties, and focuses on releasing and enhancing the monitoring and evaluation (M&E) culture (processes, mechanisms and methodologies). Eventually the IAU will have an active role with the donor community.

The mandate of MoPIC 's IAU is to do the following:

- Institutionalize the evaluation process to become one of the main procedures during the lifetime of a project. It will determine the required evaluation documents (such as the logic framework and evaluation plan) to facilitate evaluating and monitoring.
- Participate actively with the ministries and concerned institutions at the project document formulation stage by contributing to structuring the

Development Evaluation in Times of Turbulence

project's logic framework. This participation will address the linkages of the project objectives, expected outcomes, and impact on the concerned targets and beneficiaries.

- Evaluate selected completed programs and projects to assess their impact, and compare their objectives with their achievements.
- Actively participate with internal missions assigned by the donors for project midterm review and post-evaluation purposes. These projects are funded by the donors. IAU will participate in formulating the evaluation methodology and monitoring its implementation.
- Highlight the key and critical sector and component indicators addressed in the National Executive Development Program for the years 2011–13. This review will show any achievement delays through the quarterly reports of the project lifetime. These reports are issued by MoPIC 's Programs and Projects Directorate.
- Build the capacity of evaluation practitioners at MoPIC and other ministries by preparing and supervising evaluation training packages and participating in and implementing evaluation training programs.
- Formulate an annual evaluation plan based on project status and determine a project evaluation framework. IAU also supervises the evaluation implementation processes.
- Share the evaluation reports, which include results and lessons learned, with all concerned parties.

Status Quo Review

In the initial stages of the process, it was important for MoPIC to subscribe to the principles advocated by the Impact Assessment Global Network. MoPIC needed a greater appreciation of the impact assessment process and a better understanding of what it entails. A status quo review was made of MoPIC 's international experiences with impact assessment that provided a valuable input to the project design.

The objectives of the review were to do the following:

- Make an inventory of impact assessment tools and review MOPIC's experience with the tools;
- Compare impact assessment frameworks;
- Determine inventory impact areas, indicators, and methodologies used; and
- Identify best practices that can be adopted by the IAU.

The donors in this status quo review were those who contribute to the development process in Jordan. The review demonstrated their procedures and methodologies, thus identifying gaps within the donor community on M&E processes.

IAU reviewed a representative sample of donor projects using tools such as reviewing documents, conducting meetings, interviewing, and field visits. IAU documented and reported all the steps of the evaluation and impact-assessment stages.

The study found reliable monitoring and evaluation programs and project management within the donor community. The donor community has gone a long way in reflecting on institutional and contextual components of M&E systems. The good practices identified by the IAU were an effective introduction to building an initial framework for impact assessment in Jordan, where it is not yet institutionalized.

Some donors follow a standardized methodology in all their projects worldwide. Other donors don't have a clear evaluation methodology.

The review also found that impact studies conducted by external parties were in the context of project evaluations, with minimal involvement of MoPIC staff. These impact studies were undertaken on a per-project basis, and most were cross-sectional, one-off, and limited in geographic scope. They used a mix of qualitative and quantitative methods and were time- and resource-intensive. Such studies would place a very high demand on MoPIC if included as part of its regular activities.

Unfortunately, minimal efforts were made to draw out the implications of these impact studies for improvement or to translate their findings into points of action.

Impact Assessment Mechanism

Drafting impact assessments is a sophisticated and time-consuming exercise, and it is important to ensure that impact assessment is proportionate and does not become burdensome. In the best case, the scope and depth of impact assessments should be targeted. Even if a complete, in-depth impact assessment is recommended for all program proposals, realistically, the importance and the weight of the proposed normative act should be taken into account, and the depth of the impact assessment should be designed accordingly. Otherwise, impact assessment could face resistance from partners, such as government employees and donors, who might respond by simply checking off the required boxes rather than by engaging fully. By contrast, a system in which the scope of the impact assessment is targeted can generate understanding and compliance from the people working with it. The division into simple and complicated impact assessments, however, contains a trap: the desire for simplification. Therefore, clear guidelines should be set regarding when in-depth impact assessment is needed, and, more important, which best practices to use, as well as the role and place for the IAU within the structure of sector and program evaluations.

Next Steps

The next steps included the following:

- Establishing an IAU at the Ministry of Planning and International Cooperation
- Positioning the IAU in the organizational structure, and highlighting its operational and institutional importance by linking it to the minister
- Coordinating the IAU's standard of procedures (SoPs) with those of other related MoPIC departments and adopting the IAU SoPs as normal procedures for projects; the SoPs will determine the required evaluation documents (such as the logic framework and evaluation plan) throughout the evaluation process
- Conducting a process to raise the awareness of the involved parties about the importance of evaluation and impact assessment issues.

Evaluation and Impact Assessment Methodology

The IAU's main objective is to institutionalize evaluation and impact assessment processes at MoPIC, as well as for all partners in the field, especially the ministries and government departments. IAU adopts methodologies that can facilitate and improve the adopted and adapted evaluation and impact assessment processes and methodologies. At this stage, IAU is adopting and sharing with all parties—especially the donors—several evaluation and impact assessment techniques and methodologies for different project phases as listed and described here and in figure 8.1:

Planning phase: Conduct awareness-raising with the involved parties, assign roles, identify evaluation and impact assessment issues, build a set of documents and procedures.

Implementation phase: Conduct an evaluation at the level of monitoring in order to identify the challenges for ongoing projects.

Completion of outcomes assessment phase: Conduct an evaluation at the end of a project according to its objectives and expected outcomes, which can be included in the completion report.

Completion of impact assessment phase: Conduct a results-based post-evaluation after the completion of the project to assess the projects' impact.

Figure 8.1 Evaluation at Different Project Phases

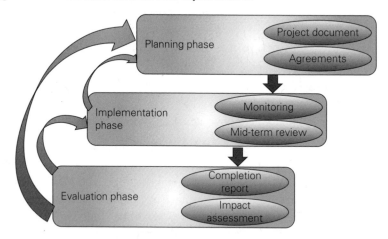

The impact assessment process takes place at three levels: the level of projects and programs, the level of sectors, and the level of the annual Executive Development Program (EDP) (box 8.1).

At the level of projects and programs, the goal is to build an integrated database of projects and programs listed in the 2011–13 EDP and financed through grants and loans, along with a representative sample of projects financed in 2011, for the purpose of evaluation and impact assessment. In selecting projects for the database, an effort was made to list projects that represent the sectors covered by the EDP and that represent most of the donors.

At the level of sectors, the IAU will select a sector from the EDP 2011–13, and hold an impact assessment study of foreign aid provided for that sector.

The IAU will also develop an M&E framework for the EDP 2011–13 itself to assess its implementation over the targeted years.

Sharing Experiences through Partners

It is hoped that benefits from MoPIC 's participation in impact assessment could be shared more widely within Jordan. Recognizing that national networks can be venues for effective learning and sharing of experiences, MoPIC hopes to raise local partners' awareness of the benefits of integrating impact assessment into regular monitoring systems. Indeed, MOPIC is committed to facilitating the process of institutionalizing impact monitoring and assessment by showcasing the IAU model and experiences.

IAU is aware of its responsibility to other ministries and government bodies in institutional and individual capacity building and will conduct and participate in specialized training workshops in evaluation and impact assessment. IAU also offers ministries an active role in participating with the donors' missions, as they get involved in the evaluation process by providing data for the evaluated programs and projects. IAU is ready to share lessons learned, successes, knowledge, and information with all its stakeholders and partners to enhance the efficient communications among all parties (figure 8.2).

Figure 8.2 Conceptual Communications of the IAU

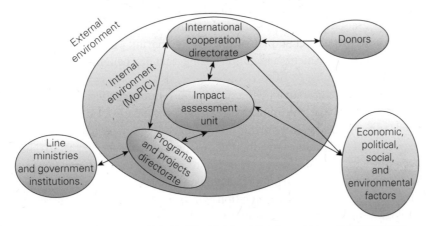

Note: IAU = Impact Assessment Unit, MoPIC = Ministry of Planning and International Cooperation.

Challenges and Issues

MoPIC's immediate challenge is to institutionalize impact assessment. Completed activities under the IAU have done much to jumpstart the institutionalization process, but making the information system work will be critical. Important to institutionalizing impact assessment will be performance monitoring and making better use of current processes as information sources

Efforts are needed to convince local stakeholders about the benefits of impact assessment activities relative to the costs and staff time because most of them still grapple with meeting financial performance targets. By building the capabilities of the field staff to collect and analyze partner information, MoPIC hopes to further build ownership of the process and develop a culture of learning from its partners. However, MoPIC is also learning that not all field staff has the aptitude for data gathering and analysis.

Later, MoPIC will incorporate partners' impact information, both qualitative and quantitative, into management information systems. Similarly, MoPIC is committed to meeting the training needs of staff, particularly those who will form the core of its impact assessment activities. The members of these teams are trained researchers and evaluators who can be called upon when there are pressing operational issues that require investigation on a local or broader scale.

Improving and promoting impact monitoring and assessment through networks is a significant challenge for MoPIC . Most of the local partners still narrowly view impact assessment as a costly undertaking that should be externally funded and controlled. Their immediate concern is its affordability, which explains their inclination to undertake impact assessment out of capital grants, but not to bother with it otherwise. Changing this attitude will require promotion and advocacy, that is, sharing MoPIC's experience with impact assessment and emphasizing that its benefits significantly exceed its costs.

Institutionalizing impact assessment will require cooperation from all partners, given that the impact assessment partner information system needs to be adapted to suit the information needs of each partner, which will require careful planning and adherence to the same process that MoPIC has been through. Building local partners' internal capacities to handle impact assessment will also be an important challenge for the network. Also critical is raising the level of staff appreciation of impact assessment tools and methodologies, and improving skills in data analysis and interpretation.

Conclusion

From MOPIC 's experience with its Impact Assessment Unit, valuable lessons have emerged in terms of institutionalizing the impact assessment process within the organization. MOPIC is also learning that, beyond internal capacities, there should be a serious commitment to institutionalize impact and partner monitoring. This commitment must be grounded in the belief that learning from partners is critical in proving effective improved organizational performance and ensuring institutional growth and sustainability.

CHAPTER 9

How Can Development Banks Boost Firms' Productivity?

Filipe Lage de Sousa

Overview

Extensive literature examines how firms' performance can be affected by trade policies, especially focusing on the gains from trade. However, there is a shortage of papers analyzing whether other government policies can affect firms' productivity, as evidenced by Grilliches, Klette, Moen, and others (2000) and Criscuolo, Martin, Overman, and Reenen (2007). This shortage of papers is not due to a shortage of methods, since other areas have already developed different ways to deal with policy impact analysis. For example, labor economics literature has made a relevant contribution by evaluating the extent to which government polices affect individuals' achievements. A survey of this literature can be found in Heckman, LaLonde, and Smith (1999). Further work should be pursued in evaluating government policies on firms' performance to provide empirical evidence for public policy design.

This chapter contributes to the literature on firms' performance and public policy by trying to understand to what extent government interventions affect firms' productivity. Banerjee and Duflo (2005) provide evidence that firms in many developing countries face credit constraints, by using a sample of countries including Brazil. Therefore, Brazilian firms might be credit constrained, especially for long-term projects. Terra (2003) provides evidence that Brazilian firms are definitely credit constrained. Financial restrictions for long-term projects are considered among the most important market failures in the Brazilian economy as they hamper the entrepreneurial efforts of local firms.

As a partial remedy, the Brazilian government provides long-term loans through the Brazilian Development Bank (Banco Nacional de Desenvolvimento Economico e Social; BNDES).[1] The statutory goal of this institution is to improve Brazilian economic competitiveness without neglecting broader social aspects. BNDES invests in several areas including research and development, infrastructure, export support, and regional and urban development. In the case of manufacturing, BNDES finances long-term projects aimed at the creation of new plants, the enlargement of existing ones, the restructuring and the modernization of production processes, innovation and technological development, and export promotion. Overall, the importance of BNDES in the Brazilian economy is sizeable: in 2011 its disbursements reached US$82.3 billion, representing 17.5 percent of aggregate investment.[2]

Although BNDES project analysis involves several dimensions including social and environmental aspects, it is nonetheless interesting to assess its overall impact on the competitiveness of Brazilian firms. The aim of this chapter is to contribute to this assessment by investigating the impact of BNDES activities on the productivity of Brazilian manufacturing firms. This impact is a central issue from a policy perspective: "Productivity isn't everything, but in the long run it is almost everything.... Compared with the problem of slow productivity growth, all our other long term economic concerns—foreign competition, the industrial base, lagging technology, deteriorating infrastructure, and so on—are minor issues" Krugman (1992, 13, 18).

Considering the relevance of productivity to fostering economic development and evaluating how it might be improved by government policies is a challenging and important investigation. A range of papers investigates BNDES effects, such as BNDES (2002), Monteiro Filha (1994), Pereira (2007), Puga and Torres Filho (2006), Reiff and others (2007), and Sousa (2003), but none has addressed productivity. Ottaviano and Sousa (2008) were the first to analyze whether BNDES financial support might affect firms' productivity, but their results call for further work to evaluate how BNDES financial supports improve firms' productivity. The methodology used in this chapter distinguishes it from Ottaviano and Sousa (2008).

Theoretically, the aim of this chapter is to understand which cost reduction is able to boost firms' productivity. Specifically, a firm must evaluate two types of cost when it decides to make investments to develop a new good for the market: (1) research and development (R&D) sunk cost to develop the new product, and (2) production costs of the new good.

Depending on which cost is reduced, the effect on productivity diverges. In the first case, R&D sunk cost, reducing costs has a positive effect, while in the second, production costs, the effect is negative. The main economic intuition is that when production costs are reduced, less-efficient firms become profitable, which pushes down overall economic productivity. When R&D fixed costs are reduced, there is a procompetitive effect in the market, in which more firms decide to innovate, and, thus, only the more efficient ones are able to survive. This theoretical framework is the first difference between this chapter and Ottaviano and Sousa (2008), which investigates the effects on productivity depending on which type of technology—old technology or new technology—is financially supported.

Another difference is in how a control group was created. Whereas Ottaviano and Sousa (2008) matched a financed firm with a similar nonfinanced one, this chapter uses the Kernel matching method. The Kernel approach permits comparing supported firms with all other firms by weighting nonfinanced firms by how similar they are to those that are financed. The main advantage of this strategy is that it allows the use of all the information in the dataset.

Empirical results show that, on average, granted firms do perform better than nongranted firms after being awarded a BNDES loan. However, it is not clear whether this improvement in productivity is associated with BNDES loans. No effect of BNDES loans on firms' performance is detected by using the difference-in-differences approach after comparing them with similar firms. Therefore, granted firms perform identically to other similar firms. This may represent that the criterion for making the decision on which firms to lend money to does not focus entirely on economic issues. Other issues, such as social, regional, and environmental impacts, might be as important (or maybe more so) as economic aspects in selecting the project, due to the amenities that each project creates. Theoretically, the government might be reducing both R&D and production costs leading to a null effect. More emphasis should be given to R&D costs to improve average productivity because reducing R&D costs provides higher social benefits to the economy.

This chapter is structured as follows. The first section begins by describing the financial support offered by BNDES to manufacturing firms, and is followed by a description of the dataset used in the following section. Next, the theoretical methodology is discussed. Descriptive statistics are presented and the empirical strategy is discussed, followed by the empirical results. Finally, concluding comments are offered.

Overview of BNDES Schemes

BNDES provides a wide range of financial tools to support Brazilian manufacturing firms: Financing and Endeavors (FINEM), Automatic BNDES, Machines and Equipment (FINAME), Leasing FINAME, International Competition FINAME (BNDES-Exim), and Subscription of Securities.

FINEM is a direct support scheme for projects with financial needs over R$10 million (US$4.7 million). Projects with financial needs below this threshold are supported indirectly through retailing banks under the Automatic BNDES scheme. Both schemes contemplate several categories of expenses covering the creation of new plants, enlargement of existing ones, restructuring and modernization of processes, innovation, and technological development.[3]

Through the FINAME and the Leasing FINAME schemes, BNDES supports the acquisition of new domestically produced machines and equipment either by buying them (FINAME) or leasing them (Leasing FINAME). The aim of BNDES-Exim is to provide financial support for exports. Subscription of Securities facilitates changes in firm ownership.

Our focus is on FINEM and Automatic BNDES, which support the discovery and the implementation of promising projects. Conversely, FINAME and Leasing FINAME do not contemplate investments in innovation and technological development. Nonetheless, it is necessary to account for them in order to isolate the role of FINEM and Automatic BNDES. BNDES-Exim and Subscription of Securities have different objectives. FINEM and Automatic BNDES are, therefore, loans that might affect firms' productivity since their expansion may be guided by improvements in production and/or creation of new and/or more sophisticated goods.

To receive either of these two loans, either FINEM or Automatic BNDES, firms must send an application with brief information on their projects to a retail bank or BNDES itself. The bank evaluates whether the projects are in line with the purpose of the loans. After their application is approved, firms are asked to send a complete and detailed project plan to be evaluated by the financial institution. This project plan is analyzed by investigating whether it is economically viable, what collateral can be used to guarantee the loan, and so forth.

The analysis culminates in a formal contract proposal in which the terms and conditions of the loan are established, including the amount, repayment period, and interest rate. After the negotiation, the loan contract is signed. It is important to note two crucial points. First, firms do not receive their loan in a single installment after signing the contract; they receive the funds gradually during the development of the project. During negotiations, disbursements are scheduled over the years of the project implementation. Second, there is a limit for BNDES participation in any project, which is 80 percent for the two loans mentioned here. Therefore, a project is not fully financed by BNDES, only a part of it is.

Once the loan has been approved, firms receive their first disbursement and remaining disbursements are made after an evaluation of the project's progress. Before the second disbursement, the company should prove whether the money of the first disbursement was invested in the items outlined in the project plan. Any violation of the loan terms leads to an investigation and disbursements can be interrupted until explanations are given. If no problems emerge, disbursements continue until the end of the project. Since these are long-term projects, the period between contract signing and the end of disbursements takes on average 4.5 years. It is generally only after all disbursements have been made that firms start to amortize their loans, including interest and principal.

Description of the Dataset

To pursue our investigation, data were drawn from a variety of sources used by Negri, Lemos, and others (2009) and Ottaviano and Sousa (2008). The dataset combines information from the Annual Industrial Research (Pesquisa Industrial Anual; PIA) of the Brazilian Institute of Geography and Statistics (Instituto Brasileiro de Geografia e Estatística; IBGE);[4] the Annual Social Information Report (Relação Anual de Informações Sociais; RAIS) of the Ministry of Labor; the Foreign Trade Secretary (Secretaria de Comércio Exterior; SECEX) of the Ministry of Industrial Development and Foreign Trade; the Foreign Capital Census and the Central Bank Register of Brazilian Capital Abroad of the Brazilian Central Bank; and BNDES itself.[5]

BNDES data are used to identify firms given loans. Information is available from 1995 to 2003.[6] During this period, 539 firms received FINEM loans and 8,505 firms borrowed under the Automatic BNDES scheme. In the latter case, it is not possible to use all firms since some of them are not available from PIA; PIA covers firms with more than 30 employees but some smaller firms are granted Automatic BNDES loans. This lack of data reduced the number of firms granted Automatic BNDES in our sample by half.

Our sample size was further reduced by three other issues. First, the focus of this chapter is on *manufacturing firms* whereas BNDES records concern all *manufacturing projects*. In other words, they report manufacturing projects by nonmanufacturing firms (for example, those of large food retailers investing in the development of their own brands) and do not cover nonmanufacturing projects of manufacturing firms (for example, in agriculture). Hence, we end up evaluating only the performance of manufacturing firms granted loans to implement projects in the manufacturing sector. A second issue is related to mergers. For example, if Firm A received a loan in 1997 and then in 2000 merged with Firm B creating a new Firm C, the initial loan would be registered to Firm C. As the past records of Firm C are impossible to reconstruct, all information on loans projects granted to firms like A and B are dropped. Finally, there is a time lag of generally two to three years before a firm enters the census database of PIA.[7] Hence, some granted firms with more than 30 employees are not recorded by PIA at the moment they receive BNDES loans.

In the end, data were available for 240 firms granted FINEM loans and more than 2,000 firms granted Automatic BNDES from 1996 to 2003. About 15,000 nongranted firms are available to construct the counterfactual group. A description of all variables used in this chapter is reported in Annex 9A.

Although the treated group had a reasonable size, potential drawbacks of conducting a policy analysis with this treated group should be addressed. First, any of these firms (granted or not) might be affected by other government interventions apart from BNDES loans. Second, there may be a time lag for any impact to be detected, since outcomes do not necessarily appear immediately after the loan has been granted. For the former problem, it will be assumed that BNDES loans are the main type of subsidies to affect the firms' productivity, since BNDES is the largest financial institution in Brazil offering loans for long-term projects. For the latter shortcoming, BNDES loans encompass six months before the project may be considered eligible for analysis; then, when the loan is approved, the project is already being implemented, and considering the effects on the current and subsequent period is not a strong assumption.[8]

Theoretical Background

Melitz (2003) provides a theoretical framework in which heterogeneous firms with different productivity levels exist in the market.[9] According to

Melitz's model, there are two crucial steps for a firm: step 1, when it invests in R&D to create a new product for the market; and step 2, when it decides whether or not to produce this new product.

To create a new product, a firm incurs a sunk cost of R&D, referred to in this model as the *fixed cost of entry*. At this stage, the firm evaluates all market possibilities and its innovative capacity. Until this moment, the firm's profitability and productivity are unknown. The decision to create a new product is called the *free-entry condition,* because there is no barrier to entry for any firm in the market.

The second step occurs after a new product is invented and its productivity is revealed. By knowing its productivity, the firm is able to evaluate how profitable it is to produce this new product. If it is profitable, the firm chooses to produce the new good to the market; otherwise it loses its R&D sunk cost.

In summary, any firm decides first whether it will develop a new good to the market by paying an R&D sunk cost. After knowing the firm's productivity level, and consequently the firm's profitability, the firm chooses whether to produce the new good. Those two decisions are represented by Melitz (2003) by two functions that define which productivity level is required to create a new good or to produce it to the market.

The first step, called the *free entry condition (FEC),* is when a firm decides whether or not to create a new variety. This step derives a function of the firm's average profit $\bar{\pi}$ on its productivity cut-off point φ^* where one of the parameters is the sunk cost to create a new variety f_e. The cut-off productivity defines whether a firm is profitable enough to produce the developed good. The formula for this condition is described in equation 1.

$$\text{FE: } \bar{\pi} = h(\varphi^*; f_e) \tag{1}$$

This function allows us to evaluate how average profit responds to cut-off productivity variation. Intuitively, the higher the productivity cut-off level, the lower the probability of success for a firm to enter in the market. Therefore, average profit in the economy should be higher to stimulate firms to develop new goods by spending resources in R&D. In other words, the derivative of this function is positive in respect to the productivity cut-off point, as shown in equation 2.

$$\frac{dh(\varphi^*; f_e)}{d\varphi^*} > 0 \tag{2}$$

In the second step, which is called a *zero cut-off profit condition (ZCP),* firms decide whether or not to produce to the market. Again, we can derive a function of the firm's average profit $\bar{\pi}$ on its productivity cut-off point φ^*, but now the parameter is the fixed cost of production f. This condition ·may be represented by equation 3.

$$\text{ZCP: } \bar{\pi} = g(\varphi^*; f) \tag{3}$$

In this case, the relation between average profit and productivity cut-off inverts. The lower the productivity cut-off in the economy, the more firms will be able to survive in this market. Average productivity decreases as less efficient firms survive in the market. Since firms' profits are decreasing as a function of rivals' productivity, average profits will be higher. As more firms are able to operate in the market, there will be an increase in competition and thus the average firm's profit must be lower. Then, ZCP function is downward sloping in terms of productivity cut-off as represented in equation 4.

$$\frac{dg(\varphi^*; f)}{d\varphi^*} < 0 \tag{4}$$

By taking into account both functions, it is possible to draw a graph of average profit in relation to productivity cut-off (figure 9.1).

It is feasible that the point at which the two lines cross on the graph in figure 9.1 defines not only the average productivity cut-off but also the average profit in this economy. In other words, firms with a productivity level below this threshold are not able to survive in this market as they will not produce their goods profitably. Therefore, if a firm develops a new good and later discovers its productivity level is under the cut-off, the firm will give up producing the good because it is not profitable. Conversely, a firm will be stimulated to produce any new good that is profitable.[10]

The question is: how is the productivity cut-off point affected when there is government support to reduce R&D sunk costs or production costs? When

Figure 9.1   Average Profit versus Cut-Off Productivity

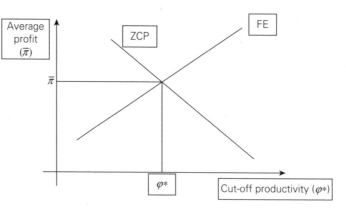

Development Evaluation in Times of Turbulence

R&D cost is reduced, government creates an incentive for more firms to risk developing new goods, since economic agents are generally risk averse. Because there are more firms innovating, more productive firms will enter the market creating a procompetitive effect. As a result, only more competitive firms will be able to survive in a more innovative market. Thus, productivity cut-off rises. This situation is represented in equation 5.

$$\frac{d\bar{\pi}}{df_e} > 0 \text{ and } \frac{d\varphi^*}{df_e} < 0 \tag{5}$$

Conversely, when government reduces the fixed cost of production, the opposite occurs. If their production costs are decreased, more firms are able to survive in the market, since even the less-efficient firms are able to compete with the others. As less-efficient firms remain in the market, the productivity cut-off drops. Equation 6 describes these phenomena.

$$\frac{d\bar{\pi}}{df} > 0 \text{ and } \frac{d\varphi^*}{df} > 0 \tag{6}$$

These results help us highlight how government policy can affect productivity of the economy when heterogeneous firms are producing in the market. If government reduces the fixed costs of production, even less productive firms can survive in the market; therefore, the average productivity level of the economy will be lower (as represented by the shift of the curve from ZCP_0 to ZCP_1). In contrast, if government intervention diminishes the fixed cost of entering the market, then firms have incentives to innovate and create new products ensuring that the more-productive firms remain in the market through a procompetitive effect; then average firms' productivity increases (as can be seen, from FE_0 to FE_1).

When government reduces both costs in similar magnitudes, an interesting result occurs: both curves are shifted down (from FE_0 to FE_1 and ZCP_0 to ZCP_1) and the net effect might be null. In other words, by reducing R&D costs jointly with production costs, government subsidies might have no effect on average productivity in the economy. These shifts are visualized in figure 9.2.

Both loans analyzed in this study (FINEM and Automatic BNDES) have financeable items that reduce both costs: innovation and technological development (R&D fixed cost) and restructuring of processes (fixed production cost). Therefore, all projects have a mixture of reducing fixed costs for both innovation and production. According to the theory, the effects of government intervention in reducing fixed costs presents different outcomes depending on which cost is addressed. Therefore, if a treated group of firms (those granted by BNDES loans) improves its productivity

Figure 9.2 Government Reduces Projects' Implementation Costs

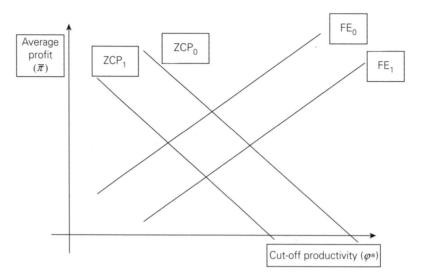

above a nontreated group, then these firms are investing more in R&D. If BNDES finances this type of cost, then more emphasis is given to reducing R&D costs compared with production costs. If the treated group improves its productivity less than nontreated firms, then more emphasis is given to production cost and BNDES is simply making firms more able to survive in the market.

Therefore, there is an identification problem in what type of cost was given emphasis by BNDES loans. Policy analysis can answer this question by evaluating productivity of the firms granted these loans, as it may be possible to identify by the results whether the bank is supporting projects related to investment in innovation or just making it easier for firms to remain in the market.

Even though the government subsidy policy may not produce the desired increase in economic productivity, it could still benefit consumers. The reason is helping less-productive firms survive in the market leads to a greater variety of goods available to consumers, making them better off.[11]

Descriptive Statistics

Two channels were explored to evaluate how BNDES loans are distributed in the Brazilian economy: by rich regions versus poor regions[12] and by manufacturing sector. Information is available for 1998–2007. Since the loans investigated occurred from 1995 to 2003, only the average from 1998 until 2003 is presented for analysis.

Figure 9.3 presents the average percentage of disbursement between rich and poor regions in Brazil. As shown, 78 percent of BNDES disbursement ended up in rich regions from 1998 to 2003; however proportionately, these areas represented 83 percent of the Brazilian GDP and 81 percent of manufacturing firms during the same period. Therefore, it is safe to conclude that BNDES loans proportionately favor poor regions since poor regions received a greater share than their actual participation in the economy.

With respect to the manufacturing sector's share, table 9.1 presents the average share of each sector in BNDES disbursement as well as their shares in manufacturing GDP. Generally, BNDES loans reflect sector shares, but two sectors escape this rule: transport equipment and petroleum refining and related industries. With respect to the latter, although many multinationals operate in this sector, the Brazilian government oil company, Petrobras, plays a substantial role.

The majority of Petrobras' investments is implemented without BNDES support since it has as much access to financial support from international banks as BNDES does. The transport equipment sector heavily invested in the development of cars that could run on either ethanol or gasoline (or even a mixture of the both) during this period. Due to the environmental amenities generated by those projects, BNDES provided a substantial part

Figure 9.3   Share of Disbursements, GDP, and Manufacturing Firms between Rich and Poor Regions

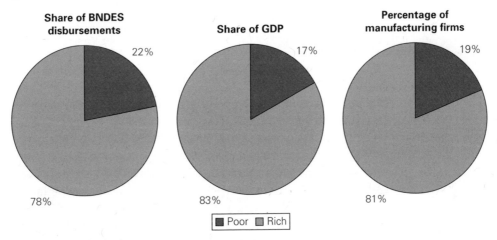

Source: BNDES and IPEA data.

Note: BNDES = Brazilian Development Bank, GDP = gross domestic product.

Table 9.1 Manufacturing Sectors Receiving BNDES Disbursements and Their Share of GDP (percent)

Manufacturing sector	BNDES	GDP
Food and kindred products	15	17
Tobacco products	0	1
Textile mill products	3	3
Apparel and other finished products made from fabrics and similar materials	1	2
Lumber and wood products, except furniture	2	1
Paper and allied products	6	4
Printing, publishing, and allied industries	0	4
Petroleum refining and related industries	1	12
Chemicals and allied products	7	12
Rubber and miscellaneous plastics products	2	4
Leather and leather products	1	2
Stone, clay, glass, and concrete products	2	4
Primary metal industries	9	7
Fabricated metal products, except machinery and transportation equipment	2	3
Industrial and commercial machinery and computer equipment	7	7
Electronic and other electrical equipment and components, except computer equipment	2	5
Transportation equipment	41	9
Miscellaneous manufacturing industries	1	3
Total	100	100

Source: BNDES and IBGE data.

Note: BNDES = Brazilian Development Bank, GDP = gross domestic product.

of their financial needs. Flex-fuel cars are now available for Brazilian consumers contributing to a cleaner environment.

Summing up, results show that BNDES loans are biased toward poor regions and the transportation equipment sector. Conversely, rich regions and the petroleum refining and related industries are underrepresented.

The key question is whether BNDES loans are instrumental in relaxing the financial constraints faced by Brazilian firms. A positive answer to this question requires checking first whether granted firms improved their performance after receiving a loan. Value added per worker (labor productivity) is used as the measure of firm performance.[13] Table 9.2

Table 9.2 Comparing Productivity of Granted and Nongranted Firms

	Nongranted firms		Granted firms					
Year	Average productivity (R$)	Number of firms	Year granted	Number of firms	Average productivity before (R$)	Productivity premium before	Productivity in 2003 ($R)	Productivity premium[a] in 2003	Annual percent increase in productivity premium
1996	51,357	21,533	1997	1,375	73,071	1.42	63,450	2.19	6
1997	57,440	20,815	1998	1,127	92,699	1.61	82,316	2.84	10
1998	50,123	22,510	1999	706	118,823	2.37	84,719	2.93	4
1999	53,034	23,143	2000	801	108,462	2.05	84,452	2.92	9
2000	43,829	23,284	2001	808	100,307	2.29	87,469	3.02	10
2003	28,949	23,159	Average	963	98,672	1.95	80,481	2.78	8

Source: Brazilian Statistical Institute and BNDES.

a. "Productivity premium" of granted firms was calculated as the ratio of the average value added per worker of these firms to that of nongranted firms. A higher number indicates greater productivity.

reports the average values of this variable for granted and nongranted firms in the years in which the former received their loans and in the last year of observation, 2003. The first three columns present figures of nongranted firms, while information on granted loans is shown in the last six columns. For better understanding, a "productivity premium" of granted firms was calculated as the ratio of the average value added per worker of these firms to that of nongranted firms. A higher number indicates greater productivity.

Table 9.2 shows that granted firms are generally more productive than nongranted firms. One year before their loans were approved, the productivity premium of granted firms ranged from 1.42 for firms granted in 1997 and 2.37 for those granted in 1999. On average, firms selected to be financed were twice as productive as those not selected. Moreover, BNDES loans selected even more productive firms over the years, since the productivity premium increased from 1.42 to 2.29.[14] On average, the productivity premium of granted firms increased by 8 percent annually over nongranted firms (see last column).

Results from descriptive statistics seem consistent with the idea that BNDES financial support has helped Brazilian firms relax their credit constraints: granted firms performed 8 percent better annually than nongranted firms. However, this evidence may not survive closer econometric scrutiny, which will be presented in the next section.

Empirical Strategy

To assess the impact of BNDES schemes on firms' performance, ideally one would compare granted and nongranted firms that are identical in all respects when loans were awarded to the former. Propensity score matching (PSM) allows one to pursue such an ideal comparison by matching each granted firm with a nongranted one exhibiting similar observable characteristics. This method artificially generates a "control group" of nongranted firms to be compared with the "treated group" of granted firms to assess the impact of "treatment" by BNDES schemes. The comparison can then be made in terms of productivity levels.

There are different ways to implement PSM[15]; this chapter uses the Kernel method, which creates a counterfactual group by pairing each granted firm with all nongranted firms weighted by how similar they are. In other words, weights are allocated to nontreated firms according to how alike they are compared with supported firms. The main advantage of this method is that all information in the sample can be used, which will lead to a control group with more than 15,000 firms.[16]

Matching is based on the following pretreatment characteristics: productivity, age, number of employees, average salary of employees, market share, total revenues, percentage of highly skilled workers (at least undergraduate degree), sector, location, educational level of employees (years of schooling), ratio of financial costs over total revenues, ratio of exports over total revenue, ratio of imports of capital goods over investment, ratio of imports of intermediaries over cost of production, and multinational status.[17]

Although this method establishes a control group similar to the granted group in terms of observable characteristics, nonobservable characteristics might affect granted and control group performance differently. One example is the firms' management. To control for unobservable time-invariant characteristics, evaluation of the treatment effect is performed by differences-in-differences according to the following specification used in Bronzini and Blasio (2006):

$$y_{it} = \beta\, BNDES_i + \sum_t \alpha_t D_t + \sum_t \delta_t (BNDES_i \cdot POST_t) + X_{it}\gamma + \varepsilon_{it}, \quad (7)$$

where y_{it} is value added per employee, $BNDES_i$ is a dummy variable indicating whether the firm received any loan in the period of observation, D_t is a year dummy, $POST_t$ is a set of dummies for each year after receiving the loan, and X_{it} is the vector of control variables. The parameter of interest is delta which estimated value measures the impact of BNDES schemes on firm productivity over time. The estimation of equation 7 allows one to assess not only whether BNDES loans affect firm productivity, but also when the impact materializes.

Before presenting the results, some additional comments are worth mentioning. One shortcoming of using value-added per worker is that it also captures improvements in productivity created by investments in capital. However, some controls are able to capture these things, such as capital imports and FINAME loans. The latter represent most of the improvements by domestic capital goods, since more than 80 percent of all manufacturing firms have financed their capital investment by borrowing from FINAME during the period analyzed. The former represent all capital goods imported by any Brazilian firm at each year in this period. In other words, it is a record of how many capital goods were imported by any firm in every year during the period analyzed. Therefore, investments in capital goods are able to capture any increase in productivity not related to the investigated loans.

A second issue worth discussing is that some firms were granted FINEM or Automatic BNDES loans more than once in the period of observation. Although more than 90 percent of all granted firms received only one loan, repeated treatments may distort the overall picture. To tackle this problem, any firm granted FINEM or Automatic BNDES loans more than once was removed from the sample to eliminate double treatment.

Last, but not least, control variables include various firm characteristics besides acquisition of capital goods: age, wage, number of employees, their skill and education levels, market share, revenues, financial status, exports, intermediate imports, and multinational status.[18]

Empirical Results

To see where policy interventions may have a stronger impact, two channels were explored: location of the project (poor or rich regions) and project size (small or large projects).[19] Therefore, results presented in this paper show not only how these loans affect Brazilian manufacturing firms, but also whether the loans had a greater impact on small projects and/or whether firms in poor regions benefited more from these financial supports.

The aim of PSM is to create a counterfactual group of nongranted firms ("control group") that are identical in every respect to the granted firms ("treated group") when they received loans ("treatment"). This method controls for potential nonlinearities in the relation between control variables and firm productivity.

The implementation of PSM is not possible for all years. On the one hand, some time should be allowed to check the full effect of the treatment. Since Automatic BNDES and FINEM last for at least five years,[20] a period beyond a five-year horizon should be allowed for impact. This period allows the model to check BNDES' effects not only during but also after the treatment. Given the time spanned by our dataset (1996 to 2003), the impact period is clearly not feasible for loans granted from 1998 onward. On the other hand, to build the control group for firms treated in a certain year, one needs to have at least one previous year of observation for PSM. Hence, the impact of BNDES schemes can be scrutinized through PSM only for firms granted Automatic BNDES and FINEM loans in 1997, which therefore defines our treated group. Moreover, to avoid concerns regarding repeated treatment, all firms treated more than once from 1995 to 2003 were excluded. Lastly, the construction of the control group was based on all firms active in 1996 that were never granted loans during the period of observation from 1995 to 2003 and have survived during the whole period. In the end, 291 treated and 15,127 nontreated firms were left on which to perform PSM.[21]

After matching nontreated firms with treated firms, the difference-in-differences approach of equation 7 was used to infer whether BNDES loans had any effect on firms' productivity by eliminating any time-invariant characteristic. Different specifications were tried distinguishing between small and large projects as well as poor and rich regions with or without controls. For parsimony, table 9.3 reports only the results for the specifications in which only FINAME or all controls

Table 9.3 Results Using PSM Plus Difference-in-Differences Approach

Value added per worker	All regions		Poor regions		Rich regions	
	(1)	(2)	(3)	(4)	(5)	(6)
Policy effect in 1997	−0.07 (0.12)	−0.08 (0.10)	0.09 (0.27)	0.09 (0.14)	−0.09 (0.13)	−0.07 (0.11)
Policy effect in 1998	0.13 (0.13)	0.12 (0.11)	−0.24 (0.44)	−0.24 (0.33)	0.19 (0.13)	0.16 (0.11)
Policy effect in 1999	0.01 (0.11)	−0.17 (0.09)	0.57 (0.44)	0.37 (0.31)	−0.07 (0.11)	0.03 (0.12)
Policy effect in 2000	0.01 (0.13)	−0.03 (0.11)	−0.24 (0.29)	−0.19 (0.21)	0.04 (0.15)	−0.08 (0.12)
Policy effect in 2001	−0.09 (0.15)	−0.04 (0.13)	0.20 (0.30)	0.23 (0.20)	−0.14 (0.17)	−0.10 (0.12)
Policy effect in 2002	−0.04 (0.15)	−0.02 (0.12)	−0.16 (0.33)	−0.21 (0.20)	−0.02 (0.17)	−0.01 (0.12)
Policy effect in 2003	0.06 (0.13)	0.04 (0.09)	0.00 (0.33)	−0.11 (0.22)	0.08 (0.13)	0.05 (0.13)
FINAME	0.40 (0.04)***	0.12 (0.03)***	0.48 (0.10)***	0.02 (0.07)***	0.39 (0.04)***	0.09 (0.01)***
Age		0.05 (0.02)**		0.00 (0.07)		0.02 (0.01)**
Skill		−0.09 (0.20)		0.26 (0.50)		0.40 (0.08)
Wage		0.35 (0.02)***		0.23 (0.05)***		0.41 (0.01)
Schooling		0.10 (0.06)		0.20 (0.14)		0.03 (0.02)

(continued)

Table 9.3   (continued)

Value added per worker	All regions		Poor regions		Rich regions	
	(1)	(2)	(3)	(4)	(5)	(6)
Number of employees		−0.62 (0.02)***		−0.63 (0.03)***		−0.59 (0.01)***
Market share		0.44 (1.35)		−11.22 (5.34)**		1.42 (1.81)
Revenues		0.72 (0.02)***		0.78 (0.03)***		0.66 (0.01)***
Financial status		−0.70 (0.28)**		−1.44 (1.24)		−0.53 (0.05)***
Export		0.11 (0.07)		0.52 (0.12)***		0.15 (0.04)***
Intermediaries import		0.19 (0.11)*		0.79 (0.28)***		0.01 (0.07)
Capital import		0.19 (0.05)***		0.48 (0.14)***		0.11 (0.06)**
Number of observations	110,275	109,544	15,068	14,989	95,207	82,776
R-squared	0.02	0.38	0.02	0.47	0.02	0.36

Note: Standard errors in parentheses.
* significant at 10%; ** significant at 5%; *** significant at 1%.

are introduced. Rich and poor areas were considered jointly as well as separately.[22]

Most of the controls presented the expected sign. For example, the covariate variable used to capture FINAME was always positive and significant at the 1 percent level despite whether the firms were in rich or poor areas. Capital import is positive as well. These two results indicate that the control variables of investment in physical capital is reasonably captured by those measures. Therefore, the shortcoming of using only labor productivity was overcome by using these measures. Moreover, results suggest that those controls appear to capture any improvement in productivity related to capital investments. Other controls, such as wages and revenues, present positive and expected signs at all regressions.

Focusing on BNDES loans, despite whether firms were in a poor or rich region, results show that no impact was found from those loans on firms' productivity, since not a single parameter estimated appears different from zero. It is important to notice that the impact was evaluated not only while the project was implemented, but also some time after it was finished. It is assumed that all projects ended their implementation after five years (the average loan duration), which enabled this study to see the impact two years after implementation was completed. Even considering this period, no significant result was found.

Similar outcomes were found when splitting the sample to different project sizes, in other words, whether the project was large (FINEM) or small (Automatic BNDES). The only difference appeared to be regarding capital goods acquisition. Whereas small projects presented robust results related to domestic capital goods, large projects seemed to be more impacted by imported capital goods. This result is economically intuitive, since small projects are implemented more often by small- and medium-size firms; therefore, their projects can benefit more from domestic capital. Learning how to deal with a national capital good might be easier for a Brazilian firm because it does not face translation costs and other costs involved in international commerce. Conversely, large projects are implemented by large firms, including multinationals, which have a lower cost to learn how to operate an imported capital good.

Theoretical Explanation

There are two type of explanations for the results: one theoretical and another based on the empirical results. Theoretical justification is based on the Melitz model presented earlier, which shows that when government reduces proportionate R&D costs and production costs, both curves shift downward. Consequently, productivity level cut-off may remain at the same level. In other words, government might pursue an innocuous policy to boost productivity when both costs are subsidized. As the two financial supports investigated in this chapter (FINEM and Automatic BNDES) reduce both costs, those loans end up not being able to impact positively firms' productivity.

Another point should be emphasized related to the theoretical model. By reducing those costs, either isolated or jointly, the government increases market competition. When R&D cost is diminished, government policy induces a procompetitive effect in the economy so that more products are developed and only more successful projects are implemented. Conversely, if production costs are reduced, more firms are able to survive in the market and competition increases.

In summary, reducing both R&D and production costs increases market competition, which leads to lower profits. There is a stylized fact in the Brazilian economy that value added in the manufacturing factor has dropped over the last years. Additionally, the number of manufacturing firms has increased steadily over the same period, according to PIA. Evidence from theory and stylized facts suggests that the effect of BNDES financial support might be to increase competition in the manufacturing sector.

Explanation Based on Empirical Results

Another explanation for the results can be found in the empirical outcomes. The results suggest a positive relationship between productivity and capital goods acquisition. It might be that all labor productivity can be explained by the inclusion of new capital goods in the manufacturing process. The majority of FINEM and Automatic BNDES financial supports encompass capital goods acquisition, not only domestic but also imported. Thus, productivity gains obtained by Brazilian firms might be related only to those capital goods.

This outcome is not an isolated case in the literature. Criscuolo and others (2007) investigated the effect on industrial policy in the United Kingdom and found no significant impact on firms' productivity, even though they found effects on employment and investment. Similar results were found by Ottaviano and Sousa (2008), who explain this result differently. In theoretical terms, they argue that some firms are implementing new technologies (higher fixed costs to implement, but lower marginal costs) and other, old technologies (lower fixed cost to implement, but higher marginal costs). When government reduces implementation of both technology types, a null effect occurs as shown in this chapter.

Additionally, Ottaviano and Sousa (2008) mentioned the existence of two time issues, one before and another after the loan itself, which might help explain the result (of no impact). Major adjustments to become more productive may have occurred before applying for financial support, since BNDES policies select mainly successful enterprises, as table 9.2 reports. Therefore, firms might have already become more productive in order to be eligible for this financial support. After getting it, their performance did not change substantially. As a result, BNDES effect on firms' productivity might be prior to the announcement of the loan approval. Conversely, *ex-post* evaluation of similar institutions, such as in the European Bank for Reconstruction and Development, occurs only two years after the end of any project, as pointed out in EBRD (2006). In order words, it might be too soon to see any impact on firms' productivity within two years after the project has finished.

Concluding Remarks

This chapter has evaluated how government support might affect firms' productivity not only theoretically but also empirically. In the theoretical approach, government support might have different effects in firms' productivity: negative, positive, or even null. The crucial point is which type of cost is considered. If it is production cost, the effect of government loans on productivity is negative. However, when government loans help reduce R&D cost to launch a new good to the market, there is a positive impact. When government reduces both types of cost, the net effect might be null.

Based on a theoretical model, an empiric investigation was carried out for two BNDES loans: FINEM and Automatic BNDES. Overall, granted firms performed better after receiving BNDES loans. On average, firms improved their productivity by 8 percent annually after being treated compared with nontreated firms. However, there is no robust evidence that those improvements in productivity were related to government policies, as found in similar papers, such as Ottaviano and Sousa (2008) and Criscuolo and others (2007). One explanation is that acquisition of capital goods (either domestic or imported) related to those loans captured all productivity gains. Theoretically, one justification might be that government is reducing both implementation costs: R&D and production. For policy implications, emphasis should be given to reduce R&D sunk costs. When the government provides incentives for innovative projects, more firms decide to create a new product. Therefore, overall productivity rises due to a more competitive and innovative market.

Further conclusions can be reached. Initially, as firms perform better after receiving a loan, the economic aspects of each project appear to be relevant as one criterion decision for loans approval. As they are identical to nongranted firms and they are performing similarly, then perhaps the criterion decision on selecting projects does not focus entirely on economic issues. Other issues, such as social, regional, and environmental impacts, might be as important as economic aspects (or perhaps even more so) in project selection, due to the amenities that each project creates.

This "no treatment effect" results may be similar to the controversial issue of educational grants, in which academics question whether scholarships improve research quality or more highly skilled researchers are selected for financial support. Regardless, further work should be pursued to investigate whether these loans can eventually impact firms' productivity, especially by using total factor productivity instead of labor productivity.

Annex 9A   List of Variables

Variables from the Annual Industrial Research (Pesquisa Industrial Anual; PIA) of the Brazilian Institute of Geography and Statistics (Instituto Brasileiro de Geografia e Estatística; IBGE) regarding information from 1996 to 2003.

1. *Value Added* = total value added
2. *Number of employees* = total number of employees
3. *Sector* = sector classification defined by the Brazilian Statistical Institute at the level of CNAE 2 (National Classification of Economic Activities), which is similar to SIC 2
4. *Location* = region where the firm is located (North, Northeast, Midwest, Southeast, and South)
5. *Average salary of employees* = total wages over the number of employees
6. *Market share* = market share in CNAE 2 sectors in terms of net revenues
7. *Total revenues* = total value of net revenues, which includes taxes (different from value added)
8. *Ratio of financial costs to total revenues* = total financial costs over total revenue

Variables whose source is RAIS from the Ministry of Labor regarding information from 1996 to 2003.

1. *Percentage of high skilled workers* = percentage of workers with at least an undergraduate degree
2. *Educational level of employees* = average number of years spent in school by employees
3. *Age* = number of years in operations until 2003

Variables whose source is SECEX from the Ministry of Industrial Development and Foreign Trade jointly with some measures of PIA regarding information from 1996 to 2003.

1. *Ratio of exports to total revenues* = total exports (SECEX) over total revenues (PIA)
2. *Ratio of imports of capital goods to investment* = total capital goods imports (SECEX) over total investment (PIA)
3. *Ratio of imports of intermediaries to cost of production* = total intermediate imports (SECEX) over total cost of production (PIA)

Variable whose source is the Brazilian Central Bank from the 2000 Foreign Capital Census.

1. *Multinational status* = definition of multinational firm by the Central Bank of Brazil for each firm located in Brazil in 2000

Annex 9B Further Results

Table 9B.1 Results for Small Projects in Method 5

Dependent variable	All regions		Poor regions		Rich regions	
Value added per worker	(1)	(2)	(3)	(4)	(5)	(6)
Policy effect in 1997	−0.07 (0.10)	−0.07 (0.07)	0.04 (0.28)	0.10 (0.13)	−0.08 (0.11)	−0.09 (0.11)
Policy effect in 1998	0.09 (0.10)	0.07 (0.08)	−0.09 (0.29)	−0.07 (0.15)	0.10 (0.11)	0.09 (0.11)
Policy effect in 1999	0.06 (0.09)	0.06 (0.06)	0.06 (0.32)	−0.01 (0.19)	0.06 (0.10)	0.06 (0.12)
Policy effect in 2000	−0.11 (0.11)	−0.14 (0.08)*	0.13 (0.33)	0.03 (0.22)	−0.13 (0.11)	−0.14 (0.12)
Policy effect in 2001	−0.03 (0.12)	0.02 (0.10)	−0.02 (0.32)	0.04 (0.17)	−0.03 (0.13)	0.00 (0.12)
Policy effect in 2002	−0.07 (0.11)	−0.07 (0.09)	−0.03 (0.33)	−0.10 (0.17)	−0.07 (0.12)	−0.06 (0.12)
Policy effect in 2003	0.08 (0.10)	0.08 (0.07)	0.08 (0.35)	−0.13 (0.21)	0.08 (0.11)	0.07 (0.13)
FINAME	0.46 (0.04)***	0.05 (0.03)*	0.22 (0.09)***	−0.15 (0.06)**	0.49 (0.04)***	0.09 (0.02)***
Age		0.03 (0.02)		0.00 (0.07)		0.04 (0.02)*
Skill		0.22 (0.17)		0.26 (0.50)		0.37 (0.17)**
Wage		0.38 (0.03)***		0.23 (0.05)***		0.30 (0.03)
Schooling		0.01 (0.05)		0.20 (0.14)		−0.06 (0.06)
Number of employees		−0.63 (0.02)***		−0.63 (0.03)***		−0.63 (0.02)***
Market share		1.29 (1.02)		−11.22 (5.34)**		−1.82 (1.72)
Revenues		0.70 (0.02)***		0.78 (0.03)***		0.73 (0.02)***
Financial status		−0.25 (0.25)		−1.44 (1.24)		−0.18 (0.15)
Export		0.35 (0.05)***		0.52 (0.12)***		0.13 (0.07)***

(continued)

Table 9B.1   (continued)

Dependent variable	All regions		Poor regions		Rich regions	
Value added per worker	(1)	(2)	(3)	(4)	(5)	(6)
Intermediaries import		−0.76 (0.60)***		0.79 (0.28)***		−1.59 (0.20)***
Capital import		0.04 (0.07)		0.48 (0.14)***		0.00 (0.11)
FINEM	1.02 (0.04)***	−0.01 (0.02)	1.16 (0.17)***	0.48 (0.14)***	1.01 (0.04)***	0.21 (0.05)
Number of Obs.	12,172	12,132	1,355	1,352	10,817	10,780
R-squared	0.06	0.50	0.07	0.69	0.06	0.50

Notes: Standard errors in parentheses.
* significant at 10%; ** significant at 5%; *** significant at 1%.
Columns (1), (3), and (5) show results using only FINAME and FINEM dummy as controls. Columns (2), (4), and (6) present outcomes using all controls.

Table 9B.2   Results for Large Projects in Method 5

Dependent variable	All regions		Poor regions		Rich regions	
Value added per worker	(1)	(2)	(3)	(4)	(5)	(6)
Policy effect in 1997	0.07 (0.30)	0.00 (0.09)	−0.05 (1.15)	−0.49 (0.11)*	0.08 (0.30)	0.08 (0.38)
Policy effect in 1998	−0.03 (0.30)	−0.06 (0.11)	0.30 (0.86)	0.16 (0.13)	−0.07 (0.32)	−0.04 (0.38)
Policy effect in 1999	0.08 (0.35)	0.03 (0.21)	−0.47 (0.82)	−0.08 (0.19)	0.14 (0.37)	0.14 (0.42)
Policy effect in 2000	−0.11 (0.41)	−0.06 (0.36)	−2.14 (1.17)*	−1.74 (1.32)	0.20 (0.38)	0.17 (0.44)
Policy effect in 2001	0.27 (0.38)	0.19 (0.31)	1.82 (1.13)	1.69 (1.31)	0.02 (0.35)	0.00 (0.45)
Policy effect in 2002	−0.31 (0.37)	−0.16 (0.14)	0.29 (1.05)	0.08 (0.32)	−0.40 (0.39)	−0.28 (0.45)
Policy effect in 2003	0.12 (0.37)	0.00 (0.14)	−0.11 (1.17)	−0.13 (0.32)	0.15 (0.38)	−0.04 (0.44)
FINAME	0.01 (0.07)	0.02 (0.04)	0.42 (0.16)***	−0.01 (0.06)	−0.02 (0.06)	0.00 (0.02)

(continued)

Table 9B.2   (continued)

Dependent variable	All regions		Poor regions		Rich regions	
Value added per worker	(1)	(2)	(3)	(4)	(5)	(6)
Age		0.07 (0.05)**		−0.01 (0.08)		0.07 (0.03)**
Skill		0.19 (0.23)		1.04 (0.37)***		−0.08 (0.18)
Wage		0.11 (0.07)***		−0.23 (0.17)		0.33 (0.03)
Schooling		0.11 (0.07)		−0.12 (0.11)		0.18 (0.07)**
Number of employees		−0.73 (0.05)***		−0.84 (0.09)***		−0.61 (0.02)***
Market share		−0.99 (1.10)		−16.05 (10.07)		1.14 (1.66)
Revenues		0.81 (0.04)***		1.14 (0.13)***		0.70 (0.02)***
Financial status		−0.03 (0.14)		−1.17 (0.55)**		−0.80 (0.11)***
Export		−0.44 (0.14)***		−0.24 (0.23)		−0.55 (0.08)***
Intermediaries import		0.04 (0.06)		1.05 (0.28)***		0.05 (0.07)
Capital import		0.29 (0.17)*		0.32 (0.25)		0.21 (0.11)**
Automatic BNDES	0.07 (0.08)	0.01 (0.04)	−0.24 (0.18)	−0.18 (0.06)***	0.10 (0.08)	0.07 (0.03)**
Number of Obs.	11,537	11,435	1,269	1,265	10,268	10,170
R-squared	0.01	0.64	0.14	0.74	0.01	0.39

Note: BNDES = Brazilian Development Bank. Standard errors in parentheses.
* significant at 10%; **significant at 5%; ***significant at 1%.
Columns (1), (3), and (5) show results using only FINAME and Automatic BNDES dummy as controls. Columns (2), (4), and (6) present outcomes using all controls

Notes

1. This financial institution has similar characteristics to the World Bank and the Inter-American Development Bank, although it is sponsored by the Brazilian government.

2. IPEA and BNDES (www.ipeadata.gov.br and http://www.bndes.gov.br).

3. A complete list is available at http://www.bndes.gov.br/english /items_support .asp.

4. This is our main data source, since it contains the majority of the variables useful for this analysis, including productivity.

5. The construction of the dataset has followed procedures that guarantee the confidentiality of information so that an individual datum cannot be related to any specific firm.

6. Data on 1995 is used only to exclude any firm that received treatment in that year.

7. IBGE receives information about firms' size (number of employees) from a particular year only at the end of the following year. Thus, any new firm for the census part will provide information only after two or three years of having become eligible to be computed.

8. Firms are credit constrained to implement the whole project. However, BNDES does not finance the full project, only up to 80 percent of it.

9. It is important to emphasize that heterogeneity is driven only by productivity. All other factors are identical for all firms in the market.

10. For more information, see Melitz (2003).

11. In this model, consumers are assumed to have love-of-variety property, which means that as consumers face more variety, they are better off.

12. Rich areas are considered to be in the south and southeast regions in Brazil, whereas the North, Northeast, and Midwest are considered poor regions.

13. Potential shortcomings of using this measure are discussed in the "Empirical Strategy" section.

14. The only exception is in 1999, when productivity premium achieved its maximum.

15. PSM is used by Negri, Lemos, and others (2009) to evaluate the impact of FINEP on firm productivity and R&D investment. See also Arnold and Javorcik (2009) for a detailed implementation of PSM on foreign investment in Indonesia.

16. As mentioned previously, Ottaviano and Sousa (2008) have already investigated that phenomenon by using PSM one-to-one. Although this method has the advantage of comparing granted firms with similar nongranted firms, it has a drawback in not using all information available. Using this method restricts the control group to less than two hundred firms.

17. More details of each variable is available in Annex 9A.

18. A full description of these variables is in Annex 9A.

19. Rich and poor regions respect what was defined in the "Descriptive Statistics" section. Regarding small and large projects, any projects supported by Automatic BNDES is considered a small project, while any project supported by FINEM is considered a large project.

20. The average time for all disbursements from both loans is around 4.5 years.

21. This PSM was done by estimating firms' probability to get a loan from BNDES by using a probit model with the characteristics mentioned in Annex 9A (all of

them from the year before the granted year, in this case 1996). Weights were then given to nontreated firms by their similarity to granted firms.

22. Other results, such as including small and medium projects, are presented in Annex 9B.

References

Arnold, J. M., and Javorcik, B. S. 2009. "Gifted Kids or Pushy Parents? Foreign Direct Investment and Plant Productivity in Indonesia." *Journal of International Economics* 79 (1): 42–53.

Banerjee, A. V., and E. Duflo. 2005. "Growth Theory through the Lens of Development Economics." In *Economics Handbook of Economic Growth,* volume 1, 473–552.

BNDES (Banco Nacional de Desenvolvimento Economico e Social). 2002. "BNDES, urn Banco de Ideias–50 anos refletindo o Brasil." BNDES, Rio de Janeiro, Brazil.

Bronzini, R., and G. d. Blasio. 2006. "Evaluating the Impact of Investments Incentives: The Case of the Italian Law 488/1992." *Journal of Urban Economics* 60 (2): 327–49.

Criscuolo, C., R. Martin, H. G. Overman, and J. V. Reenen. 2007. "The Effect of Industrial Policy on Corporate Performance: Evidence from Panel Data." Unpublished. London.

EBRD (European Bank for Reconstruction and Development). 2006. "Evaluation Policy of the EBRD Evaluation-Department." EBRD, London.

Grilliches, Z., T. J. Klette, J. Moen, et al. 2000. "Do Subsidies to Commercial R&D Reduce Market Failures? Microeconometric Evaluation Studies." *Research Policy* 29 (4/5): 471–95.

Heckman, J. J., R. J. LaLonde, and J. A. Smith. 1999. "The Economics and Econometrics of Active Labour Market Programs." In *Handbook of Labour Economics*, volume 3, edited by 0. Ashenfelter, D. E. Card, and D. Card, 1865–2097. Amsterdam: Elsevier.

Krugman, P. 1992. *The Age of Diminished Expectations: U.S. Economic Policy in the 1990s.* Cambridge, MA: MIT Press.

Lemos, M. B., Negri, F. and Negri, J. A. 2009. "Impactos do ADTEN e do FNDCT sobre o Desempenho e os Esforços Tecnológicos das Firmas Industriais Brasileira." *Revista Brasileira de Inovação* 8 (1): 211–54.

Melitz, M. 2003. "The Impact of Trade on Intra-Industry Reallocations and Aggregate Industry Productivity." *Econometrica* 71 (6): 1695–1725.

Monteiro Filha, D. C. 1994. "A aplicavao de fundos compulsórios pelo BNDES na formavao da estrutura setorial da industria brasileira: 1952 a 1989." Doctoral thesis, Instituto de Economia Industrial. Universidade Federal do Rio de Janeiro (UFRJ), Rio de Janeiro, Brazil.

Ottaviano, G., and Sousa, F. 2008. "O efeito do BNDES na Produtividade das Empresas." In *Políticas de Incentivo à Inovação Tecnológica*, edited by J. De Negri and L. Kubota, 361–86. Brasilia: IPEA.

Pereira, R. 0. 2007. "Avao do BNDES sobre o emprego formal: Efeito nas empresas financiadas." *Revista do BNDES* 14 (27): 27–42.

Puga, F. P., and E. T. Torres Filho. 2006. "Empresas apoiadas pelo BNDES geram mais empregos e pagam mais." *Visão do Desenvolvimento* 17: 117.

Reiff, L. 0. d. A., L.H.R. Rocha, and G. A. G. d. Santos. 2007. "Emprego formal, qualidade de vida eo papel do BNDES." *Revista do BNDES* 14 (27): 5–26.

Sousa, F. L. d. 2003. "0 papel do BNDES na distribuivao geognifica da industria de Transformavao." *Revista do BNDES* I 0 (19): 3–20.

Terra, M. C. T. 2003. "Credit Constraints in Brazilian Firms: Evidence from Panel Data." *Revista Brasileira de Economia* 57 (2): 443–64.

PART THREE: IMPLICATIONS OF TURBULENT TIMES FOR BUILDING MONITORING AND EVALUATION CAPACITY

CHAPTER 10

A Proposed Framework to Understand Civil Society Organizations' Involvement in M&E

Marie Gildemyn

Overview

The aim of this chapter[1] is to increase our understanding of civil society organizations[2] (CSOs) involvement in monitoring and evaluation (M&E), especially in aid-dependent, developing countries. As a first step, the two main functions of M&E, accountability and feedback/learning, are unpacked relying on a broad and diverse range of literature across disciplines. The most relevant elements discussed in this review are integrated within a conceptual framework proposed at the end of the chapter. This framework not only aims to improve our understanding of CSOs' involvement in M&E, but could also inform future capacity-building initiatives for CSOs.

Introduction: M&E in the Current Aid Architecture

In the late 1990s, a new approach to aid emerged constructed around the principles of ownership, participation, harmonization, alignment, and results-based management (RBM). Important building blocks of this new aid architecture are the International Monetary Fund's Poverty Reduction Strategy Papers (PRSPs), the Paris Declaration (OECD/DAC 2005), the Accra Agenda for Action (OECD/DAC 2008), and the more recent Busan Partnership Agreement (OECD/DAC 2011). The shift in thinking, combined with the adoption of new aid modalities, such as general and sector budget support, have had enormous consequences for the M&E systems of both donors and governments. Because donors have been moving away from an ex-ante type of conditionality toward an ex-post type of conditionality, in which aid is based on a proven record of progress and results, country-led M&E systems have been subjected to an ambitious reform agenda (Holvoet and Renard 2007).

To respond to the new challenges, developing countries have been asked to better define and elaborate their national M&E systems, to make them more results-oriented and robust, and to allow participation of nonstate actors, including CSOs. Conversely, donors have been asked to harmonize and align their own M&E systems with each country's M&E system to reduce the country's administrative burden. National M&E systems thus have two main functions:

- To be accountable, particularly at the domestic level, to ensure the implementation of (pro-poor) policies and programs
- To provide feedback to support "the realization of results-oriented, iterative and evidence-based policy-making" (Holvoet and Rombouts 2008, 579).

The initial emphasis on broad-based participation within the M&E systems was motivated by three assumptions: first, that the involvement of CSOs would improve domestic accountability, which refers to the accountability relations between the government and its citizens (Hickey and Mohan 2008); second, that CSOs would have a comparative advantage because, compared with external evaluators, they are closer to the local community and able to monitor over longer periods of time, especially at decentralized levels (Goetz and Jenkins 2001); and last, that CSOs would have sound experience in the use of participatory and qualitative M&E tools, which would complement the quantitative approach that dominates most official M&E systems (Prennushi and others 2002).

In practice, however, the role of CSOs within national M&E systems is not always clear, and their participation takes place through a variety of formal and informal arrangements. Some CSOs participate within working groups, steering committees, and other more formal structures, while others carry out M&E independently. The literature supports the observation that institutionalized participation of CSOs within the official M&E system appears difficult in practice and is not systematically researched (Lucas and others 2004; Eberlei 2007; Eberlei and Siebold 2006). Available literature concentrates primarily on the involvement of CSOs in the monitoring of the first generation of PRSPs, focusing on the obstacles and opportunities they face. Conversely, more CSOs appear to carry out M&E independently and engage with government officials through other channels. This type of independent M&E carried out by CSOs is referred to as *CSO-led M&E*[3] in this chapter. Some common tools CSOs are using to carry out this type of M&E are shown in table 10.1.

Independent M&E carried out by CSOs has become increasingly popular in recent years, especially as a demand-side approach to accountability. As the name suggests, CSO-led M&E carried out under the banner of social accountability is more focused on M&E for accountability than M&E for policy/program feedback and learning, although both functions are important. Despite the huge popularity of these initiatives, little is known about their effectiveness and impact. As a first step to understanding the influence of CSO-led M&E, this chapter deconstructs the twin goals of M&E: accountability and feedback/learning. Second, the most important elements discussed are combined in a framework proposed at the end of the chapter.

Table 10.1   M&E Tools Used by CSOs According to Their Place within the Logic Model

	Input	Output	Outcome
Client satisfaction survey		X	X
Citizen report cards		X	X
Community score cards		X	X
Community monitoring	X	X	X
Public expenditure tracking	X	X	
Social audits	X	X	X

Source: Adapted from Verbeke and Holvoet 2006.

Note: CSO = civil society organization, M&E = monitoring and evaluation.

Unpacking the Accountability Function of M&E

This section examines how CSO-led M&E can contribute to accountability. The link between CSO-led M&E and accountability is clearest in the concept of social accountability, in which CSOs use M&E tools combined with other activities, such as advocacy and policy education to demand accountability from public officials and/or service providers. Before examining this link, it is important to deconstruct or unpack the concept of accountability, and to briefly discuss how accountability has been conceptualized in development discourse.

What Is Accountability?

The concept of accountability has become increasingly popular in recent years. More than 100 different definitions and types of accountability have been reported in the literature (Lindberg 2009), which has contributed to a loss of meaning and fuzziness. Despite the conceptual cacophony, the ultimate goal of accountability remains the same: to keep power under control and prevent abuses.

Within the development discourse, accountability has become a buzz-word and is often portrayed as the new panacea for failures in service delivery and weak development outcomes. This trend can be witnessed through key publications such as the *World Development Report* on improving public service delivery (World Bank 2004), the importance of accountability in the second generation of PRSPs (Hickey and Mohan 2008), and the increasing emphasis on social accountability (Malena and others 2004; McNeil and Malena 2010). Further, many donor discourses have emphasized the importance of accountability to help realize good governance, public sector reform, and, ultimately, democracy (Lindberg 2009; Newell and Bellour 2002).

To create some clarity, Lindberg (2009, 8) proposed a definition of accountability that captures the core characteristics of any form of accountability:

- An agent or institution who is to give an account (A for agent)
- An area, responsibilities, or domain subject to accountability (D for domain)
- An agent or institution P to whom A is to give account (P for principal)
- The right of P to require A to inform and explain/justify decisions with regard to D
- The right of P to sanction A if A fails to inform and/or explain/justify decisions with regard to 0.

The last two characteristics in this definition refer to the two dimensions of accountability, which are answerability and enforceability, as proposed by Schedler (1999). *Answerability* refers to the fact that accounting agents can ask power holders to provide information about their past or future actions and decisions (transparency) and their reasons for doing so (justification). "Accountability thus involves the right to receive information and the corresponding obligation to release all necessary details" (Schedler 1999, 15). *Receiving information* not only refers to obtaining data and evidence, for example, through monitoring, but also to reasoning and argumentation. *Enforceability* refers to the capacity to impose sanctions, or to the act of punishing the powerful if they fail to live up to their promises or if they engage in unlawful activities (Schedler 1999).[4] The distinction between these dimensions is important because the concept of answerability is often conflated with the concept of accountability. Without the element of enforceability or without the threat of sanction, one cannot talk about full accountability. Enforceability, thus, requires the presence of accounting actors that have enough power and/or autonomy to impose sanctions. As will be discussed, CSOs usually lack the power, legitimacy, and capacity to meet this dimension of accountability.

Although Schedler (1999) mentions that the concept of enforceability refers to both "rewarding" and "punishing," he and other authors (O'Donnell 1999; Rubenstein 2007) emphasize the element of sanction. If the goal of enforceability and accountability in general is to ensure that public officials and other actors comply with established rules, then the focus should be on creating the right incentive structure rather than on punishment alone. Ackerman (2005, 13) expresses this more nuanced version when he mentions, "The best accountability system is one that includes both punishments and rewards so that public officials have strong incentives both not to break the rules and to perform at their maximum capacity." In a similar way, Brett (2003) points out that for institutions to be accountable and perform well, both strong incentives and a real threat of sanction need to be present.

Moving away from the definition of accountability toward its typology, a common distinction is made between horizontal and vertical accountability. *Vertical accountability* can be described as the use of external mechanisms by nonstate (external) actors to hold policymakers to account (Goetz and Jenkins 2001). In vertical accountability, the relationship between the accountability holders and the power wielders is unequal. The most conventional mechanism used in vertical accountability is elections, where citizens (less powerful) can sanction or reward the current government for its past performance. Other examples are exposure of public officials' wrongdoing in the media and government lobbying. Taking into account the direction of accountability between the more powerful and the less powerful, one can talk about upward (vertical) accountability or downward (vertical) accountability. Within the aid context, upward accountability is used when governments or nongovernmental organizations (NGOs) are accountable toward donors, while downward accountability, also called domestic accountability, refers to efforts by government to become more accountable to its citizens.

Conversely, *horizontal accountability* occurs between actors with equal power. Because power is not easily measurable, Schedler (1999, 26) proposes to "translate" equal power by looking at the level of autonomy or the degree of mutual independence between the actors in question. O'Donnell (1999, 38) defines horizontal accountability as: "The existence of state agencies that are legally enabled and empowered, and factually willing and able, to take actions that span from routine oversight to criminal sanctions or agencies of the state that may be qualified as unlawful." His definition implies that within horizontal accountability there is no room for nonstate, external actors to participate directly in accountability initiatives. His narrow definition has given rise to debate among scholars and has ultimately led to the emergence of a new notion, in which CSOs are able to play a more prominent role.

CSO-led M&E and Accountability

Traditionally, the role of civil society in accountability has been located in the vertical axis. Through elections, lobbying, and other mechanisms, CSOs are able to hold governments accountable for their past performance. Nevertheless, several authors (Peruzzotti and Smulovitz 2006; Goetz and Jenkins 2005) have highlighted the weakness of voting as an instrument of accountability because of various imperfections such as information asymmetry and corruption. In addition, horizontal accountability mechanisms are deficient in many developing countries (O'Donnell 1999). New approaches toward accountability that rely on civil society engagement have gained prominence as a way to increase domestic accountability. Called *hybrid or diagonal accountability*, these approaches all "challenge the vertical–horizontal dichotomy on which understandings of accountability have been based" (Goetz and Jenkins 2001, 364). Goetz and Jenkins (2001), for example, point out that some CSOs engage in performance monitoring and financial auditing activities that are traditionally carried out by actors within the horizontal accountability axis (Goetz and Jenkins 2001, 365). Other authors (Newell and Bellour 2002; O'Donnell 1999) have pointed out that the presence of strong CSOs within the vertical accountability axis can stimulate horizontal accountability agencies to take action. For example, in Latin America, Peruzzotti and Smulovitz (2006, 10) studied how civil society and media organizations are able to "monitor public officials, expose governmental wrongdoing, and [can] activate the operation of horizontal agencies" through the use of both institutional and noninstitutional channels. Following their monitoring activities, these CSOs can apply soft sanctions, such as exposure in the media, or trigger the response of formal horizontal accountability agencies that have the capacity to enforce legal sanctions. This hybrid accountability has been called *societal or social accountability* by these authors.

In more recent years, the concept of social accountability has gained prominence and has been adopted and actively promoted by various donors, including the World Bank (2012) through its Global Partnership for Social Accountability (GSPA). The definition has also broadened over the years, sparking critiques from certain authors about the increasing fuzziness surrounding the concept (for example, Joshi and Houtzager 2012). Originally, Malena and others (2004, 3) defined social accountability as, "an approach towards building accountability that relies on civic engagement, that is, in which it is ordinary citizens and/or civil society organizations who participate directly or indirectly in exacting accountability." It is important to understand that social accountability initiatives encompass a broad range of activities initiated by various actors using various strategies. Examples of social accountability initiatives include CSOs involved in policy advocacy, budget literacy, civic education, and lobbying and coalition building, among others (Malena and McNeil 2010). The U. K. Department for International Development (DFID) proposed a different classification with the various stages of the accountability process at which CSOs can engage (see box 10.1). This chapter particularly addresses CSOs that are involved in the "investigation" phase and that are using M&E tools to "assess" government's performance and/or compliance with previously established standards.

Although new social accountability initiatives are mushrooming across the globe and funding for these initiatives is growing, little sound evidence of their effectiveness or impact is available. Several small case studies and some impact evaluations on the effect of social accountability initiatives have been done, but large-scale comparative studies are still lacking. An exception is the large-scale research in which McGee and Gaventa (2011) review various studies[5] on the effectiveness and the impact of such initiatives and try to identify contributing factors. Their results suggest that evidence about effectiveness and impact of such initiatives is uneven and inconclusive, sometimes even contradictory. Most accountability initiatives are also directed toward strengthening answerability and transparency aspects, whereas less attention has been paid to the link with existing horizontal accountability institutions.

Other, earlier research (for example Eberlei and Siebold 2006; Lucas and others 2004) point to some constraints, opportunities, and strategies CSOs are using to overcome obstacles when they carry out this type of M&E. Some of the obstacles relate to the CSOs' lack of financial resources as well as their lack of time and analytical skills to undertake M&E activities beyond the project level. In addition, many CSOs operate within a legal environment that does not guarantee the right to public information, making access to information challenging (Eberlei and Siebold 2006; Goetz and Jenkins 2001). The most challenging obstacle, however, is the unequal power relations in the accountability relation (Rubenstein 2007) and the perceived lack of legitimacy of CSOs' engagement in M&E activities.

However CSOs are using several strategies to overcome or compensate for these constraints. Some strategies, which have been reported in the literature on social accountability initiatives, include advocacy, networking with media and other organizations, and trying to trigger the response of actors who have the power and legitimacy to impose sanctions. With regard to the enforceability dimension, rather than sanctioning governments, CSOs may try to incentivize governments to take action through the use of informal, "soft" mechanisms such as exposure in the media, mobilization of public opinion, and dialogue and engagement as opposed to "naming and shaming." However, there is a lack of research on the impact of these mechanisms (Malena and others 2004; McNeil and Malena 2010).

Figure 10.1   Conceptual Framework: Accountability Dimension

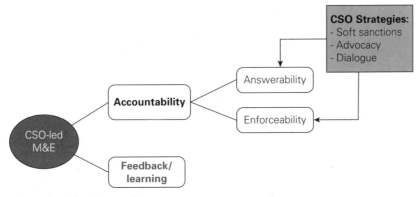

Note: CSO = civil society organization.

In sum, to understand how CSO-led M&E can contribute to improved accountability, it is important to look at both answerability and enforceability as represented in the first part of the conceptual framework (figure 10.1). Being involved in various M&E activities can provide a springboard for CSOs to hold governments accountable, but the mere act of monitoring (and evaluating) is not sufficient. Too many initiatives that support accountability are directed only toward strengthening the answerability and transparency aspects, while forgetting the enforceability dimension. For CSOs involved in accountability initiatives, additional strategies—such as soft sanctions, advocacy, and dialog—are fundamental to transforming their M&E evidence into a tool of genuine accountability.

The next section will discuss how M&E can be used to provide feedback or to influence programs and policies.

Unpacking the Feedback/Learning Function of M&E

Monitoring and evaluation, like research in general, aims to generate evidence and knowledge about programs and policies to find out what has worked and why, and to inform future decision making. *Evidence-based policy making* and *results-based management* are terms used to express the shift toward a more rational approach to policy making, in which M&E plays a crucial role. The link between research/knowledge and policy/ programs has been intensively researched by many academics and practitioners, and the field of evaluation use and influence is one of the biggest within evaluation research. The theories of *evaluation use and influence*[6] can be used to understand the influence of M&E by CSOs. In the second part of this section, links between policy and knowledge/research undertaken by researchers and organizations in developing countries will be discussed.

Evaluation Use and Influence

Research on the use of evaluation results emerged during the 1960s and 1970s when many social scientists involved in the evaluation of large-scale social welfare programs in the United States became disappointed that their research/evaluation results were not being used to improve programs and policy making. This frustration gave rise to numerous theories explaining the nonuse of evaluation results and research in general. Some earlier work concentrated on the contextual elements facilitating or inhibiting the use of evaluation results. Other research (for example Shula and Cousins 1997) proposed a classification of different types of use.

The basis for evaluation theory was developed with the definition of three main types of evaluation use: instrumental, conceptual, and political/symbolic (Leviton and Hughes 1981). *Instrumental use* refers to the direct use of evaluation results for decision making; *conceptual use*, also called *enlightenment*, refers to the subtle influence of evaluations or "the percolation of new information, ideas and perspectives into the arenas in which decisions are made" (Weiss 1999, 471). *Political or symbolic use* occurs when evaluation findings are used to legitimate positions or decisions that have already been made (Kirkhart 2000). A fourth type, called *process use*, was described by Patton (1997). Process use refers to the fact that not only evaluation findings, but also the process of participating in an evaluation can have effects or lead to outcomes, such as feelings of empowerment and organizational learning. Thus, there are many ways in which M&E can be used beyond instrumental use. Paradoxically, despite the fact that instrumental use is rather exceptional, the direct use of evaluation findings to improve programs and decision making is still considered one of the main goals of evaluation.

More recently, following an article by Kirkhart (2000), researchers have proposed a shift in terminology from *evaluation use* to *evaluation influence*. The overall argument behind this shift is that the term "use" implicitly has an intentional, instrumental connotation whereas M&E can have effects or consequences in a plethora of ways. The term *evaluation influence* is a broader concept that captures the unintentional, longer-term consequences of M&E. Evaluation consequences can occur as a result of the findings, the process, or a combination of both (Kirkhart 2000). Although there is no consensus on the proposed switch, some authors have endorsed the concept of evaluation influence and taken it one step further (Henry and Mark 2003, Mark and Henry 2004; Christie 2007).

Mark and Henry (2004, 39), for example, developed a "Comprehensive Theory of Evaluation Influence" (see figure 10.2) that offers a "more specific framework and typology of influence." They propose a theory of change that explains the link between evaluation inputs (first column) and the long-term desired outcome of evaluation, social betterment (far right column).

Their theory explains how available evaluation inputs (such as resources and time available to carry out the M&E) will influence the type of evaluation activities carried out, and the type of knowledge or M&E evidence produced with its attributes (such as credibility and timeliness). The policy setting in which M&E activities take place and the broader context can facilitate or inhibit certain aspects of the evaluation process. Central to the theory are the different categories of influence mechanisms (dark grey boxes in figure 10.2; see table 10.2 for more details) that occur as a result of the evaluation findings and/or the evaluation process. This menu of possible influence mechanisms[7] (table 10.2) thus explains the different underlying processes through which evaluations can have an effect (Henry

Figure 10.2   A Comprehensive Theory of Evaluation Influence

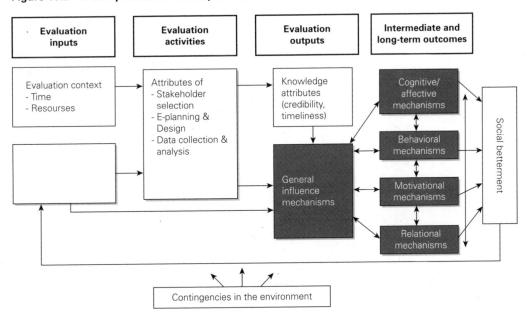

Source: Adapted from Mark and Henry 2004 and Mark 2006.

A Proposed Framework to Understand Civil Society Organizations' Involvement in M&E

Table 10.2   Model of Alternative Mechanisms That May Mediate Evaluation Influence

Types of process/ outcomes	Level of analysis		
	Individual	Interpersonal	Collective
General Influence	Elaboration Heuristics Priming Skill acquisition	Justification Persuasion Change agent Minority-opinion influence	Ritualism Legislative hearings Coalition formation Drafting legislation Standard setting Policy consideration
Cognitive and affective	Salience Opinion/attitude valence	Local descriptive norms	Agenda setting Policy-oriented learning
Motivational	Personal goals and aspirations	Injunctive norms Social reward exchange	Structural incentives Market forces
Behavioral	New skill performance Individual change in practice	Collaborative change in practice	Program continuation, change, or cessation Policy change Diffusion
Relational	Self-perception of empowerment	Networks shifts in power relations	Democratic forum Learning organizations Social justice

Source: Adapted from Mark and Henry 2004 and Mark 2006.

and Mark 2003). To explain these underlying mechanisms, the authors have relied on established research from social and behavioral sciences, which "can be a powerful source of methods, measures and hypotheses" (Mark and Henry 2004, 51). The framework of mechanisms distinguishes among three levels of analysis—the individual, interpersonal, and collective levels—indicating the locus of the change process, and five mechanisms or types of processes: general influence, cognitive and affective, motivational, behavioral (Mark and Henry 2004, 39), and, more recently, relational (see column and row headings of table 10.2). Entries in table 10.2 can be both *outcomes* of the evaluation and *mechanisms* that stimulate other outcomes: "Because the elements [...] can play the dual roles of an outcome of evaluation and mechanisms that stimulates other outcomes, we often refer to them as processes" (Mark and Henry 2004, 43). A certain combination of different influence mechanisms can then form a pathway toward a longer-term

Development Evaluation in Times of Turbulence

outcome, such as better education or health, which is captured in the term *social betterment*.

Like any theory, this theory has advantages and disadvantages. One of its limitations, especially for CSO-led M&E, is the lack of attention to external factors that influence the process. External factors are acknowledged, through the concept of contingencies and the decision-making context, but for use in developing countries, more details are necessary, which will be discussed in the next section. Empirical applications of this theoretical framework are also limited (Christie 2007; Weiss and others 2005), especially in a developing-country context. Conversely, because the theory is still a work in progress, it can easily be adapted to provide the foundations for context-specific, local theories of evaluation influence (Henry and Mark 2003). However, the most important contribution of the theoretical framework is the attention it draws to the broad range of ways in which M&E can have an effect at different levels beyond direct, instrumental use. Table 10.2 entries show that program and policy change are only two among many possible influence mechanisms.

Understanding the Knowledge/Research–Policy Interface in Developing Countries

Because the theories and frameworks discussed above have not yet been studied in the context of developing countries, and to better understand which factors are mediating the relationship between M&E and program/policy, the broader literature on the interface between knowledge/research and policy was consulted. M&E can be considered a type of research because it relies on techniques and methods from social sciences. More specifically, the experience of the Research and Policy in Development (RAPID) group at the Overseas Development Institute (ODI) and the work of the International Development Research Centre (IDRC) were examined. The frameworks proposed by both research groups partially overlap but also complement each other. The RAPID framework draws attention to a broad range of factors that are relevant for understanding the relationship between research and policy. The work of IDRC focuses on the specific strategies CSOs and research institutions are adopting to increase the influence of their research on policy.

The RAPID Framework
The RAPID framework (figure 10.3) was developed by ODI to map the four broad areas that play a role in the research–policy link: external influence, political context, the evidence, and the links. M&E research falls at the intersection of the political and evidence "circles" (see arrow in figure 10.3).

Figure 10.3   The RAPID Framework

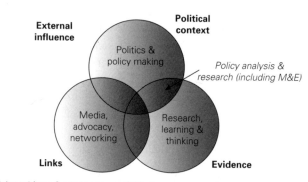

Source: Adapted from Court and Young 2004, 2.
Note: RAPID = Research and Policy in Development.

The four elements shed light on the link between CSO-Ied M&E and its feedback function. *External influence* (figure 10.3) refers to elements within the broader, international context in which CSOs operate, such as the Paris Declaration and the Millennium Development Goals, as well as more general influences, such as the move toward evidence-based policy making and the presence of donors in developing countries. The *political context* refers to national-level political processes, such as the political structure of a country, and/or the way policy making occurs within a certain sector. For most of the factors in this category, data on a range of indicators exists. Examples are the Freedom of Press Index as a proxy for media freedom in a country and the governance indicators published by the World Bank.[8] With respect to policy making, there are differences in openness across policy domains. Some sectors, such as the education sector, are more open to sources of evidence that are generated by external actors such as CSOs, whereas others, such as macroeconomic policies, are more closed (Jones and others 2009, 16).

The category *evidence* (figure 10.3) relates to both the characteristics of the evidence and the communication strategies employed (Court and Young 2003; Court and Young 2004). Evidence can be generated in many ways beyond academic research, for example, through participatory research and storytelling, but also through M&E (see arrow in figure 10.3). However, there is a hierarchy of different types of evidence. In addition, there is variation in the attributes of evidence, such as credibility, validity, and reliability, which will facilitate or inhibit its uptake within policy making. The way evidence is communicated also plays an important role and will be discussed in more detail when explaining the key elements of the IDRC framework.

The last element of the framework may be the most important and is closely related to the influence of CSO-Ied M&E. To bridge policy and

Development Evaluation in Times of Turbulence

evidence, *links* (figure 10.3) act as a key facilitator and can be created through the development of networks, advocacy, and others. Compared with individual evaluators, CSOs undertaking M&E have an advantage here because they are more experienced in such types of activities. This element reappears in the IDRC framework, described below.

The IDRC Framework

The IDRC developed a framework, referred to as a "realist perspective of policy influence" (figure 10.4), based on an in-depth evaluation of 23 best-practice cases about the influence of research on policy in developing countries (Carden 2004, 2009).

The framework and underlying empirical evidence are discussed extensively in Carden (2009). Although it is beyond the scope of this chapter to explain them in detail, key elements relevant to understanding the influence of CSO-Ied M&E will be highlighted. The framework shows similarities with the RAPID framework regarding research and context (figure 10.4). Under *context*, decision context is emphasized and broken down into five receptivity categories to explain the openness of government/policy makers toward research findings. These decision context categories will influence the strategies researchers and organizations adopt to draw attention to their research. As Carden (2009, 25) explains, "each of these classes of receptivity calls for definable strategies by which researchers and research advocates can maximize their prospects of influencing public policy and development action." The relationship between an adopted strategy, or combination of strategies, according to the decision

Figure 10.4 Realist Perspective of Policy Influence

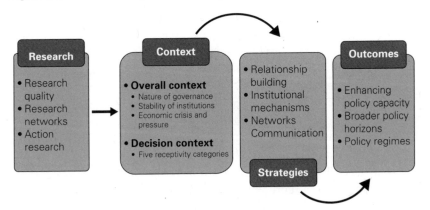

Source: Adapted from Carden 2010.

context and the outcome is not linear and predictable, however, because other contextual elements can interfere.

For the purpose of this chapter, the *strategies* (figure 10.4) of relationship building, networks, and communication are especially important. Having a good communication strategy is crucial and goes beyond mere dissemination of results. The establishment of a permanent dialogue forum, for example, has been shown to be conducive for policy influence because it promotes the continuous exchange of information between researchers and policymakers (Carden 2009). As discussed in the previous section, establishing dialogue is also crucial to strengthening domestic accountability. Further, professional mobility, networks, and personal relations are important informal channels of communication that foster the exchange of ideas.

In sum, CSO-led M&E has consequences that go beyond the instrumental use of M&E findings. M&E generated by CSOs can exert influence in many ways as suggested by Mark and Henry. In addition, CSOs use a variety of strategies to increase the influence of their work, as visible from the ODI and IDRC literature. Given that both main functions of M&E have been deconstructed and linked, where possible, to CSO-led M&E, the most important elements will be combined into a conceptual framework explained in the conclusion of this chapter.

Bringing Everything Together: Toward an Understanding of CSOs' Involvement in M&E

Some of the most important elements discussed in this chapter are summarized below. These elements can be considered the building blocks for a conceptual framework, whose aim is to contribute to a better understanding of CSOs' involvement in M&E.

Following the introduction, the concept of accountability was unpacked, highlighting its two dimensions—answerability and enforceability—and some of its main types—vertical, horizontal, and hybrid/diagonal or social. The concept of social accountability was analyzed because of its usefulness in understanding how CSOs, especially CSOs involved in M&E activities, can strengthen domestic accountability. The literature has highlighted obstacles and opportunities CSOs face when trying to demand answers from government or, more importantly, create the right incentive structure for government to take action. The two dimensions of accountability and the strategies CSOs employ to turn M&E evidence into a tool for domestic accountability are represented in the framework shown in figure 10.5. The figure lists factors related to the broader political context in which the

Figure 10.5   Understanding CSOs' Involvement in M&E

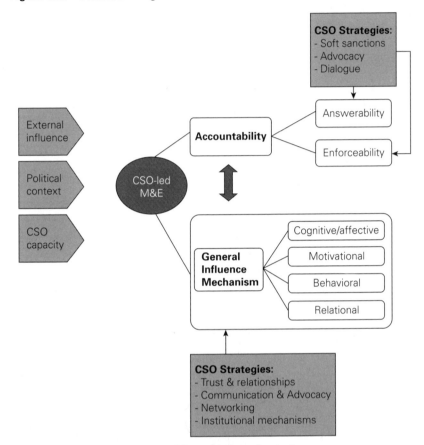

Note: CSO = civil society organization, M&E = monitoring and evaluation.

CSOs operate and factors related to the capacity of CSOs to undertake this type of independent M&E.

The second part of this chapter explained the feedback function of M&E by relying on the literature about evaluation use and influence and the knowledge/research–policy interface discussed in the context of developing countries. The literature broadens the understanding of the concept "evaluation use and influence" beyond instrumental use. Most evaluations do not result in concrete program or policy changes but generate important changes at the conceptual or cognitive level. In addition, the Comprehensive Theory of Evaluation Influence offers a framework to examine the different underlying processes through which evaluation influences broader outcomes at the cognitive, motivational, behavioral, and relational levels, which should ultimately result in social betterment. The underlying mechanisms of the Comprehensive Theory of Evaluation Influence are also represented in the proposed conceptual framework (see figure 10.5).

Finally, the literature on the knowledge/research–policy interface draws attention to the factors that play a role in the knowledge/research–policy interface, as well as strategies CSOs are using to bring M&E evidence to the attention of policy makers.

In conclusion, the proposed framework takes into account the importance of context to understanding the environment in which CSOs are carrying out M&E activities, the type of M&E they are carrying out, and their capacity to transform the gathered M&E evidence as a tool to increase accountability and to influence (pro-poor) programs and policies. The framework draws its strength from the fact that it reflects elements from a broad range of literature, and takes into account both the accountability and the feedback function of M&E.

The framework is still a work in progress and future research and fieldwork on CSO-Ied M&E are necessary to fine-tune its elements. For example, this chapter was structured to discuss the two main functions of M&E separately. Nevertheless, as indicated by the dark grey arrow in figure 10.5, dynamics and trade-offs between both functions exist. CSOs that are engaged in expenditure tracking, for example, to ensure the good use of program resources, may be able to introduce improvements in that program through a combination of their M&E evidence, advocacy, and dialogue. Further, some influence mechanisms like "agenda-setting" or "change in practice" (see table 10.2) are indicators of a greater answerability and responsiveness of public officials. Additional research, especially empirical research, is needed to further explore the interaction between both functions. Despite this challenge, the proposed framework is a good starting point to study CSO-Ied M&E in different settings, and, hopefully, a source of inspiration for further research on the topic.

Notes

1. This chapter is a revised, shorter version of Gildemyn 2011.
2. For the purpose of this chapter, the term *civil society organizations* refers to a wide variety of organizations, beyond nongovernmental organizations (NGOs), such as trade unions, think tanks, community-based organizations, and others.
3. The term CSO-led M&E is adopted here to refer to the array of M&E activities in which CSOs are involved at the program and policy level. These M&E activities go beyond the (internal) M&E activities CSOs are undertaking at the level of their own projects and programs.

4. There is debate among authors regarding the concept of enforceability. Some authors (for example Hickey and Mohan 2008 and Schedler 1999) argue that noncompliance with agreed standards can lead to sanctioning, while others (Lindberg 2009) have argued that sanctions should only be applied if power holders fail to provide answers or justification.

5. Not all studies on social accountability made an explicit distinction between the different types of accountability initiatives. The results discussed here apply to social accountability initiatives as a whole, not only those that have M&E at their core.

6. Evaluation use and influence primarily looks at "the consequences" of evaluation and, implicitly, of monitoring as well. Monitoring and evaluation are two distinct but complementary processes. Although the theory was developed to explain evaluation influence, it has also been applied to performance monitoring (Mark and Henry 2004) and to study the influence of indicators (Lehtonen 2012).

7. For a detailed explanation of the different types of influence mechanisms see Henry and Mark 2003; Mark and Henry 2004; Mark 2006.

8. These indicators are available at : *www.govindicators.org*

References

Ackerman, J. M. 2005. "Social Accountability in the Public Sector: A Conceptual Discussion." Social Development Papers 82, World Bank, Washington DC.

Brett, E. A. 2003. "Participation and Accountability in Development Management." *The Journal of Development Studies* 40 (2): 1–29.

Carden, F. 2004. "Issues in Assessing Policy Influence on Research." *International Social Science Journal* 179: 135–51.

———. 2009. *Knowledge to Policy? Making the Most of Development Research.* International Development Research Centre. Ottawa: Sage Publications.

Christie, C.A. 2007. "Reported Influence of Evaluation Data on Decision Makers' Actions: An Empirical Examination." *American Journal of Evaluation* 28 (8): 8–25.

Court, J., and J. Young. 2003. "Bridging Research and Policy: Insights from 50 Case Studies." Working Paper 213, Overseas Development Institute, London.

———. 2004. "Bridging Research and Policy in International Development: An Analytical and Practical Framework." Research and Policy in Development Programme Briefing Paper 1, Overseas Development Institute, London.

DFID (U.K. Department for International Development). 2007. "Civil Society and Good Governance: A DFID Practice Paper." DFID, London.

Eberlei, W. 2007. "Accountability in Poverty Reduction Strategies: The Role of Empowerment and Participation." Social Development Papers 104, World Bank, Washington, DC.

Eberlei, W., and T. Siebold. 2006. *Stakeholder Involvement in PRS Monitoring.* http://inef.uni-due.de/page/documents/eberlei/Eberlei-Siebold-Monitorin_ Juni2006.pdf (accessed November 5, 2010).

Gildemyn, M. 2011. "Towards an Understanding of CSO-Led M&E: Unpacking the Accountability and Feedback Function of M&E." Discussion Paper 2011-03, University of Antwerp.

Goetz, A. M., and R. Jenkins. 2001. "Hybrid Forms of Accountability: Citizen Engagement in Institutions of Public-Sector Oversight in India." *Public Management Review* 3 (3): 363–83.

Goetz, A.M., and R. Jenkins. 2005. *Reinventing Accountability*. Hampshire: Palgrave MacMillan.

Henry, G. T., and M. M. Mark. 2003. "Beyond Use: Understanding Evaluation's Influence on Attitudes and Actions." *American Journal of Evaluation* 24 (3): 293–314.

Hickey, S., and G. Mohan. 2008. "The Politics of Establishing Pro-Poor Accountability: What Can Poverty Reduction Strategies Achieve?" *Review of International Political Economy* 15 (2): 234–58.

Holvoet, N., and R. Renard. 2007. "Monitoring and Evaluation under the PRSP: Solid Rock or Quicksand?" *Evaluation and Program Planning* 30 (1): 66–81.

Holvoet, N., and H. Rombouts. 2008. "The Challenge of Monitoring and Evaluation under the New Aid Modalities: Experiences from Rwanda." *Journal of Modern African Studies* 46 (4): 577–602.

Jones, N., A. Datta, and H. Jones. 2009. *Knowledge, Policy, and Power. Six Dimensions of the Knowledge-Development Policy Interface.* http://www.odi.org.uk/resources/download/3790.pdf (accessed November 10, 2010).

Joshi, A., and P. P. Houtzager. 2012. "Widgets or Watchdogs? Conceptual Explorations in Social Accountability." *Public Management Review* 14 (2): 145–162.

Kirkhart, K. E. 2000. "Reconceptualizing Evaluation Use: An Integrated Theory of Influence." *New Directions for Evaluation* 88: 5–23.

Lehtonen, M. 2012. "Indicators as an Appraisal Technology: Framework for Analyzing the Policy Influence of the UK Energy Sector Indicators." In *Sustainable Development, Evaluation and Policy-Making: Theory, Practise and Quality Assurance,* edited by A. Von Raggamby and F. Rubik, 175–208. Cheltenham: Edward Elgar Publishing.

Leviton, L. C., and E. F. X. Hughes. 1981. "Research on the Utilization of Evaluations: A Review and Synthesis." *Evaluation Review* 5 (4): 525–48.

Lindberg, S.I. 2009. "Accountability: The Core Concept and Its Subtypes." Africa Power and Politics Programme Working Paper 1, Overseas Development Institute, London.

Lucas, H., D. Evans, and K. Pasteur. 2004. "Research on the Current State of PRS Monitoring Systems." Discussion Paper 382, Institute of Development Studies, Brighton.

Malena, C., and M. McNeil. 2010. "Social Accountability in Africa: An Introduction." In *Demanding Good Governance: Lessons from Social Accountability Initiatives in Africa,* edited by M. McNeil and C. Malena. Washington, DC: World Bank.

Malena, C., R. Forster, and J. Singh. 2004. "Social Accountability: An Introduction to the Concept and Emerging Practice." Social Development Papers 76, World Bank, Washington, DC.

Mark, M. M. 2006. "The Consequences of Evaluation: Theory, Research and Practice." Presidential address at the Annual Meeting of the American Evaluation Association, Portland, OR.

Mark, M. M., and G. T. Henry. 2004. "The Mechanisms and Outcomes of Evaluation Influence." *Evaluation* 10 (1): 35–57.

McGee, R., and J. Gaventa. 2011. "Shifting Power? Assessing the Impact of Transparency and Accountability Initiatives." Working Paper 383, Institute of Development Studies, Essex.

McNeil, M., and Malena, C., eds. 2010. *Demanding Good Governance: Lessons from Social Accountability Initiatives in Africa.* Washington, DC: World Bank.

Newell, P., and S. Bellour. 2002. "Mapping Accountability: Origins, Contexts and Implications for Development." Working Paper 168, Institute of Development Studies, Brighton.

O'Donnell, G. 1999. "Horizontal Accountability in New Democracies." In *The Self-Restraining State: Power and Accountability in New Democracies,* edited by A. Schedler, L. Diamond, and M. F. Plattner, 29–51. London: Lynne Rienner Publishers.

OECD/DAC (Organisation for Economic Co-operation and Development/Development Assistance Committee (OECD/DAC). 2005. "The Paris Declaration on Aid Effectiveness." OECD/DAC, Paris.

———. 2008. "Accra Agenda for Action." OECD/DAC, Paris.

———. 2011. "The Busan Partnership for Effective Development Co-operation." OECD/DAC, Paris.

Patton, M. Q. 1997. *Utilization-Focused Evaluation: The New Century Text.* Thousand Oaks, California: Sage.

Peruzzotti, E., and C. Smulovitz. 2006. "Social Accountability: An Introduction." In *Enforcing the Rule of Law: Social Accountability In the New Latin American Democracies,* edited by E. Peruzzotti and C. Smulovitz, 3–33. Pittsburgh: University of Pittsburgh Press.

Prennushi, G., G. Rubio, and K. Subbarao. 2002. "Monitoring and Evaluation." In *A Sourcebook for Poverty Reduction Strategies,* edited by J. Klugman. Washington, DC: World Bank.

Rubenstein, J. 2007. "Accountability in an Unequal World." *The Journal of Politics* 69 (3): 616–32.

Schedler, A. 1999. "Conceptualizing Accountability." In *The Self-Restraining State: Power and Accountability in New Democracies,* edited by A. Schedler, L. Diamond, and M. F. Plattner, 13–28. London: Lynne Rienner Publishers.

Shula, L. M., and J. B. Cousins. 1997. "Evaluation Use: Theory, Research and Practice since 1986." *Evaluation Practice* 18 (3): 195–208.

Verbeke K., and N. Holvoet. 2006. "Glossary of Selected M&E Instruments and Methods." Report for the Directorate General for Development Cooperation, Antwerp.

Weiss, C. H. 1999. "The Interface Between Evaluation and Public Policy." *Evaluation* 5 (4): 468–86.

Weiss, C.H., E. Murphy-Graham, and S. Birkeland. 2005. "An Alternate Route to Policy Influence: How Evaluations Affect D.A.R.E." *American Journal of Evaluation* 26 (1): 12–30.

World Bank. 2004. "Making Services Work for Poor People." In *World Development Report*. Washington, DC: World Bank.

———. 2012. "Global Partnership for Social Accountability and Establishment of a Multidonor Trust Fund." World Bank, Washington, DC.

CHAPTER 11

Monitoring and Evaluation in a New Environment

Case Study of Jordan's Ministry of Social Development

Rasha Qudisat

Objective

This chapter introduces the success factors of establishing a monitoring and evaluation (M&E) system in a new environment: Jordan's Ministry of Social Development (MoSD). It examines the support needed, the setting, the practice, and the use of the system. It illustrates the process of applying monitoring outcomes to creating a managerial policy tool. By piloting and evaluating the system in one department of the ministry, the authors were able to justify the need for M&E in other areas. The chapter also explains the use of M&E tools to provide an early warning system, which can alert decision makers to the need to review plans and strategies at certain points.

This chapter does not assess MoSD's social services, nor its plans and strategies. It is intended to highlight the importance of and need for M&E in the social sector.

Country Context

Jordan is a lower middle-income country with a population of 6 million and a per capita gross domestic product (GDP) of US$4,504 as of 2010. The population is about 80 percent urban and is one of the youngest among lower middle-income countries, with 70 percent under the age of 30. The country is not rich in natural resources (potash and phosphate are its main export commodities); its agricultural land is limited; and water is scarce—Jordan is the fourth water-poorest country in the world. The economy is well integrated with the rest of the region through trade, remittances, foreign direct invest (FDI), and tourism and has especially strong links to the Arab Gulf economies. Jordanian policy makers hope to use the country's demographic opportunity of a well-educated, young population to build a dynamic, knowledge-based economy.

Jordan has made significant investments in social development; however, households continue to be vulnerable to multiple risks. Despite its middle-income status, Jordan's economic achievements are fragile, and it is vulnerable to external shocks, such as commodity-price fluctuations and global economic turndowns. The global economic crisis has contributed to a slowdown in growth accompanied by a deteriorating fiscal situation. This situation makes it increasingly difficult for Jordan to provide adequate social protections. The global financial crisis highlights the importance of reinforcing the fundamentals of the kingdom's social protection system.

Jordan is on track to reach most of its Millennium Development Goals (MDGs), with regional disparity among its governorates. Yet, Jordan faces considerable challenges in strengthening its social protection system. Good social indicators (including low levels of maternal and infant mortality, high vaccination rates, universal primary education and high adult literacy, declining fertility, and increasing life expectancy) exist beside high levels of poverty. Approximately 781,000 Jordanians live in poverty, representing 13.3 percent of the population in 2008, a decline from 21 percent in 1989 (figure 11.1). However, this decline in the poverty rate is tenuous and could be easily reversed because a large share of the population lives just above the poverty line and 10 percent are vulnerable to falling into poverty. At the same time, many of the poor live just below the poverty line. Thus, low-cost but well-targeted social protection interventions could move a significant

Figure 11.1 Poverty Rates, 1989–2008

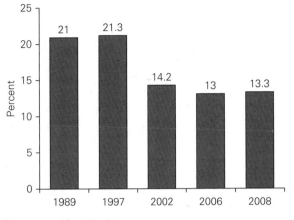

Source: Jordan Department of Statistics data.

share of the poor out of poverty and protect a significant share of the near poor from falling into poverty.

Regarding education, Jordan's primary and secondary enrollment, primary completion, illiteracy rates, and female enrollment have reached their goals for 2015 (Government of Jordan 2010). In terms of the gender indicators, Jordan lags in female representation in the Parliament and in employment in nonagricultural sectors. Clean drinking water is available to 98 percent of Jordan's population compared with 86 percent in low- and middle-income countries and 8 percent in the Middle East and North Africa region.[1] Although Jordan invests heavily in human capital, its best-trained people migrate abroad while foreign laborers take many jobs in the country. Commensurate with high growth in investments and GDP, job creation in Jordan has been strong.[2] However, unemployment among nationals has remained high, fluctuating between 12.5 and 14.5 percent over the last decade (figure 11.2). The percentage on unemployed women has declined slightly from 25.9 to 22.8 percent, while the percentage on unemployed men has gone from 12.8 percent to 10.8 percent. Among the factors explaining simultaneous high job growth with persistent unemployment among Jordanians is the mismatch between the high expectations of the unemployed (due, in part, to the existence of high-wage jobs in Gulf countries) and the prevailing low wages of available jobs in Jordan (World Bank 2008).

Expenditures on social assistance in Jordan were estimated at JD 459.7 million (US$656.7 million) in 2009, representing 2.8 percent of GDP. The largest share of social assistance spending (29 percent) went for untargeted

Figure 11.2   Unemployment Rates, 2005–March 2011

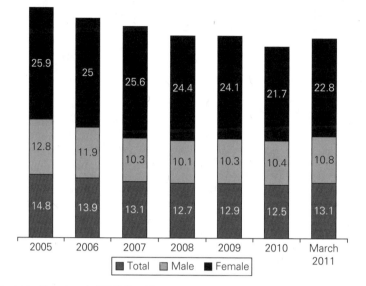

Source: Jordan Department of Statistics data.

Note: The unemployment rate in March 2011 was 13.1, and it remained steady throughout 2011.

general subsidies; cash transfers (the most tightly targeted outlay) accounted for about 20 percent of spending. Social care services and education-related transfers together accounted for less than 5 percent of social assistance spending.[3] Jordan has all the elements of an appropriate social protection system, yet, weaknesses in results-based program design and implementation limit its effectiveness.

The major pillars of Jordan's economic adjustment programs in the most recent period of reform have been the pursuit of macroeconomic stabilization by managing the demand side of the economy while implementing structural reforms to strengthen the supply side of the economy. Specific objectives of the plans were to reduce both budget and current-account deficits, control inflation, build up foreign reserves and, more broadly, to achieve sustainable economic growth.

In the 1990s, planning was oriented toward program planning, attaining macroeconomic stability, and rectifying fiscal imbalances,[4] whereas, in about 2001, there was a shift to comprehensive planning focusing on long-term sustainability and based on targeted objectives and indicators using an indicative planning approach to increase development and performance. This type of planning is achieved by developing action plans that include priorities for the main sectors starting with Jordan's Socioeconomic

Transformation Program for 2002–04. However, challenges still face the economy and new requirements have emerged that necessitated a rigorous review of the reform agenda for the period 2004–06,[5] which aimed at achieving and sustaining GDP growth rates of 6 percent per annum by the year 2006 and a growth of per capita income of 3.6 percent by the same year. The National Agenda 2006-15, which created a master plan for the reform, future growth, and development of Jordan, was translated into an executive program with the first phase from 2007 to 2009 and second phase from 2010 to 2013 (figure 11.3).

Effects of the Economic Crisis on Jordan

The global and regional downturn strongly affected the Jordanian economy, and growth slowed considerably in 2009. In particular, reduced oil prices and bleak global demand slashed Jordan's GDP growth to 2.3 percent, down from 6.7 percent in the 2000–08 period and 8.1 percent in 2004–08. Financial services, wholesale and retail trade, and manufacturing were especially hard hit, while the public sector and construction grew countercyclically as a result of the government's swift response to the crisis. Economic growth was expected to recover gradually over the medium term in 2010 (at about 3.3 percent) and to reach 6 percent in 2013 (figure 11.4).

The Government of Jordan has been working on accelerating structural reforms (fiscal reforms, business environment, financial sector reforms, and social protection reforms) and on short-term policy actions to address the

Figure 11.3   Main Socioeconomic Reforms, 1990–2013

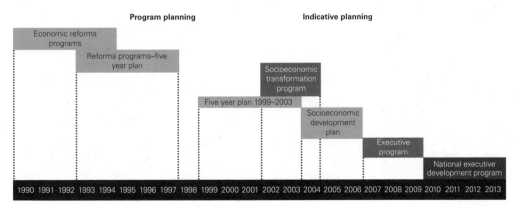

Figure 11.4   Jordan's Medium-Term Outlook
percent

	2008	2009	2010	2011	2012	2013
Outlook	Actual	Actual	Estimated	Projected		
National Accounts						
Real GDP Growth	7.6	2.3	3.3	5.0	5.5	6.0
Real Gross Domestic Investment Growth	8.3	−34.8	36.8	15.5	15.1	8.7
Nominal-GDP (US$ million)	22,744	25,156	27,198	26,662	32,479	35,565
Prices						
GDP Deflator (Change in percent)	18.8	8.1	47	3.9	3.8	3.3
Consumer Price Index (%change)	14.9	−0.6	7.9	2.0	3.1	2.8
Imports Price Index (%change)	20.5	4.5	−2.6	−0.8	0.4	−0.1
Money & Banking						
Growth of Money Supply	17.3	9.3	19.2	12.0	12.6	11.4
Total Deposits—Resident (% of GDP)	97.3	107.5	110.4	113.5	115.5	124.0
Lending to the Public Sector to Total Banks Assets (in percent)	19.7	17.0	18.4	18.9	18.9	18.4
External Accounts						
Balance of Trade in Goods & Services (% of GDP)	−30.0	−21.5	−23.4	−202	−18.5	−17.3
Current account balance (% of GDP)	−9.6	−5.1	−10.9	−7.8	−7.3	−6.9
Foreign Direct Investments (% of GDP)	14.9	6.7	10.8	11.1	10.0	8.8
Remittances (US$ million)	3,166	3,126	3,295	3,230	3,216	3,199
International Reserves (US$ million)	8,568	11,471	11,701	12,542	13.283	14,387
Fiscal Accounts						
Total revenues	**29.4**	**25.4**	**25.2**	**24.9**	**24.1**	**24.6**
Domestic revenues	25.0	23.5	23.2	23.5	23.0	23.6
Grants	4.5	1.9	1.9	1.4	1.1	1.0
Total expenditures	**33.7**	**33.8**	**30.5**	**29.9**	**28.2**	**27.7**
Primary current expenditures	25.6	23.5	22.6	21.8	20.6	20.3
o/w wages and salaries	4.5	4.3	4.4	4.1	3.8	3.7
o/w oil & food subsidies	2.4	0.7	0.5	0.5	0.4	−3.2
o/w capital expenditures	**6.0**	**8.1**	**5.1**	**5.7**	**5.2**	**5.2**
Total interest expenditures	**2.2**	**2.2**	**2.8**	**2.4**	**2.4**	**2.2**
Fiscal balance excluding grants	−8.8	−10.3	−7.3	−6.4	−5.2	−4.2
Fiscal balance including all grants	−4.3	−8.5	−5.3	−5.0	−4.1	−3.2
Primary balance excluding grants	−6.6	−8.1	−4.5	−4.0	−2.7	−1.9
Primary balance including all grants	−2.1	−6.3	−2.6	−2.6	−1.7	−0.9
Gross public debt over GDP	58.3	61.5	62.2	62.1	60.8	58.7
Net public debt over GDP	53.1	54.2	55.4	55.9	54.8	53.3
Memo items						
Average International Oil Prices (US$ per barrel)	97.0	61.8	78.1	74.6	73.9	73.0
Primary Balance of Stabilization	−13.3	−3.4	−1.8	−2.8	−3.0	−3.0

Source: International Monetary Fund, country report, Jordan.

Note: GDP = gross domestic product, o/w = of which.

immediate adverse impacts of the economic crisis, while keeping a focus on social reforms. The reform policy follows the comprehensive principle of the "treatment-protection-prevention-promotion" approach at the economic, social, and political levels. The *treatment* section is focused on poverty issues; direct cash transfers are provided to poor people who are unable to work. In the fiscal area, an example of *prevention* and *promotion* is reducing public expenditures to achieve a more balanced budget. Social insurance is an example of *protection* because it empowers poor and vulnerable groups who are able to work.

Development of Social Assistance in Jordan

Although voluntary social works in Jordan date to the early 1920s, formal social works were begun in 1948 with the establishment of a special directorate for social affairs in the Ministry of Interior Affairs (MoI). The MoSD was established in 1956, to reduce poverty, encourage employment, empower women, provide a social safety net, and coordinate with organizations in the social field (box 11.1).

These major goals are to be achieved through several sectorial goals: develop and implement a comprehensive social policy, provide inclusive

---

Box 11.1   Ministry of Social Development

The major goals of the Ministry of Social Development, established in 1956, are as follows:

- Reduce poverty in a comprehensive manner, shifting from cash-based assistance (welfare) to sustainable economic empowerment of the poor, taking into consideration the individual characteristics of the poor who are unable to work.
- Enhance poverty reduction through local development.
- Strengthen principles of social justice and equal opportunity.
- Empower women (economic, social, public life, and cultural).
- Improve protection of women and children.
- Provide an effective and comprehensive social safety net (social care and protection, social security, health insurance, education, employment) to the poor, consistent with best practices.
- Enhance corporate social responsibility in the private sector and encourage civic engagement of local communities.

---

social care and protection, enhance the productivity of the capable poor, and empower women and provide them with opportunities of advancement. MoSD is considered the most decentralized ministry in the country, as it is responsible for 186 administrative units and directorates at the field level, including field and departmental directorates and offices in governorates and civil-society development centers.

Developmental planning in Jordan also dates to the middle of the 20th century, beginning with project-based planning, which evolved in the 1970s into sectorial planning. By 2000, planning in Jordan shifted into a new era, adopting the indicative planning approach (indicators-based planning) (as shown in figure 11.3). Accordingly, Jordan endorsed the principles of M&E as M&E began to evolve at the international level. Consequently, MoSD is adopting a more systematic approach to create a new organizational culture that institutionalizes governmental accountability for its developmental and social obligations.

MoSD focuses on two major themes: (1) protection and care that targets vulnerable groups (women, children, disabled persons) though providing integrated social services; and (2) poverty reduction by providing cash assistance to the poor, enabling them to break out of the poverty circle (especially those who are able to work) through empowerment and awareness. This comprehensive strategy includes continuous efforts to build the capacity of MoSD, as well as the capacity of social workers and of civil society organizations, and to build up the National Aid Fund (NAF), an independent organization that provides financial assistance, health insurance, and vocational training to the poor.

Furthermore, MoSD is working to enhance its technical and institutional capacity to improve its M&E systems to ensure efficient and effective operations and impact on the beneficiaries and their communities. However, despite significant progress, MoSD's resources are overburdened by the increasing demand for social services, largely due to an increase in people's awareness of their rights for social protection and to the growing credibility of the social protection program.

Through 2008, MoSD had no official M&E unit; however, it maintained a huge amount of information related to the services it has provided and to its beneficiaries. Despite this mass of data, MoSD did not have an institutionalized database that could track daily (or even periodically) the social services provided to various target groups. MoSD began developing its M&E methods to ensure integration within policy-making and social-development planning processes, starting with the establishment of an M&E unit in the ministry in 2009.

M&E in Social Development

Institutionalization of an M&E system in a broad-outreach institution like MoSD was a substantial initiative that necessitated organizational, managerial, and cultural alterations in the structure of the ministry. It required communicating the vision, purpose, and importance of an M&E system at the outset, and ensuring a participatory approach to guarantee ownership of the M&E system so that it would be used and adapted throughout the ministry. The M&E system was implemented through six steps as shown in figure 11.5: (1) securing political support, (2) identifying the purpose of M&E, (3) a desk review and interviews, (4) a pilot project, (5) dissemination of the system, and (6) continuing to assess the M&E system in practice.

Securing Political Support and Identifying the Purpose

The first, and most vital, step in establishing the system was gaining solid political support from the minister. The plan was to first erect an infrastructure for the "M" (monitoring), which would pave the road for the "E" (evaluation). This first step legitimated the rules for the game, focused on

Figure 11.5   Steps in Establishing an M&E System

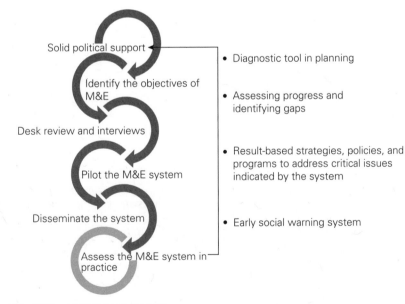

Solid political support

Identify the objectives of M&E

Desk review and interviews

Pilot the M&E system

Disseminate the system

Assess the M&E system in practice

- Diagnostic tool in planning

- Assessing progress and identifying gaps

- Result-based strategies, policies, and programs to address critical issues indicated by the system

- Early social warning system

Note: M&E = monitoring and evaluation.

> **Box 11.2 Four Uses of M&E**
>
> Monitoring and evaluation (M&E) can be used for any of the four objectives as described below.
>
> As a *tool for change*: Through M&E, an organization can identify the strengths and weaknesses of a project, program, or department so it can invest in the strengths and correct the weaknesses.
>
> In response to a *demand-driven* situation: A critical situation, such as a sudden increase in beneficiaries, may need to be evaluated and understood in order to respond quickly.
>
> As part of the *decision support system*: M&E results can guide a minister to provide the support for a program or directorate in terms of resources and decisions to enhance its performance.
>
> As an *early-warning system*: M&E techniques can be used to forecast the availability of resources (financial and human) versus the demand for services and the ability to provide them.

key issues (considering the limited resources), anticipated utilization and deadlines, and eventually achieved high-level support. Once the support was granted, the second step was to identify four possible M&E objectives (box 11.2). M&E can be used as a "tool for change" in addressing institutional capacity needs through identifying the strengths and weaknesses of an institution; in response to an evolving situation ("demand driven"); or as part of a "decision support system" in the institutions responsible for planning and implementation of result-based strategies, policies, and programs. It also can be used as an "early warning system," as demonstrated later in this chapter. Indeed, the different needs of planning, program implementation, social demand, and the need to enhance social services are generating demand for evaluation.

Desk Review

The third step was a desk review of current services and practices and interviews with stakeholders. It included collecting information on beneficiaries (women, children, juveniles, panhandlers, elderly, poor people), services provided, and programs implemented. MoSD quantitative and qualitative reports from the central office, directorates, and field offices were reviewed and data and information collected. Interviews with stakeholders and staff at different levels of management were conducted to assess their understating of M&E concepts. Surprisingly, there was a lack of knowledge of M&E

concepts among lower and middle management, many considering it barely useful and even a waste of time and effort. Changing this mentality and creating a culture of M&E to establish an enabling environment for evaluation was a challenge.

Testing the System

To deal with the 3F crisis, which affected the lives of many Jordanians, Jordanian authorities enhanced the social safety net, which is largely administered by MoSD and its Social Defense Directorate. Increased financial resources were provided in 2009, largely channeled through MoSD.

The Social Defense Directorate, a major directorate within MoSD (box 11.3), piloted an M&E system. Local trainings[6] were held to introduce senior and junior staff members to the theories and applications of M&E. Performance indicators at the input, output, and outcomes levels were put in place and the staff fully involved to guarantee ownership and accurateness.

The indicators were assessed to identify which were critical for future evaluations. Once the system was put in place, a reporting mechanism was agreed on. The Social Defense Directorate produced its first monitoring report, which presented the major challenges and recommendations to enhance its performance in terms of service provision, human resources, and financial resources and highlighted the need for further capacity building in M&E.

Quarterly, monthly, and annual monitoring reports highlight critical factors and anticipate future problems. The M&E system reporting framework includes the main activities related to objectives, indicators, recurrence of measurement (annual, semiannual, quarterly, and monthly),

---

Box 11.3   Beneficiaries of the Social Defense Directorate

The Social Defense Directorate in the Ministry of Social Development works with the following groups:

- Juveniles
- Children in conflict with the law
- Children in need of protection and care
- Battered women and their children
- Panhandlers
- Beneficiaries in rehabilitation centers.

---

baseline value (2009), target value (2010), and actual (total computed) and achievement percentages. The latter show the percent of achievement; when achievement is fully met, the cell is fully colored, otherwise, it is partially colored. The other section shows the actual achievement monthly and quarterly, where actual and targeted achievement are compared.

Dissemination

Although realizing that one size does not fit all, organizers found that the pilot provided valuable information in moving forward to disseminate the M&E system to the other directorates and finalize the documentation of the M&E unit in terms of vision, mission, tasks, staffing, and standard procedures. The M&E system can serve as a useful guide or "diagnostic tool" in planning, assessing progress, and identifying gaps. It can be used as a communication vehicle and catalyst to introduce M&E as an innovative, knowledge-building idea that can be applied in the most difficult environments, in the toughest times, and with limited resources. It can help high-level stakeholders identify appropriate strategies, policies, and programs to address critical issues, even without the need for a technical comprehension of this automated M&E reporting system.

Triangulation

Data triangulation in social systems is considered a challenge; Jordan's MoSD is no special case, especially with its 186 decentralized directorates and offices. Once the conception, theories, and application of the M&E system were constructed within the central MoSD, there was still a need to triangulate the data and to set up the system at various levels of application.

Decentralization is an advantage in that matter; it was easy to triangulate the M&E data at the field, directorate, district, governorate, and regional levels through the MoSD center. M&E concepts, theories, systems, and purposes have been transferred to the field level. Since the offices all provide the same services, they report the same indicators to the MoSD center, where a computerized system develops national indicators of services provided.

The connection between the MoSD center and its many offices has enabled MoSD's stakeholders to identify any sudden change in a particular indicator at the national level, and then find the exact local geographic area that caused this change and the reasons behind the change, such as an increase in beneficiaries, an increase in violence in neighborhoods, or unhealthy behaviors in a particular area. The system allows policy makers, planners, and managers to identify field locations that are experiencing certain problems or field offices that are showing certain weaknesses in their responses so they can review the plans and programs at these locations and identify strengths upon which to build. (See figures 11.6 and 11.7.)

Beneficiaries' Index

Analyzing the results of the M&E system at the MoSD center level showed that resources available for programs are constantly changing to meet the

Figure 11.6 Monitoring System, Governorate–Regional Level

Indicator	North Region					Middle Region					South Region				
	Irbid	Ajloun	Mafraq	Jarash	Total	Amman	Zarqa	Balqa'	Madaba	Total	Karak	Tafeleh	Ma'an	Aqaba	Total
Social defense															
Transferred to juvenile cases the courts The number of juvenile reconciliation cases transferred Juvenile Police offices to the were Number of reported cases in need of protection and care transferred to social service offices at the Family protection offices															
Family and childhood															
Children admitted in institutions Children reintegrated within their families Elderly people admitted within MoSD centers															
Disabled people															
Disabled people admitted in the MoSD centers Disabled people reintegrated within their communities															
NGOs															
NGOs supported financially by MoSD NGOs working in voluntarism															
Housing															
Poor people who benefited from Housing for the Poor Program Families who benefited from housing rehabilitation program															
Family productivity enhancement															
Families who benefited from EPP Community Centers working in voluntarism Revolving funds granted															

Note: EPP = Enhanced Productivity Program, MoSD = Ministry of Social Development, NGO = nongovernmental organization.

Figure 11.7 Monitoring System, Governorate–District Level

Indicator	Western Amman	Eastern Amman	Al Jeezeh	Marka	Wadi Al sair	Naour	Middle Badya	Total
Social defense								
Transferred to the courts juvenile cases								
The number of juvenile reconciliation cases transferred to Juvenile Police offices were the								
Number of reported cases in need of protection and care transferred to social service offices at the Family protection offices								
Family and childhood								
Children admitted in institutions								
Children reintegrated within their families								
Elderly people admitted within MoSD centers								
Disabled								
Disabled people admitted in the MoSD centers								
Disabled people reintegrated within their communities								
NGOs								
NGOs supported financially by MoSD								
NGOs working in voluntarism								
Housing								
Poor people who benefited from Housing for the Poor Program								
Families who benefited from housing rehabilitation program								
Family productivity enhancement								
Families who benefited from EPP								
Community Centers working in voluntarism								
Revolving funds granted								

Note: EPP = Enhanced Productivity Program, MoSD = Ministry of Social Development, NGO = nongovernmental organization.

unprecedented demand of social services caused by the fast pace of changing circumstances inside and outside the country. To measure the level of beneficiary satisfaction with the services provided by the Social Defense Directorate, a beneficiaries' index was developed. Reviewing and updating the system in the current fast pace of change is seen as an ongoing process. Dynamic and fixed indices were used, as a managerial policy tool, to measure beneficiaries' responses to social services in terms of interactivity and changes in services and beneficiaries, as well as in provision of financial resources.

Dynamic index

The Dynamic Index (weighted) (figure 11.8) explains the interactivity among beneficiaries and MoSD social services. It measures the degree of response between beneficiaries and services.

Development Evaluation in Times of Turbulence

Figure 11.8 Social Defense Beneficiaries' Dynamic Index

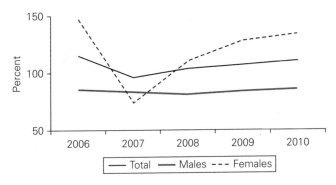

Source: MoSD Social Defense Directorate data.

The figure shows a sharp decrease of female beneficiaries from 2006 to 2007 (an in-depth qualitative study is needed to explain this decrease); however, the percentage of females using social services increased dramatically from 2007 to 2010. The increase was likely caused by expanded services and awareness. In 2007, MoSD established Dar AI Wefaq (women's protection shelter) which provides integrated services for battered women and their children in terms of health, legal, and social services, family reconciliation, and so on. In parallel with the establishment of Dar AI Wefaq, MoSD ran an awareness campaign on domestic violence. Accordingly, more violence cases were reported, and more social services were provided.[7]

Fixed index

The Fixed Index (weighted 2005=100) (figure 11.9) measures the change in the number of beneficiaries served over time. Overall, the number of beneficiaries increased gradually from 2006 to 2010. This increase was due to direct reasons such as the enhancement of the quality of MoSD social services through new strategies and policies. In addition, awareness-raising programs about MoSD services resulted in an increased demand for services. An increase in the 2009 budget allowed new centers, projects, and services to be included in the MoSD system, which provided a larger outreach to beneficiaries in terms of quality and quantity.

Legal reforms played a major role in the social protection systems; with the encouragement of MoSD, the government of Jordan enacted several laws in the last two years to handle family violence cases in a just and decent way, and to ensure the promotion and protection of all vulnerable groups'

Figure 11.9   Social Defense Beneficiaries' Fixed Index

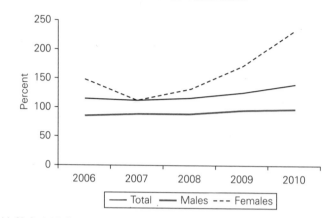

Source: MoSD Social Defense Directorate data.

rights and dignity, as well as their full participation in the society on an equal basis with others. MoSD was instrumental in passage of the family violence law, reviewed the juvenile law, and helped pass a bylaw to open protection houses for battered women and victims of violence. A helpline was established to report family violence cases. In addition, based on an increase in juvenile delinquency in Jordan, MoSD developed a new approach to protect at-risk youth using the juvenile justice system in cooperation with various partners. In addition, it created a system of prevention policies and programs targeting at-risk youth in disadvantaged areas.

M&E as an Early Warning System

A comparison between the financial resources and services provided was conducted to investigate the trend of increasing expenditures on social defense services. Despite Jordan's tight macroeconomic policy stance, mainly in the area of public expenditures, the royalty initiated a dramatic increase in financial resources in the social sector in the year 2009 in response to a growing need.

Considering the increased demand for social services, MoSD's budget was increased to enhance current services, provide new services with wider outreach, purchase services from nongovernmental and community organizations, and establish new buildings and infrastructure for MoSD social centers. For example, MoSD created six additional offices at rehabilitation centers.

An analysis compared the increase in beneficiaries (demand) with the available financial resources. It was conducted for two scenarios: one without resources targeted for physical buildings and one with those resources. Scenario 1 (figure 11.10) excludes building expenses from the analysis. Figure 11.11 shows that in mid-2010, the increase in beneficiaries was projected to meet with the increase in financial resources provided by the 2009 increases from royalty initiatives. In the years following 2010, when the budget returns to normal, the analysis shows a gap between the number of beneficiaries and financial resources, which may increase the burden on the ministry and its capacities to fulfill the demand and may affect the quality and quantity of social services provided. At this point, a question should be raised as to whether the government will be capable of creating ad hoc strategies to meet its commitments. This analysis provides an early warning for policy makers about a possible need to reconsider allocations and services to comply with changing demand and supply.

Scenario 2 (figure 11.11), which includes building-related expenses, shows a much smaller gap between beneficiaries and resources after mid-2010 compared with scenario 1. It shows another positive intersection in 2012. However, the increase in financial resources that causes this intersection is due to a high budget for new buildings. By providing increased funding for facilities, the ministry is increasing the number of centers and shelters providing services to beneficiaries in their localities rather than transporting

Figure 11.10   Scenario 1: Demand vs. Supply, Excluding Buildings

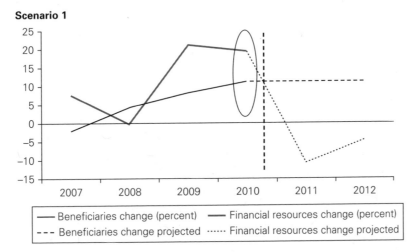

Source: Jordan Social Protection Directorate, Public Budget Report data.

Figure 11.11 Scenario 2: Demand vs. Supply, Including Buildings

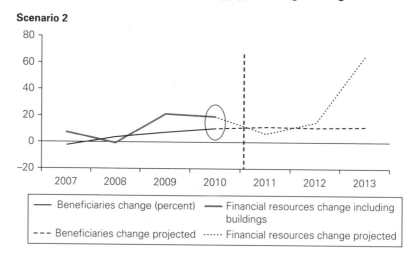

Scenario 2

Legend:
— Beneficiaries change (percent)   — Financial resources change including buildings
--- Beneficiaries change projected   ⋯⋯ Financial resources change projected

Source: Jordan Social Defense Directorate, Public Budget Report data.

them to the main centers where they are separated from their families. The increase in facilities will also create an environment with fewer beneficiaries per building to comply with international standards. It is hoped that the increase in local facilities will enhance beneficiaries' satisfaction and improve their lives in the long run.

However, including the finances for building new centers in long-term projections may not show a true picture of whether the ministry is providing good quality services into the future. More in-depth qualitative study is needed in this area.

Responding to an early warning

Figures 11.10 and 11.11 show that the government should review its policies and possibly design new strategies to avoid facing a tough financial situation after 2012.

Figure 11.11 shows that the nonbuilding financial resources decline after 2012 despite the fact that increasing the number of service centers will require more staff, as well as other expenses to operate these facilities.

If the number of beneficiaries continues to grow, there may not be sufficient resources to provide them with services, given current projections. Thus, in addition to increasing the capacities of the ministry to provide social services, it is imperative to establish preventive policies and programs that invest in human capital to decreases the demand for social services.

Lessons Learned and Conclusion

Two important lessons were learned though the establishment of an M&E system. The first lesson was that when the system was being established there was considerable resistance from employees due to a lack of knowledge and understanding of M&E, as well as to a reluctance to changing the culture of the daily work routine. Many employees considered M&E an extra work burden. Employee ownership of the system is imperative to success. Regular meetings and interaction with the employees raised the level of awareness regarding the need to forecast and plan based on trends in progress and availability of resources. Ownership and participation in developing the system, collecting data, and identifying weaknesses and strengths were essential in getting the staff to understand the value of M&E. They were able to see the change in practice rather than simply reading compiled reports. They were able to appreciate their own performance and encouraged to enhance their work. According to their first M&E report, the staff used the result-based management approach to develop new procedures and strategies to enhance the quality of services provided, which served as guidance for the minister to approve new approaches recommended and were successful in the following year.

As a result of educating employees on the benefits of M&E, the same employees who initially resisted the system now consider it an indispensable part of their work. For example, Amer Hyasat of the Social Defense Directorate, where the system was piloted, said, "The monitoring and evaluation system has enabled us to improve performance, better understand the problems, and offer better interventions at the right times. . . . We need to move forward on this system and to connect it electronically with all directorates and field offices."

The second lesson was that there is a need for regular review and updates of the current status, especially when dealing with dynamic situations such as social development. Considering MoSD's wide mandate in serving Jordan's citizens, its role should be strengthened to develop comprehensive evidence-based social protection policies, programs, and projects with a special focus on vulnerable groups, grounded in an ongoing monitoring system. Monitoring and evaluation methods can benefit high-impact MoSD programs such as Social Defense and Family Productivity Enhancement.

In conclusion, since the purpose of an M&E system at MoSD is to create a decision support system for social policies, it is recommended that the government proceed in using M&E systems for MoSD, disseminate MoSD's experience in developing an M&E system and analysis procedure to other social development institutions and agencies concerned with social development and services, and provide the stakeholders of these agencies with the guidance of optimum integrated social policies.

Financial resources should be allocated to avoid negative gaps between supply and demand of social services, which would create a deficit for MoSD and limit the services it is able to provide. To cover potential negative gaps, MoSD may consider outsourcing or increasing its allocation from the public budget. Another approach is to develop strategies and programs to decrease the number of beneficiaries through preventive programs to help vulnerable groups avoid or escape the circle of poverty. Another strategy is to enhance the roles of civil society and nongovernmental organizations to create treatment and preventive programs to decrease the number of vulnerable groups and empower them to be independent, which would lessen the financial burden on MoSD. M&E forecasting is a good tool to provide policy makers with a guide to which approaches to implement.

Notes

1. Data from the Water Authority of Jordan.
2. Jordan's economy created 70,000 net jobs in 2007; 65,000 in 2008; 69,000 in 2009; and 26,000 in the first half of 2010.
3. Data are from the National Aid Fund Report 2010 and the Ministry of Finance General Report, January 2010.
4. See Jordan's *Socioeconomic Transformation Plan 2002–2004*.
5. See Jordan's *Social and Economic Development Plan 2004–2006*.
6. Based on the technical background of the participating staff in the training sessions and level of ownership.
7. The number of battered women is not cumulative; it was taken at a moment in time.

References

Government of Jordan. 2010. "Keeping the Promise and Achieving Aspirations," Second National Millennium Development Goals Report. Government of Jordan.

World Bank. 2008. "Resolving Jordan's Labor Market Paradox of Concurrent Economic Growth and High Unemployment." Policy Note 39201, World Bank, Washington, DC.

CHAPTER 12

National Performance Reporting as a Driver for National M&E Development

The Experience of Botswana

Robert Lahey

Introduction

For more than a decade, developing countries have expressed considerable interest in introducing a results-oriented monitoring and evaluation (M&E) capability. Efforts at introducing a systematic approach to M&E have been aligned with reporting on progress against the objectives of a country's Poverty Reduction Strategy Paper (PRSP) or against the Millennium Development Goals (MDGs). Both efforts have provided some incentive to measure and report on key national-level performance indicators.

Project-specific M&E is older and has been spurred by donor requirements for greater performance measurement, driven in part by the donor country's own requirements for accountability and reporting on performance.

Although neither comprehensive nor systemwide, these project evaluations have resulted in the creation of discrete pockets of M&E knowledge in developing countries (often in the health sector, for example). What has not always happened, though, is a level of coordination and harmonization across various donor-funded project- and program-level M&E efforts.

Building a national evaluation or M&E system[1] must be thought about in more than technocratic terms or in the historical pattern of M&E in the context of development aid. A new paradigm is emerging centered around national ownership and M&E capacity that is linked to the national vision of the country, accountability, and good governance (Menon 2010).

If an M&E system is to be owned by a country, it needs to be linked to the country's national development plan and integrated into the operations and culture of government institutions and ministries. To create a sustainable M&E system, governments must believe in the utility of the system and understand its benefits. To do that, they must eventually own the system. National ownership implies a particular cultural, social, and political context (Segone 2010).

Moving from concept to reality in M&E development and implementation typically raises a number of hurdles for any country. Both a broad vision and a practical approach that will suit the circumstances of the country and its public sector are needed (Lahey 2012).

This chapter examines the case of Botswana, a country that has recently taken steps to strengthen its M&E capacity to better manage for results. The chapter explores how Botswana has used the development of its first national performance report, *Vision 2016 Botswana Performance Report*, not only to raise the profile of M&E and identify gaps in M&E for future capacity-building efforts, but also to help create a demand for M&E across all sectors of society.

Botswana's story of how its national performance reporting efforts served as a driver for M&E capacity building should have broad application to the international community.[2] This chapter highlights some of the lessons learned.

Framework for Developing a National M&E System

M&E should be considered within a broad "system" context, that is, recognizing that M&E is not an end in itself. This section discusses the underpinnings of such a system, identifying the essential building blocks that serve as the basis for a successful M&E system.

Four Essential Building Blocks for a National M&E System

A national M&E system rests on two overriding influences: (1) the political will for change within a country and (2) the pace of development of the M&E infrastructure. On these two foundation pieces, one could imagine four essential building blocks, listed below and in figure 12.1 (Lahey 2006 and Lahey 2007).

1. A vision of the leadership in the country
2. An enabling environment in which an M&E system can develop and function
3. The capacity to supply M&E information, that is, the technical capacity to measure performance and provide credible information in a timely way
4. The capacity within the system to demand and use M&E information, key users being government institutions, ministries, citizens, the media, and other stakeholders.

Political support is an essential driver to launch and resource the M&E exercise. It leads the change in organizational culture that may be needed; provides the champion(s); ensures an enabling environment; deflects resistance to the introduction of M&E and the changes that this might imply; and provides the basis to help ensure that the M&E system is sustainable over the long term.

The successful development and implementation of an M&E system takes more than political support, though. Even with a commitment to invest in M&E development, technical hurdles may require a lengthy process to develop credible data systems, train M&E specialists, and educate managers throughout the system on how and where M&E information will

Figure 12.1   Four Essential Building Blocks for an Effective National M&E System

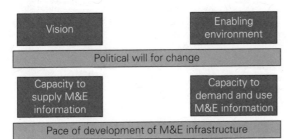

Note: M&E = monitoring and evaluation.

be used. This process is generally lengthy and iterative, as the experience of most countries using M&E systems would attest, and one in which allowance for continuous learning and improvement through oversight mechanisms is particularly beneficial.

Critical Success Factors for National M&E System Development

Although each country faces its own challenges in growing an M&E system, the framework in figure 12.1 identifies broad considerations for developing and implementing an M&E system in the public sector. The framework is elaborated in box 12.1.

Important considerations for national M&E system development (also shown in Box 12.1) are:

- A broad set of players need to be involved in developing an M&E system for it to be both effective and sustainable.
- The goal is not simply to create an M&E capability, but to use performance information to improve public-sector management and governance.
- The use of (or demand for) M&E information will function if there are effective incentives built into the system.

Box 12.1   Four Essential Building Blocks Elaborated

Vision

- Provides an understanding of how monitoring and evaluation (M&E) information can assist public sector managers, decision makers and the country in moving to achieve its national goals
- Requires strategic leadership and clear understanding of the basic concepts and potential uses of M&E

Enabling Environment

- A fundamental commitment not only to launch an M&E exercise, but also to sustain it over the long term
- A commitment to resource development of an M&E system, as well as to allowing it to develop and mature
- A commitment to support the values and ethics that underlie a successful M&E system—transparency, objectivity, accountability—and a commitment to a results orientation and good governance
- A willingness and ability to challenge current culture within organizations

(continued next page)

Box 12.1 *continued*

Capacity to Supply M&E Information

- The technical capacity and infrastructure "to do"
- Credible and relevant data and information-gathering systems
- Skilled personnel to gather, analyze, and report on the performance of government policies and programs; assistance can come from partners within the country, such as universities, and research institutes
- A national statistical agency to facilitate a national data-development strategy and assist ministries and agencies in data capture and storage
- Infrastructure to help ensure a systematic, comprehensive, and credible approach to M&E
- Infrastructure would include policies and standards intended to clarify roles, responsibilities, and accountabilities for performance monitoring and evaluation; establish expectations across the system regarding the timing and nature of evaluation, monitoring, and performance reporting; and establish quality standards for M&E conduct
- Organizational structure to conduct and/or manage M&E exercises
- A central "policy center" to provide policy direction, oversight, and assistance for the systemwide development of M&E

Capacity to Demand and Use M&E Information

- Capacity within government institutions to incorporate and use M&E information as part of the normal process of business
- Clarity of expectations regarding where and how M&E information can and will be used within the government (for example, planning, policy, or program development; decision making; budgeting), which this can evolve over time
- Nontechnical personnel (for example, program managers) with a suitable appreciation of M&E concepts and an orientation to the utility and use of M&E information
- Adequate incentives (carrots and sticks) within organizations and across the system to ensure that managers use M&E information and report credible information in a timely fashion
- Formal or informal vehicles and fora for reporting and sharing M&E information
- Access-to-information laws to increase transparency and the potential that M&E information will be made readily available to the media, civil society, etc., for their participation in the national system

- Although the collection and analysis of performance information generally requires the assistance of technically trained analysts and data specialists, the use of this performance information is generally carried out by nontechnical managers. Though they do not require a technical comprehension of M&E methods, it is important for these managers to understand and appreciate how and where M&E information can help them manage their programs and policies.

Moving from Concept to Reality—Assessing Botswana's M&E Aspirations and Readiness

This section describes the case of Botswana, where, despite political support and an enabling environment, the realities of technical capacity gaps resulted in a need to develop a strategy that incorporated short-term and longer-term components as the way forward for M&E system development.

Botswana's National Vision (Vision 2016) Drove the Need for a National M&E System

In 1996, Botswana developed its Vision 2016 through a national consultation process with the express purpose of defining a long-term vision for Botswana. The work to develop this vision was led by a presidential task group that represented all sectors of Batswana society, including political parties, parastatals, private sector organizations, nongovernmental organizations (NGOs), trade unions, and religious organizations. Through a broad consultation with the public, a succinct statement was developed that reflected both the aspirations of the nation and key priority issues on which Botswana would need to focus to move forward as a people, a nation, and within the global economic environment.

The result, *A Long Term Vision for Botswana*, identified seven pillars defining direction for "the way ahead" to the year 2016, the 50th anniversary of independence for the country. Box 12.2 identifies the seven pillars—broad goals that must be met if the country is to achieve "prosperity for all" by 2016. It also shows key result areas (KRAs) that represent a succinct identification of the nation's expectations for each of the seven pillars.[3]

As part of the institutional arrangements to monitor and report on the progress of Vision 2016, two key bodies were established: a Vision Council and a Vision Secretariat. The Vision Council was set up as an independent and nonpartisan body to monitor and assess the performance, progress, and achievements of Vision 2016 activities until 2016 and beyond.

It has 19 members drawn from all sectors of Batswana society including government, the private sector, and civil society. The Vision Secretariat is led by the Vision Coordinator, who, with a team of about five professionals, supports the mandate of the council.

In the delivery of its mandate, the council is guided by the following terms of reference:

- To drive and monitor the implementation of Vision 2016 and to address problems and challenges that may be faced during implementation
- To generate sustained ownership of the vision by all stakeholders, and a national consensus on national directions and strategies
- To harmonize and promote cooperation among various sectoral objectives, and bring them within the larger national interest
- To call for information, and to conduct public hearings or special investigations
- To coordinate stakeholder feedback for effective policy implementation
- To monitor the implementation of national development plans as vehicles of the vision
- To commission the translation of the materials relating to the vision into Setswana and other languages
- To regularly review the membership and functions of the council in response to changing circumstances.

With a clear mandate for monitoring and evaluation, the Vision Council and its secretariat have worked over the past decade aiming to develop a comprehensive national M&E system. However, major challenges (both technical and institutional) have yielded mixed results. In 2008, a new attempt was launched to establish a national M&E framework; it began with the conduct of an M&E readiness assessment, an approach strongly recommended by the World Bank as a good-practice first step toward M&E framework development (Kusek and Rist 2004). The framework process provided an opportunity to assess the presence and strength of the four M&E building blocks described in figure 12.1 and box 12.1, which was important in determining an appropriate country strategy for M&E system development.

Political Will and an Enabling Environment for National M&E System Development

The M&E readiness assessment pointed out the drivers behind the desire for developing an improved approach to national M&E in Botswana. It included not only the Vision Council's efforts to develop a capability to carry out an oversight role for Vision 2016, but also the public sector reform agenda being led by the Office of the President. The reform agenda had resulted in several cross-government initiatives launched over the past decade that aimed to bring more accountability into the public sector; improve management and governance of individual ministries and across ministries; encourage systematic macro- and sector-specific planning; and raise the focus of monitoring and management decision making from "expenditures" and "activities" to "results."

Clearly, in 2008 Botswana was experiencing a supportive environment for M&E capacity building that reflected not only the independent, nonpartisan Vision Council, but also the political level. The Office of the President was advocating results-based management (RBM) across the public sector and, together with the Ministry of Finance and Development Planning, was crafting an "M&E chapter" for the tenth version of its medium-term national development plan (NDP 10) that identified the need for ministries to embrace results-oriented M&E. Additionally, the Office of the President created a new unit intended to provide M&E oversight across the public sector.

For its part, the Vision Council felt a need to respond to the fundamental question being raised among Batswana: "Where are we?" in regard to performance and progress against the targets set in the seven Vision 2016 pillars. The fact that Botswana was headed toward the last leg of Vision 2016 added to the urgency to improve its ability to measure and report on performance.

Issues of Technical Capacity: Establishing Short-Term and Long-Term Strategies for M&E Development

Although there were senior leadership champions for M&E, as well as an apparent commitment to develop a national M&E capability in Botswana, an M&E readiness assessment revealed critical deficiencies in both the capacity to supply and to use M&E information. Key constraints in the capacity to supply M&E information included: insufficient human resources with M&E or analytical skills; substantial data problems, primarily lack of credible, quality, results-oriented data supplied in a timely fashion, and, when needed, at a subnational level; and little or no experience with the conduct of evaluation studies.

Regarding the capacity to demand and use M&E information, although there was a broad-based demand for national performance reporting (championed by the Vision Council and its secretariat), ministry-level use of M&E was less clear. As box 12.1 points out, the expectations of where and how M&E information can and will be used within government (for example, to support planning, policy, or program development, decision making, or budgeting) is a fundamental requirement of an effective M&E system. These expectations can, of course, evolve over time.

Faced with serious deficiencies yet immediate needs, Botswana adopted a strategy to move ahead on national M&E development with a two-pronged approach encompassing the short and long term. In the short term, the aim was to develop a comprehensive national performance report that responded to the needs of Vision Council to answer the question "Where are we?" in terms of the Vision 2016 goals. In the long term, the aim was to build the needed M&E infrastructure to fill capacity gaps across the system associated with the ability to supply and to use M&E information.

Whereas the short-term exercise was being viewed as a "quick win" because it would produce very public results (a national performance report), the much-less-visible longer-term objective needed an action plan and an expectation to demonstrate results against its longer timeline. The short-term exercise was expected to take no more than six months, while the longer-term project was expected to be carried out over three to five years. Moreover, the broader project would require a substantial investment, particularly in data development and analytical capacity, across Botswana's public sector.

Developing a National Performance Report as a Driver for M&E Capacity Building

Developing a national performance report on Botswana's Vision 2016 goals, which came to be known as *Botswana's Performance Report* (2009), was set up as a separate exercise from the longer-term development work.

Strategy for Performance Measurement and Reporting

The M&E readiness assessment showed that monitoring the Vision 2016 pillars was hampered by a lack of systematic data to populate and report against indicators on "results achieved." It was hoped that the M&E capacity-building efforts for the longer-term plan (ideally generated during Botswana's mid-term plan) would, over time, yield a more comprehensive results-oriented information base.

Hampered by a paucity of data, the inaugural edition of *Botswana's Performance Report*[4] used a broad-based approach to draw relevant data and information from a variety of sources across the public sector, private sector, and civil society, as well as from international sources.

The measurement strategy drew on areas of strength that had been iden-tified during the readiness assessment, rather than focusing on weaknesses and capacity gaps in the system. "Pockets" of M&E strength and analyti-cal expertise included M&E units in a few ministries (such as Agriculture) where there was generally limited experience and often unfilled positions, but a potential for future M&E efforts. Additionally, a growing number of officials (mostly, but not exclusively public servants) had received train-ing at the International Program for Development Evaluation Training (IPDET), held annually in Ottawa, Canada, as a joint venture between the World Bank and Carleton University. These IPDET graduates were useful contacts for relevant M&E information and can in the future form the basis of an M&E network for Botswana. All of this serves to build a foundation in the understanding of results-based management and the role of M&E across the public sector.

An important institution for any national M&E system is the national statistics office: the data experts. In Botswana, the Central Statistics Office (CSO) was the keeper of the original Vision 2016 M&E system, a first attempt developed in 2001 with the assistance of the United Nations Devel-opment Programme (UNDP). Whereas the failures of the original Vision M&E system were well documented, CSO still has an important role to play in ensuring that data development across Botswana is carried out in a cost-effective fashion that will support future M&E efforts, including national performance measurement and reporting. The elements described above are needed to build a future M&E system.

For the immediate needs of developing a national performance report, there was a greater sense of urgency, created in large part by the high-level audience—the president of Botswana and his high-level consultative com-mittee. To meet the short-term objective, a new approach to performance reporting was adopted—one that told a "performance story" for Botswana by relying on both quantitative and qualitative information and incorporat-ing success stories to illustrate where, how, and to what extent progress was being made for each Vision 2016 pillar.

Telling Botswana's "Performance Story" with Limited Data

Measuring and reporting on performance for each of the seven Vision 2016 pillars meant clarifying the intent of each Vision pillar. The original Vision 2016 document offered a set of 43 "expectations for the nation" that could be succinctly articulated as a set of 18 KRAs. The 43 statements are shown in annex 12A and the KRAs reflected in Vision 2016 are listed in box 12.2.

Box 12.2 The Vision 2016 Pillars and Key Result Areas

Vision 2016 pillar	Key result area expected
Pillar 1: An educated, informed nation	• A system of universal, continuing, and quality education • An informed society • An IT-literate society
Pillar 2: A prosperous, productive, and innovative nation	• Rapid economic growth and diversification • Sustainable development • Full employment
Pillar 3: A compassionate, just, and caring nation	• Eradication of absolute poverty and more equitable income distribution • Accessible and good-quality health services • No new HIV infections
Pillar 4: A safe and secure nation	• A safe and secure society • A professional public security service
Pillar 5: An open, democratic, and accountable nation	• Responsible and accountable leadership • Open and transparent government
Pillar 6: A moral and tolerant nation	• A discrimination-free society • National moral and cultural values
Pillar 7: A united and proud nation	• National unity • Social stability • A strong family institution

Source: Presidential Task Group for a Long Term Vision for Botswana 1997.

Note: HIV = human immunodeficiency virus, IT = information technology.

It is important to note that the expectations for the nation were important in clarifying the intentions of the goals and subgoals of Vision 2016 and were particularly helpful in identifying appropriate performance indicators.

The process for arriving at a template for the reporting format for *Botswana's Performance Report* is illustrated in figure 12.2.

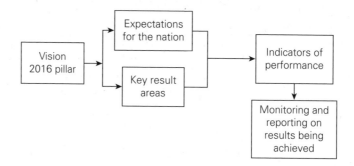

The critical problem turned to how to actually measure results. Indicators not only had to be relevant to the expected results for the particular pillar, they required the existence of relevant data. For many indicators, too little quality data relevant to the results were readily available. Additionally, little subnational (district level) data were available, which hampered an understanding of performance.

Given the data limitations, the approach taken in the report was to tell a "performance story" about each of the Vision pillars and associated KRAs, relying on several indicators of results and using both qualitative and quantitative data and information. Box 12.3 shows the distribution and use of both types of indicators in measuring KRAs, noting that in all, some 77 indicators were used in *Botswana's Performance Report.*

Multiple lines of evidence were used to gather information, including: data drawn from the M&E system maintained by the CSO to support monitoring and reporting of both Vision 2016 and the Millennium Development Goals; a review of relevant government documents and ministry reports, including progress reports for each sector of the government's medium-term plan; focused interviews with subject experts from a broad cross-section of officials in the public sector, private sector, civil society organizations, as well as international experts; consultations with members of the Vision Council and the Vision fora established for each of the seven Vision pillars; a document and literature search and review (using both Botswana and international sources) to focus on issue-specific research and studies; and focus groups with members of the three Vision fora where traditionally there has been limited data (that is, Pillars 5, 6, and 7).

Throughout the process, the Vision Council's M&E committee monitored this exercise and the Vision Coordinator and secretariat played an

Box 12.3   Type and Number of Indicators Used to Measure Performance against Key Results Expected under Each Vision 2016 Pillar

Vision 2016 pillar	Key result area expected	Nature of indicator		Number of indicators
		Quantitative	Qualitative	
Pillar 1: *An educated, informed nation*	A system of universal, continuing, and quality education	✓		9
	An informed society	✓	✓	4
	An IT-literate society	✓	✓	4
Pillar 2: *A prosperous, productive, and innovative nation*	Rapid economic growth and diversification	✓	✓	6
	Sustainable development	✓	✓	3
	Full employment	✓		4
Pillar 3: *A compassionate, just, and caring nation*	Eradication of absolute poverty and more equitable income distribution	✓	✓	5
	Accessible and good-quality health services	✓		5
	No new HIV infections	✓		4
Pillar 4: *A safe and secure nation*	A safe and secure society	✓		6
	A professional public security service	✓	✓	3
Pillar 5: *An open, democratic, and accountable nation*	Responsible and accountable leadership		✓	5
	Open and transparent government	✓	✓	3

(continued next page)

Box 12.3 *continued*

Vision 2016 pillar	Key result area expected	Nature of indicator		Number of indicators
		Quantitative	**Qualitative**	
Pillar 6: *A moral and tolerant nation*	A discrimination-free society	✓	✓	2
	National moral and cultural values	✓	✓	5
Pillar 7: *A united and proud nation*	National unity		✓	3
	Social stability			
	A strong family institution		✓	2
		✓	✓	4
Total number of indicators used to measure and report on performance				77

Note: HIV = human immunodeficiency virus, IT = information technology.

active role in reviewing and vetting the analysis and reporting on each of the Vision pillars. Once complete, a final "challenge" exercise was undertaken to review and vet each of the report's conclusions.

The baseline for reporting was established as 1996, when Vision 2016 was established. The intent was to measure and assess progress from that point to the most recent year for which data was available, aiming for 2008. In reality, this target was not feasible for all indicators.

Reporting on progress on performance of the nation for each of the seven pillars of Vision 2016 involved three components:

1. A presentation of "performance context" that showed, for each KRA, detailed information on trends observed for the relevant indicators
2. A narrative that provided an overview and interpretation, identifying major achievements, concerns, or challenges facing a particular KRA, and benchmarks on performance, against both Vision 2016 targets and regional and international comparisons
3. Inclusion of success stories to illustrate ways that people in Botswana (individually and collectively) have responded to Vision 2016.

As an example, box 12.4 shows the indicators used in reporting on "performance context" for the "economic growth and diversification" KRA. For each indicator, a socioeconomic "trend" was established using available data (both quantitative and qualitative) as the basis for assessing how Botswana was performing over time.

Box 12.4 Performance Context: Key Measures of Long-term Progress for the "Economic Growth and Diversification" Key Result Area

Trend*	Indicator	Overview
Improving ∩	Economic growth (rate of gross domestic product [GDP] growth in real terms)	While the economy has been growing, the rate of GDP growth in real terms has fluctuated significantly, at times above the Vision 2016 goal of 8% per year and at other times well below this rate: 1.7% (2002); 9.6% (2003); 2.8% (2004); 9.5% (2005); 0.6% (2006); 6.2% (2007). Over these six years, the average annual growth was 5.1%.
Improving ∩	GDP per capita	In the five-year period 2002–06, GDP per capita increased from P10,725 in 2002 to P12,673 in 2006, an increase of 18%. This level is still well below the Vision 2016 target of P24,219 (in 1993–94 constant prices), or a growth rate of 6% per year. In fact, over the 2000s, the average annual growth in GDP per capita was 3.3%.
No Trend ☐	Diversification in the Economy (% share of mining + government GDP to total GDP)	Mining and government are the two key sectors of the economy, accounting for 58% of GDP. This percentage has not changed appreciably from 2002–06: 55.8% (2002); 56.9% (2003); 56.0% (2004); 58.8% (2005); 57.9% (2006).
Declining ☷	Investment (capital formation rate)	The rate of investment is well below the 41% target of Vision 2016. Moreover, the capital formation rate has been in decline over the five-year period where data is available: 25.1% (2001); 24.0% (2002); 22.3% (2003); 19.8% (2004); 18.3% (2005).
Improving ∩	Competitiveness relative to other countries (Global Competitiveness Index)	Over the past five years, the country's ranking among 134 countries and its Global Competitiveness Index rating [in brackets] have fluctuated: 72 [3.94] (2005); 81 [3.79] (2006); 76 [3.96] (2007); 56 [4.25] (2008). In 2008, the ranking climbed to 56 out of 134 countries. Bostwana is the third highest ranking country in Africa and the second highest in the Southern African Development Community (SADC).

Source: Adapted from Botswana Vision Council 2009.

Note: *Trend refers to whether the situation for the country is improving (↑), worsening (↓), or not showing a definitive trend (D).

A two-page discussion accompanied the table in box 12.6 in *Botswana's Performance Report*, providing interpretation and analysis of the performance of the "economic growth and diversification" KRA under three broad headings:

- An overview of progress
- Concerns and challenges about economic growth and diversification
- Benchmarking how Botswana is performing

Performance was assessed not only in terms of progress over time, but also by using different benchmarks, subject to data availability, reporting performance against a Vision 2016 target, and comparing Botswana's performance to that of other countries in the region; in Africa; and where relevant, in the world.

The final element in the report on performance was the inclusion of success stories. Three success stories from the private sector were shown in the discussion on the "economic growth and diversification" KRA.

This component of *Botswana's Performance Report* was intended to celebrate success as well as help demonstrate the contributions made by all sectors of Botswana society toward achieving the goals of Vision 2016. Success stories identified in the national performance report were drawn from the private sector (11 success stories); civil society (11); and the public sector (18). Box 12.5 illustrates one of the success stories included with the "economic growth and diversification" KRA.

As data becomes more readily available and improves in quality, there may be changes to some of the indicators used for reporting on progress. Some may be dropped, others added, and all should benefit from a richer and more robust data base.

Next Steps–Using National Performance Reporting to Leverage M&E Capacity Building

Vision 2016 has provided all Batswana with a comprehensive set of socioeconomic dimensions that reflect their targets and expectations for the nation. It continues to be a very public document, reported on regularly in the media and given attention through the ongoing communication efforts of the Vision Secretariat.[5]

Such exposure and media attention reinforce the transparency and expectations for performance reporting to answer the question, "Where are we?" in relation to each of the Vision pillars and targets. *Botswana's Performance Report* has been widely distributed to schools and libraries around the country, not just to selected public administrators and bureaucrats.

> **Box 12.5   The Business Place Project: A Vision Pillar Success Story Reflecting the "Economic Growth and Diversification" Key Result Area**
>
> Established as a nonprofit organization, the Business Place aims to foster entrepreneurship in the country, by assisting small and microenterprises by providing affordable and accessible services such as developing business plans and financial proposals. In this way, it works to help aspiring entrepreneurs towards reaching their business goals. It is funded and directed by a public–private partnership that includes: Investec, Barloworld, Kgalagadi Beverages Trust, Community of Economic Development Association, Motor Centre Group, University of Botswana, University of Botswana Foundation, Department of Culture and Youth, and First National Bank.
>
> To date, the project has helped over 2,045 clients to develop business plans, 173 clients start their businesses, and 16 to secure funds from reputable sponsors. Currently, eight projects are in the process of being funded. Of those who have been assisted, 60 percent are male and 40 percent are female. The majority of those assisted (some 80 percent) are under 35 years of age.

Additionally, it has received attention and discussion at the highest levels in Botswana. The president and his high-level consultative committee were a key audience during the initial roll-out of *Botswana's Performance Report*. Moreover, the Vision Coordinator is automatically included in broad consultations dealing with the medium-term plan for the nation and Vision 2016 goals, and results-oriented KRAs form the focus of these plans.

Some obvious elements emerge from a reading of the national performance report. Included on the short list of "key challenge areas" is the concern for "data and information to assist monitoring and evaluation":

> The greatest deficiency impairing the Vision Council's ability to monitor and report on progress of the Vision 2016 Pillars is a general lack of data. That is, the "right data," data that relates to "results" of programmes or policies; data that has been collected in a consistent and systematic way; data that can be collected, recorded and classified in more detail at a local level; and so on (Botswana Vision Council 2009, 7).

Identified in the report's executive summary as one of six major challenges for the future for Botswana, this concern for data and M&E was presented along with the five other key challenges: economic growth and diversification; transformation of agriculture; poverty; human immunodeficiency/acquired immune deficiency syndrome; and the impact that the pace of change is having on the transformation of Batswana society. The importance of this placement is to bring recognition to the fact that, through improved data and strengthened M&E, Botswana will be better able to deal with its key social and economic challenges. It highlights the capacity gaps and reinforces the need for M&E capacity building in the country.

As a public document with wide exposure, such messaging can be powerful in leveraging future M&E capacity-building efforts. Whether or not this report has any influence on events to follow, it is encouraging to note that a transformation is taking place with the national data office. During 2011 and 2012, CSO was being transformed into Statistics Botswana with a new structure and mandate. It is premature to know what effect this change will have on data development across the country, but this is an important first step in the right direction for Botswana.

In addition to drawing attention to the need for data development, an area often ignored by countries, the national performance report identified areas for possible future evaluation or special issue-oriented studies. Through both a narrative and an easy-to-read "Status at a Glance," the executive summary clearly points out areas where future efforts should be targeted.

The "Status at a Glance" showed a three-level rating of progress for each of the 43 KRA/expectation combinations that underlie Vision 2016. Although somewhat simplistic (though appealing to those who seek a simple "dashboard" reading of performance), Botswana's key challenge areas become immediately apparent. The rating reinforces the obvious conclusion that there is a need to examine more closely (via evaluation or special study) the policies and programs in areas that continually cause the country problems despite a high level of investment in government programs.

Given the country's limited capacity for evaluation, this rating helps focus on where the greatest gains (best "bang for the buck") can likely be achieved through targeted evaluation efforts. It also identifies stakeholders (such as government ministries and agencies) that should be targeted for evaluation capacity-building efforts, at least in the short term. Annex A provides a slightly modified version of the "Status at a Glance" in *Vision 2016 Botswana Performance Report*.

Lessons Learned for National M&E System Development

The challenges in building a national M&E system are great, and considerable lessons can be drawn from the experience of both developed and developing countries.[6]

Box 12.6 identifies some key challenges and lessons for national M&E capacity development drawn from country experiences over the past two decades. The list incorporates lessons drawn from Botswana's recent experience with national performance measurement and reporting.

Box 12.6   Lessons Learned for National M&E System Development

Understand the political environment

Recognize the importance of senior leadership and political support to champion and drive change, especially when accountability has not traditionally been an important element of public sector management.

A serious effort to build a national monitoring and evaluation (M&E) system starts with a substantive government demand for M&E information. It requires a political will and sustained commitment. Central leadership and a plan are very important.

Manage the expectations and impatience of senior officials

Educate senior officials on M&E. They are an important audience.

Ensure that senior officials recognize that M&E development is long term and iterative. It is generally not possible to achieve in one or two years what some others have been working at for many years. Bring a reality check.

Provide "quick wins" (such as *Botswana's Performance Report*) to demonstrate the utility of M&E.

Know the importance of data development

Do not wait for perfection.

Rely on both qualitative and quantitative information to populate indicators.

Plan and work to use both the "E" and the "M" to measure performance.

Finding too little "quality" data likely means that a national data development strategy and plan need to be developed. Ensure that the country's national data agency is a part of this exercise.

Data development needs to be recognized as a long-term investment.

Avoid the danger of overengineering

Overengineering an M&E system could produce a proliferation of indicators and/or a large set of uncoordinated data systems across ministries. Data development is important, but not costless, and needs leadership from the central ministry, the national data office, and relevant ministries.

(continued next page)

Box 12.6 *continued*

Too few human resources skilled in M&E

Recognize that training is a long-term investment.

Establish a training and development strategy aimed at target audiences, such as M&E analysts, government managers, and senior officials, that is, both the providers and users of M&E information.

With limited resources, seek to partner and network with "pockets" of analytical expertise and opportunities for training such as International Program for Development Evaluation Training (IPDET), mentoring programs, professional associations or networks, and universities.

If there are too few skilled human resources, it is better to do a pilot implementation rather than attempt a governmentwide roll-out of M&E.

Carrying out evaluations

Ensure that the "E" in an M&E system is not overlooked, even in the planning stages.

Developing an evaluation policy center and an evaluation strategy helps position and resource the function.

Start modestly—one or two evaluations a year.

Select areas of high priority for the government.

Work to ensure that momentum is not lost once the evaluation study is completed; that is, keep a focus on follow-up to the evaluation to ensure that results get used in policy and program development.

Create greater understanding of why evaluation is important to government and how it can be used.

Implementing a national M&E system

Implementation of results-based M&E is often overlooked. Proponents need to detail and resource a plan to move from concept to reality.

Since countries' M&E systems are generally developed incrementally, it is important to monitor progress and make adjustments along the way. This oversight role can be a part of the mandate of a central agency.

Rolling out an M&E system needs to be seen as far more than a technical issue. Policy makers need to understand the importance of positioning M&E as a mechanism to support public sector management.

(continued next page)

Box 12.6 *continued*

M&E information is not an end in itself. That is, a supply of good evaluations is not enough; a reasonable demand for evaluation is key.

Internal infrastructure is usually insufficient to sustain an M&E system. A number of formal requirements associated with its use (at the ministry level, the central level, and in the context of both management and accountability) will force managers and senior officials to take the time and effort to invest in M&E development.

M&E system development requires building capacity to *use* M&E information within and across organizations (in addition to building capacity to *do* M&E).

Annex 12A   Status at a Glance

An overview of progress being made against the "Expectations for the Nation" for each Vision pillar

☆ Progress being made and a conducive environment exists for continued progress

☺ Some concerns, even though progress being made

⊠ Major challenges

Key Result Area	Expectations for the Nation	Progress being made?*
Vision Pillar One: An Educated and Informed Nation		
Universal, continuing, and quality education	1. The system of education will be both accessible and provide for quality education.	☺
	2. Vocational or technical training will serve as an alternative to mainstream education.	☆
	3. Different languages and cultural traditions will be recognized, supported, and strengthened within the education system.	⊠
Informed society	4. Botswana will become a regional leader in the production and dissemination of information.	☺
	5. There will be a culture of transparency and accountability in government, private sector, and other organizations in Botswana.	☺

(continued next page)

Key Result Area	Expectations for the Nation	Progress being made?*
IT-literate society	6. All schools will have access to a computer, and to computer-based communications such as the Internet.	☆
Vision Pillar Two: A Prosperous, Productive, and Innovative Nation		
Economic growth and diversification	1. By 2016, Botswana will have an environment where business and entrepreneurial activities are encouraged and supported.	☆
	2. Botswana will have a vibrant and energetic economy that is able to meet the competitive demands of the 21st century and attract investors.	☺
	3. There will be partnership arrangements between local and foreign investors that will have empowered citizens and developed investments, and substantially increased resource ownership and management by citizens.	☺
Sustainable development	4. Agriculture in Botswana will be productive, profitable, and sustainable, and will make a full contribution to economic development, poverty alleviation, food security, improvement of the quality of life, and the sustainable utilization of our natural resources.	⊠
	5. Renewable resources will be used at a rate that is in balance with their regeneration capacity. Nonrenewable resources such as minerals will be used efficiently, and their depletion will be balanced by enhanced physical and labor capital. There will be a fully integrated approach toward conservation and development.	☺
	6. The key natural resources and assets of the country will be equitably distributed between its people. Communities will be involved in the use and preservation of their environmental assets and will benefit directly from their exploitation.	☆
	7. The wildlife of Botswana will be managed for the sustainable benefit of the local communities and in the interests of the environment as a whole.	☆
	8. Botswana will have taken strong measures to limit the pollution that would otherwise result from rapid industrialization.	☆
Employment	9. Botswana will have reached full employment, where the total number of jobs available in the formal or informal sectors is in balance with the number of job seekers.	⊠

(continued next page)

Key Result Area	Expectations for the Nation	Progress being made?*
	10. The gender distribution among the employed will be equitable and fair at all levels, including those of decision makers and middle management.	☆
	11. Batswana will be able to obtain access to good quality basic shelter, either in the urban or in the rural areas.	☆
Vision Pillar Three: A Compassionate, Just, and Caring Nation		
Poverty and income distribution	1. There will be policies and measures that increase the participation of poorer households in productive and income earning activities.	☆
	2. Botswana will have eradicated absolute poverty, so that no part of the country will have people living with incomes below the appropriate poverty data line.	⊠
	3. Botswana will be a compassionate and caring society, offering support and opportunity to those who are poor and including all people in the benefits of growth.	☆
	4. All people will have access to productive resources, regardless of ethnic origin, gender, disability, or misfortune. Botswana will have succeeded in helping people to escape from the poverty trap and play a full part in society.	☺
	5. There will be a social safety net for those who find themselves in poverty for any reason. Partnership with the private sector and NGOs, aimed at vulnerable groups such as the elderly, disabled, orphans, and terminally ill will be established.	☆
Quantity and quality of health services	6. Botswana will have access to good quality health facilities, including both primary and curative services within reasonable traveling distance. Mental health treatment will be accessible to all.	☆
	7. All people who are suffering from AIDS-related illnesses will have access to good quality treatment in the health facilities, community, or the workplace so that they can continue to live full and productive lives for as long as possible.	☆
Combating HIV/AIDS	8. By the year 2016, the spread of HIV virus that causes AIDS will have been stopped so that there will be no new infections by the virus in that year.	⊠

(continued next page)

Key Result Area	Expectations for the Nation	Progress being made?*
	Vision Pillar Four: A Safe and Secure Nation	
Crime, safety, and security	1. By the year 2016, serious and violent crime and the illegal possession of firearms will be eliminated as will the distribution and use of addictive drugs.	⊠
Professional public security services	2. Violation of the physical well-being and human rights of individuals will have been eliminated. The abuse of spouses and children will be completely eradicated.	⊠
	3. The high incidence of deaths and serious injuries arising from the irresponsible use of vehicles, inadequate fencing of animals, or poor road marking will be substantially reduced by the year 2016.	☆
	4. The public will have sufficient confidence in law enforcement agencies and in public protective services to report crimes.	☺
	5. A small, alert, well-trained, disciplined, and fully accountable Botswana A Defence Force will serve the nation, protecting its security and stability.	☆
	Vision Pillar Five: An Open, Democratic, and Accountable Nation	
Responsible and accountable leadership	1. The Botswana of 2016 will emphasize the accountability of all citizens, from the state president down to community leaders, for their actions and decisions.	☆
	2. A morally and ethically upright, educated society will be matched by a leadership of the same qualities, which will provide role models for its younger generation and an instrument to implement democracy.	☺
	3. Botswana will have increased political tolerance and legal sanctions against those who violate the principles of accountability at all levels of leadership, including the state presidency.	☺
Open and transparent government	4. The role of the House of Chiefs and other traditional leaders will be clearly defined to suit the changing circumstances of Botswana. The co-operative relationship between traditional leaders and elected political leaders will promote social tranquility and orderly governance.	☆
	Vision Pillar Six: A Moral and Tolerant Nation	
Discrimination-free society	1. No citizens of the future Botswana will be disadvantaged as a result of gender.	☆
	2. The future Botswana will have eradicated negative social attitudes toward the status and role of women.	☺

(continued next page)

Annex 12.A *continued*

Key Result Area	Expectations for the Nation	Progress being made?*
National moral and cultural values	3. The Botswana of the future will have citizens who are law abiding.	☺
Vision Pillar Seven: A United and Proud Nation		
National unity	1. By the year 2016, Botswana will be united and proud, sharing common goals based on a common heritage, national pride, and a desire for stability.	☆
Social stability	2. The country will still possess a diverse mix of cultures.	☆
	3. We will have achieved ethnic integration and full partnership to create a nation in harmony with itself. From this partnership will have sprung an equitably distributed prosperity in a caring environment born of loyalty.	☺
Strong family institution	4. The family will be the central institution for the support and development of people in Botswana.	☺
	5. The strength of the family will have been reinforced in response to the rapid social changes that are sweeping the country.	☺
	6. The emphasis on a strong family unit will encourage responsible parenting and the institution of marriage. It will provide the social foundation for the eradication of problems such as the high incidence of teenage pregnancies.	☺

Source: Botswana Vision Council 2009. *Vision 2016 Botswana Performance Report.*

Note: AIDS = acquired immune deficiency syndrome, HIV = human immunodeficiency virus, IT = information technology. *Progress being made? is a subjective rating of progress based on both quantitative and qualitative information. It is a global rating and, as such, is imprecise. More detailed information is provided in *Botswana's Performance Report* on each Vision pillar.

Notes

1. "M&E" is a somewhat ambiguous term. What may be deemed to be a country's "National Evaluation System (NES)" may have little to do with the practice of evaluation per se. The more widely used term in developing countries is "Monitoring and Evaluation (M&E) System," where, in many instances, the prime focus is on the "M," with little or no investment in the "E." In this chapter, the use of the term M&E is intended to include the application of both monitoring and evaluation.

2. The author worked with Botswana's Vision Council during 2008 and 2009 to develop the inaugural version of *Botswana's Performance Report*, that serves as the template for future national performance reporting.

3. Annex 1 provides a detailed elaboration of the "Expectations for the Nation" drawn from Vision 2016.

4. www.vision2016.co.bw/tempimg/media/mediac_WORD.
5. A variety of communication efforts have exposed Batswana to the goals and expectations of Vision 2016. For example, the original Vision 2016 document has been crafted into popular versions intended for primary and secondary school children. An annual launch of the Vision 2016 campaign every September as part of "Vision month" brings all sectors together in communities across the country, reinforcing the messages of Vision 2016 and aiming to encourage the participation of civil society in Vision 2016 projects and activities.
6. See, for example, Mackay 2010, Lahey 2010 and Lahey 2011.

References

Botswana Vision Council, Vision 2016. 2009. *Vision 2016 Botswana Performance Report: A Report on the Progress Being Achieved against the Vision 2016 Goals.* Gaborone: Government of Botswana.

Kusek, Jody Zall, and Ray C. Rist. 2004. *Ten Steps to a Results-Based Monitoring and Evaluation System: A Handbook for Development Practitioners.* Washington, DC: World Bank.

Lahey, Robert. 2006. "The Broad Consequences of Evaluation Capacity Building: Experience of Developing Countries." Presentation to the 2006 Annual Conference of the American Evaluation Association, November 1–4, Portland, OR.

———. 2007. "A Framework for Developing a Monitoring and Evaluation System: Lessons from International Experience." Presentation to the Conference on International Experiences on Institutionalizing Monitoring and Evaluation Systems and the Application and Use in Ukraine, February 21–22, Kyiv, Ukraine.

———. 2010. "The Canadian Evaluation M&E System: Lessons Learned from 30 Years of Development." Evaluation Capacity Development Series 23, World Bank, Washington, DC.

———. 2011. "The Canadian Monitoring and Evaluation System." PREM Note 11, special series on "The Nuts and Bolts of M&E Systems." World Bank, Washington, DC.

———. 2012. "Guidance for National Evaluation Capacity Development: A Report for the United Nations Evaluation Group (UNEG) Task Force on National Evaluation Capacity Development." International Labour Office: Geneva.

Mackay, Keith. 2010. "Conceptual Framework for Monitoring and Evaluation." PREM Note 1, special series on "The Nuts and Bolts of M&E Systems," World Bank, Washington, DC.

Menon, Saraswathi. 2010. "A Perspective from the United Nations on National Ownership and Capacity in Evaluation." In *From Policies to Results: Developing Capacities for Country Monitoring and Evaluation Systems,* edited by Marco Segone. Geneva: UNICEF.

Presidential Task Group for a Long Term Vision for Botswana. 1997. *Vision 2016: Towards Prosperity for All.* Government of Botswana.

Segone, Marco, ed. 2010. *From Policies to Results: Developing Capacities for Country Monitoring and Evaluation Systems.* New York: UNICEF.

CHAPTER 13

A Pilot Experience for Evaluating M&E Systems for Social Programs in Latin America

Juan Abreu, Marie-Helene Boily, Idania Fernández, and Frederic R. Martin

M&E Systems and Social Programs in Latin America

As a continent, Latin America has experienced times of great change and turbulence. The region overall experienced a decade of growth in the early years of this century, obviously in emerging economies like Brazil and Chile, but also in other countries such as Panama. At the same time, old issues of structural poverty and inequality pervaded and actually grew because of the unequal distribution of growth benefits among social categories. Latin America is now largely integrated in the world economy. It experiences the opportunities as a global food and fuel exporter as well as the shocks from international financial markets, although the region went through the recent financial crisis relatively well. Over the medium term, its economies have experienced the growing competition of the Asia powerhouses. Over the long term, the growing number and amplitude of crises linked to climatic change and resulting higher public costs (van den Berg 2013) can be felt. Faced with these recurrent problems and the challenges of the new turbulent times, the opposition parties in Parliament, citizens, civil society, and the private sector are pressuring governments to address critical issues and create greater value for public money.

The response of governments in the region has been significant and has involved major changes in economic and social policies, striving simultaneously for economic growth and poverty reduction, as exemplified by the success story of the Lula administration[1] in Brazil. A key measure of Lula's policies included the adoption and/or generalization of social protection programs largely accessible to poor and vulnerable groups, in particular conditional monetary transfer programs. Those programs started in Mexico (Progreso in 1982, which became Oportunidades in 2000) and were later adopted by many countries, including Brazil (Bolsa Familia within the Programa Fome Zero in 2000), Chile (Chile Solidario in 2004), Honduras (Bono 10000, Programa de Asignacion), El Salvador (Programa de Apoyo Temporal al Ingreso Familiar), and Panama (Red de Oportunidades in 2006).

Setting up, scaling up, and efficiently managing social-protection programs are significant challenges for governments. These programs are often complex involving many actors and partnerships and multiple activities to conduct, coordinate, and monitor. They face difficult issues in identifying and following up with beneficiaries, ensuring cost-effectiveness of delivery mechanisms, and demonstrating outcomes and impacts, especially in a context of increased external and internal shocks. Hence, governments feel the need for a solid results-based monitoring and evaluation (M&E) system as a key component of the implementation of results-based management (RBM) of those programs.

Most governments in Latin America have initiated and progressively institutionalized M&E systems (May and others 2006, Castro and others 2009, Medina Giopp 2007, Rios Hess 2007, Falcão Martins 2007, Villareal Navarro 2007). However, with significant variations across countries, sectors, and programs, M&E has been globally identified as one of the weakest pillars of RBM in Latin America (García López and García Moreno 2010). National M&E systems are often designed, but are less often fully operationalized for a variety of reasons. The demand for M&E results depends on the leadership of authorities who may not champion a culture of results but rather make decisions on the basis of other considerations. The staff members in the public sector may be reluctant to implement M&E if it is perceived as an added workload with limited benefits for them. There are problems in the design of strategies, programs, and projects with no base-line and weak logical frameworks linking outputs to outcomes to impacts. M&E human capacities are often limited, with some M&E staff positions going unfilled as a result of rapid staff rotation or being occupied by junior staff members, who lack credibility with ministerial technical departments. Training opportunities exist but often are neither practical nor adapted to the local institutional environment, thereby limiting their usefulness and applicability. Data quality issues and multiple complex and costly informa-tion systems hamper many M&E systems. Financial resources allocated to M&E systems are often not up to ambitions set by authorities and official laws and decrees. In poorer countries with weaker public institutional envi-ronments, multiple, ad hoc, and donor-driven M&E systems may under-mine the development of a national M&E system. There is now a realization that the full operationalization and institutionalization of a national M&E system is a long-term, multistep process, with a variety of technical and institutional issues to be addressed along the way. Thus, proponents see the need to regularly assess the state of implementation of a results-based M&E system and to propose an action plan to further improve the system.

Analytical Framework to Diagnose M&E Systems

Rist (2009) identifies three main areas that need to be assessed in a results-based M&E readiness diagnostic for social protection agencies:

1. Incentives and demands for designing and building a results-based M&E system
2. Roles and responsibilities and existing structures for assessing perfor-mance of the government
3. Capacity-building requirements for a results-based M&E system.

He proposes a set of key questions to be asked in a readiness assessment:

- What potential pressures are encouraging the need for the M&E system within the ministry and why?
- Who is the advocate for such an M&E system?
- What is motivating the champion to support this change effort?
- Who will own the system? Who will benefit from the system? How much information do they really want?
- How will the system directly support better resource allocation and the achievement of program goals?

- How will the organization, the champions, and the staff react to negative information generated by the M&E system?
- Where does capacity exist within the ministry to support a results-based M&E system?
- How will the M&E system link the project, program, sector, and national outcomes and impacts? ·

Rist and others (2011) identify eight domains to assess within an M&E system: the crossing of institutional, human, technical, and financial capacities with demand and supply sides. Lahey (2013) identifies four building blocks for a national M&E system: the vision, an enabling environment, the capacity to supply M&E information, and the capacity to demand and use M&E information.

The challenge of conducting an operational diagnostic of an M&E system against the standard of a fully developed results-based M&E system is to incorporate all of these elements in a single assessment grid that will organize the information in a systematic way; capture the essential elements; be adjustable to country and institutional situations; and be manageable in terms of time, human expertise, and budget.

To meet this challenge, five dimensions were identified to assess the degree of compliance of any given M&E system with the gold standard of a fully developed results-based M&E system:

- First, some preconditions in terms of planning, budgeting, performance measurement framework, accountability mechanisms, and demand for M&E will affect the feasibility and the performance of a results-based M&E system (Dimension 1).
- Then the M&E system must be institutionalized within a legal and institutional framework (Dimension 2).
- M&E is a management function that needs to be planned and budgeted (Dimension 3).
- Finally, the implementation of the system is assessed through a review of current monitoring practices (Dimension 4) and evaluation practices (Dimension 5).

Each dimension includes several subdimensions addressing specific issues, including the existence of key elements of a results-based M&E system (for example, an M&E plan), the quality of those elements, and finally, their actual use by stakeholders.

The diagnostic should also distinguish clearly among the capacities at three levels: national (or subnational) government, sector level, and program/project level. The proposed assessment framework in table 13.1 presents the five dimensions and a number of subdimensions.

Development Evaluation in Times of Turbulence

Table 13.1 The Five Dimensions to Assess the Degree of Compliance of an M&E System with a Fully Developed Results-Based M&E System

Subdimensions	National level[a]	Sectoral level	Program level[b]
Dimension 1: Preconditions for a Results-Based M&E System			
Existence, quality, and use of a strategic national development plan			
Existence, quality, and use of a strategic sectoral plan			
Existence, quality, and use of a program document			
Existence, quality, and use of a performance measurement framework			
Existence, quality, and use of an operational plan			
Existence, quality, and use of a results-based budget of the operational plan			
Coordinated and results-based management			
Availability, quality, and use of financial information on expenditures			
Existence of a demand for M&E			
Dimension 2: Legal and Institutional Mechanisms for M&E			
Existence, quality, and use of a legal framework and national evaluation policy			
Existence, clarity, and implementation of a description of roles and responsibilities of entities involved in M&E			
Existence, clarity, and implementation of the job description of key personnel of entities involved in M&E			
Existence, quality, and use of an incentive system that promotes quality M&E			
Existence, quality, and implementation of a training plan in M&E or with an M&E component			
Dimension 3: Planning and Budgeting for M&E			
Existence, quality, and use of a monitoring and evaluation plan			
Availability of human resources for the implementation of the monitoring and evaluation plan			
Availability of financial resources to implement the monitoring and evaluation plan			

(continued)

Table 13.1   (continued)

Subdimensions	National level[a]	Sectoral level	Program level[b]
Dimension 4: Current Monitoring Practices			
Existence, quality, and use of physical implementation monitoring			
Existence, quality, and use of financial implementation monitoring			
Existence, quality, and use of results monitoring			
Existence and quality of the information system for monitoring			
Dimension 5: Current Evaluation Practices			
Existence, quality, and use of baselines and situational reports			
Existence, quality, and use of program *ex-ante* evaluations			
Existence, quality, and use of yearly performance reports			
Existence and quality of mid-term and final evaluations on national development plan implementation			
Existence and quality of mid-term and final evaluations on sectoral strategic plan implementation			
Existence and quality of program mid-term, final, and impact evaluations			
Existence and use of M&E data quality assessments			

Note: M&E = monitoring and evaluation.

a. Also valid at subnational level (for example, state, province).

b. Also valid at project level.

Moving from the Conceptual Framework to an Operational Approach

In this section, the conceptual framework discussed earlier is translated into an operational approach, and a tool is presented to conduct a diagnostic of an M&E system and formulate an action plan.

Operational Approach

Each country can decide on the proper institutional and organizational approach to conduct the diagnostic and formulate the action plan. In all cases, the approach should be practical, results-oriented, structured, quick, participatory, and constructive. Typically, three institutional mechanisms are

(a) a steering committee for overall coordination and validation of the work done by the technical working group; (b) a technical working group (TWG) that will play the key role in the diagnostic of the M&E system and the formulation of the action plan; and (c) a consultative forum that will involve all stakeholders for information, consultation, and results dissemination.

Since setting up and scaling up a results-based M&E system is a medium-to long-term process the following phases are recommended:

- Conduct a structured and participatory diagnostic of the M&E system.
- Formulate an action plan to improve the performance of the system over the next few years.
- Implement the action plan. Provide adequate resources, training, coaching, and technical support, and monitor this implementation.
- Repeat this exercise every few years for a stepwise improvement in the M&E system.

There is neither a unique blueprint nor a fixed duration to implement this process. However, typically, phases 1 and 2 are conducted over a 4–6 week period and include the activities described in the following section.

Diagnostic phase:

- Set up documentation review, preliminary data collection at central level, and short visits to selected regions to capture M&E realities in the field.
- Set up institutional mechanisms for the diagnostic process.
- Train the technical working group and parameterize the tool.
- TWG implements the diagnostic phase of the tool, including meetings with key stakeholders, in-depth interviews with a semistructured interview guide and focus groups, and preparation of a preliminary diagnostic of the M&E system.
- Consultative forum meets to discuss the preliminary diagnostic, which typically involves a one to one-and-a-half day workshop of all stakeholders.[2]
- TWG revises the diagnostic to incorporate results of the consultative forum meeting.
- Steering committee officially validates the results of the diagnostic.

Action plan phase:

- Identify the elements of an action plan to improve the M&E system in a technical workshop.[3]
- TWG prepares the preliminary version of the action plan.

- Consultative forum meets to discuss and prevalidate the action plan.
- TWG revises the action plan to incorporate results of the consultative forum meeting.
- Steering committee officially validates the action plan.

Diagnostic Tool

The IDEA-AIM4R (Assessing and Improving M&E for Results) tool[4] includes two modules dealing with the diagnostic and the formulation of the action plan, respectively. The diagnostic module follows the analytical framework presented earlier and in table 13.1 and expands its five dimensions with 24 subdimensions and 94 indicators. The tool uses the same subdimensions, but offers the possibility of adjusting the wording of indicators based on the context in each country, sector, or program. A grade is given to each indicator using a three-level ordinal grading scale: 1, no, not at all; 2, partially; 3, yes, completely.[5] The objectivity of the evaluation relies on (1) the evaluation approach, which is constructive and nonpersonal, promoting a greater openness to share information about M&E practices; (2) the formulation of indicators dealing with factual evidence (for example, the existence of a document or the presence of specific quality characteristics); (3) the careful selection of TWG participants with proven expertise in the domain and independence of judgment;[6] (4) the consensus achieved in the consultative forum of stakeholders around the value given to a specific indicator; and (5) the justification and empirical evidence provided for the grade given to each indicator.

The second module of the tool guides the formulation of an action plan to improve the M&E system over the short and medium term. It involves (1) the identification of existing relevant actions; (2) the identification and prioritization of additional desirable actions; and (3) the characterization of selected priority actions (tasks, roles and responsibilities, timetable, budget, and funding needs) with more details provided for the first year of the action plan.

Pilot Application of the Operational Approach in Central America

Objectives and Process

The operational approach and tool described above have been tested and improved over time in several countries, sectors, and programs.[7] The case study presented here is from a project called Strengthening Results-Based Management of the Social Protection Sector in Central America, conducted by the Secretaria de la Integración Social Centroamericana (SISCA) from April 2010 to April 2012 and supported by the World Bank.

The process included the following stages:

- Writing a concept paper on the evaluation of M&E systems (Rist 2009)
- Adapting the IDEA-AIM4R generic tool to the specific context of social programs in Central America with the participation of professionals from SISCA, the three pilot countries—El Salvador, Honduras, and Panama— and the World Bank
- Using the adapted tool, called EME/Soc, to conduct a pilot assessment of the M&E system of three key conditional cash-transfer social programs in the Central America region: Programa de Atención Temporal al Ingreso in El Salvador, Programa Bono 10 Mil in Honduras, and Programa Red de Oportunidades in Panama.

Results from the Pilot Application

The overall grade given to the existing M&E systems in the three pilot countries (Moreno 2011, 2012; Rodriguez Waldo 2011, 2012; Vázquez Lobo 2011, 2012) varied between low and medium-low, confirming the analysis by García López and García Moreno (2010) and reflecting the limited importance given to M&E in practice. The performance of the M&E system was found to be positively affected by the institutional capacity of the country and program, the duration of program implementation, and the involvement of external funding. Results were better for monitoring than for evaluation even though monitoring, especially results monitoring, was far from fully performing. There is still limited planning of M&E activities. The emphasis has been on setting up institutional mechanisms and creating tools, but the entities responsible for the M&E systems are not yet at the stage of improving the quality and use of M&E products. This situation is partly related to limited M&E capacities at the strategic and/or operational levels. The capacities at regional levels are even weaker and are a major bottleneck to improving the completeness and timeliness of reporting based on quality data.

Lessons Learned from the Pilot Application

The diagnostic process was faced with two main challenges. First, the identification and participation of stakeholders was an issue. At times, it was

Figure 13.1   Main Results of the Diagnostic of the M&E System of the PATI Program in El Salvador

Dimension 1: Pre-conditions for results-based M&E system

1.1 Existence, quality, and use of a strategic plan in the social protection domain

1.7 Existence of a demand for M&E of the program

1.2 Existence, quality, and use of a set of performance indicators coming from a results matrix or a logic model for the program

1.6 Availability, quality, and use of the financial information on program expenditures

1.3 Existence, quality, and use of an operatinal plan for the program

1.5 Coordinated and results-based management of the program

1.4 Existence, quality, and use of a results-based budget for the program

Dimension 2: Legal framework and institutional mechanisms for the M&E of the program

2.1 Existence, quality, and use of a legal framework or evaluation policy for public program

2.4 Existence, quality, and implementation of a training program related to the M&E of the program

2.2 Existence, clarity, and implementation of a description of roles and responsibilitites of the actors involved in the M&E of the program

2.3 Existence, quality, and use of an incentive system that promotes a quality M&E of the program

Dimension 3: Program M&E plan and budget

3.1 Existence, quality, and use of a monitoring plan/strategy of the program

3.5 Availability of financial resources for the implementation of the program M&E workplan

3.2 Existence, quality, and use of an evaluation plan/strategy of the program

3.4 Availability of human resources for the implementation of the program M&E workplan

3.3 Existence, quality, and implementation of a yearly workplan for the implementation of the M&E plan/strategy of the program

Development Evaluation in Times of Turbulence

Figure 13.1 (Continued)

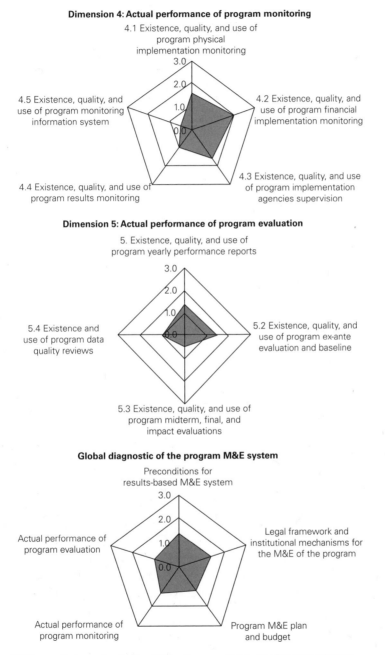

Dimension 4: Actual performance of program monitoring

4.1 Existence, quality, and use of program physical implementation monitoring

4.5 Existence, quality, and use of program monitoring information system

4.2 Existence, quality, and use of program financial implementation monitoring

4.4 Existence, quality, and use of program results monitoring

4.3 Existence, quality, and use of program implementation agencies supervision

Dimension 5: Actual performance of program evaluation

5. Existence, quality, and use of program yearly performance reports

5.4 Existence and use of program data quality reviews

5.2 Existence, quality, and use of program ex-ante evaluation and baseline

5.3 Existence, quality, and use of program midterm, final, and impact evaluations

Global diagnostic of the program M&E system

Preconditions for results-based M&E system

Actual performance of program evaluation

Legal framework and institutional mechanisms for the M&E of the program

Actual performance of program monitoring

Program M&E plan and budget

Note: M&E = monitoring and evaluation, PATI = Programa de Atención Temporal al Ingreso.

difficult to obtain the full participation of all stakeholders to avoid a closed-quarter exercise conducted by public-sector professionals and to expand the ownership of the process and the tool to more stakeholders. This challenge is related to the limited culture and tradition of M&E within the public sector. Second, high staff turnover and the resulting limited institutional memory complicated the diagnostic. Those challenges were reinforced by weaknesses in knowledge management within the public sector limiting the impact of efforts made to improve individual capabilities. There is room to improve the institutionalization of M&E functions in government institutions.

The tool was found to be applicable and user-friendly. It provided, with a limited amount of time and resources, a systematic assessment of the compliance of the M&E systems with the standard of a fully developed results-based M&E system. The tool also helped structure the action plan within a results framework, which facilitated the monitoring of its implementation and the assessment of progress over time. Specific methodological issues addressed during the application included the following:

- *The generic versus tailor-made nature of the tool.* The project team experienced a tension between the pressure to adjust the tool to the specifics of the country and program and the desire to keep a standard evaluation grid to allow for comparisons and benchmarking across countries and programs for aggregation at the regional level. This tension was resolved by keeping the same dimensions and subdimensions, but allowing some flexibility in indicator wording.
- *The optimum degree of disaggregation of the diagnostic.* The TWG discussed the optimum number of indicators and a compromise was struck to limit indicators to a manageable number (less than 100 for the whole tool).
- *The choice of grading scale.* The TWG discussed the proper range of the grading scale and agreed with a three-level scale for simplicity and objectivity.
- *The control of subjectivity in initial answers.* Controlling subjectivity in some indicator grades given by tool users required, at times, that tool administrators better relate each indicator grade to a specific situation.
- *The incorporation of risk indicators in the M&E system.* Risk indicators enable evaluators to account for unpredictable and exogenous factors that could adversely impact the performance of the M&E system.

Conclusion and Way Forward

In a context of increased accountability of governments and increased turbulence at national and international levels, the need for a solid results-based M&E system is at the fore. Countries in Latin America and the Caribbean have gone a long way in establishing M&E systems. The proposed analytical framework and operational process and tool to conduct a diagnostic of an existing M&E system's compliance with the standards of a fully developed results-based M&E system, and ability to design a short- and medium-term action plan has proven its usefulness and adaptability while respecting time and resource constraints. Obviously there is room to improve both the process and the tool, in particular to ensure proper participation of all stakeholders, including private-sector and civil-society organizations,[8] and to further parameterize the tool to formalize a full-fledged application. There is a strong need for operational tools to help guide governments, ministries, and programs in the implementation of results-based M&E and its related domains of strategic planning, operational planning, and budgeting to help them move up the scale of results-based management implementation.

Notes

1. Luiz Inácio Lula da Silva served two terms as Brazil's President from 2002 to 2011.
2. If a workshop cannot be organized, an alternative is to organize meetings with the entity responsible for the M&E system and other key stakeholders.
3. Steps 7 to 9 can be combined with step 6 in a single three-day workshop or presented in a separate workshop, time and resources permitting.
4. IDEA-AIM4R is part of the IDEA-TOOLS suite, a series of applications designed to facilitate the implementation of RBM pillars.
5. There are also N/A (not applicable) and N/I (not enough information) options. For several indicators, the intermediate grade of 2 is eliminated because the choice is binary: "No," which corresponds to a grade of 1; "Yes," which corresponds to a grade of 3.
6. Professionals from the entity who are involved in M&E may be part of the TWG to provide insider's information, but they should not lead it or control it. The lead evaluators should be external.
7. Among others, through the project "Diagnostic of M&E Systems of Programs Supporting Orphans and Vulnerable Children (OVCs)" in six African countries (Botswana, Cameroon, Côte d'Ivoire, Lesotho, Swaziland, and Uganda) through the support of UNICEF; in Zambia with the Ministry of Finance with the

support of the World Bank; and in six country programs supported by the Millennium Challenge Account (Benin, Lesotho, Morocco, Mozambique, Senegal, and Tanzania).

8. See Gildemyn 2013.

References

Castro, Manuel Fernando, Gladys Lopez-Acevedo, Gita Beker Busjeet, and Ximena Fernandez Ordonez. 2009. "El sistema de M&E en México: Un salto del nivel sectorial al nacional." Independent Evaluation Group, Document de trabajo 20, World Bank, Washington, DC.

Falcão Martins, Humberto. 2007. "Sistema de Monitoramento do Plano Plurianual, Sistema de Monitoramento de Metas Presidenciais Sistema de Monitoramento e Avaliação de Políticas e Programas Sociais, Sistema de Avaliação Externa de Programas Governamentais Brasil." In *Fortalecimiento de los sistemas de monitoreo y evaluación (M&E) en América Latina,* case study 3. Caracas and Washington, DC: Centro Latino de Administración para el Desarrollo and World Bank.

García López, Roberto, and Mauricio García Moreno. 2010. *Managing for Development Results: Progress and Challenges in Latin America and the Caribbean.* Washington, DC: Inter-American Development Bank.

Gildemyn, Marie. 2013. "Toward an Understanding of CSO's Involvement in M&E: Unpacking the Accountability and Feedback Function of M&E." In *Development Evaluation in Times of Turbulence: Dealing with Crises That Endanger Our Future,* edited by Marie-Helene Boily, Frederic R. Martin, and Ray C. Rist. Washington, DC: World Bank.

Lahey, Robert. 2013. "National Performance Reporting as a Driver for National M&E Development: The Experience of Botswana." In *Development Evaluation in Times of Turbulence: Dealing with Crises That Endanger Our Future,* edited by Marie-Helene Boily, Frederic R. Martin, and Ray C. Rist. Washington, DC: World Bank.

May, Ernesto, David Shand, Keith Mackay, Fernando Rojas, and Jaime Saavedra. 2006. "Toward the Institutionalization of M&E Systems in Latin America and the Caribbean." Proceedings of a World Bank/Inter-American Development Bank Conference, Washington, DC.

Medina Giopp, Alejandro. 2007. "El Sistema Nacional de Monitoreo y Evaluación de la Gestión Pública en México." In *Fortalecimiento de los sistemas de monitoreo y evaluación (M&E) en América Latina.* Caracas and Washington, DC: Centro Latino de Administración para el Desarrollo and World Bank.

Moreno, Ilka. 2011. "Informe Diagnóstico del Sistema de Monitoreo y Evaluación del Programa Red de Oportunidades de Panamá." Secretaria de la Integración Social Centroamericana, Ciudad de Panamá.

———. 2012. "Plan de Acción para el Mejoramiento del Sistema de Monitoreo y Evaluación del programa Red de Oportunidades de Panamá." Secretaria de la Integración Social Centroamericana, Ciudad de Panamá.

Ríos Hess, Salvador. 2007. "Diagnóstico de los sistemas de monitoreo y evaluación en Chile." In *Fortalecimiento de los sistemas de monitoreo y evaluación (M&E) en América Latina.* Caracas and Washington, DC: Centro Latino de Administración para el Desarrollo and World Bank.

Rist, Ray. 2009. *Results-based Readiness Assessment Diagnostic Tool for Social Protection Agencies.* Washington, DC: World Bank.

Rist, Ray, Marie-Helene Boily, and Frederic Martin. 2011. "Introduction." In *Influencing Change: Building Evaluation Capacity to Strengthen Governance.* Washington, DC: World Bank.

Rodriguez Waldo, Floralba. 2011. "Programa de Atención Temporal al Ingreso—PATI: Aplicación de la Herramienta de Diagnostico del Sistema de Monitoreo y Evaluación y Diseño del Plan de Acción para su Mejoramiento: Diagnostico." Secretaria de la Integración Social Centroamericana, San Salvador.

———. 2012. "Programa de Atención Temporal al Ingreso—PATI: Aplicación de la Herramienta de Diagnostico del Sistema de Monitoreo y Evaluación y Diseño del Plan de Acción para su Mejoramiento." Secretaria de la Integración Social Centroamericana, San Salvador.

Villareal Navarro, Julio. 2007. "Colombia y el sistema de monitoreo y evaluación, Sistema Nacional de Evaluacion y Gestion por Resultados (SINERGIA)." In *Fortalecimiento de los sistemas de monitoreo y evaluación (M&E) en América Latina.* Caracas and Washington, DC: Centro Latino de Administración para el Desarrollo and World Bank.

van den Berg, Rob D. 2013. "Evaluation in the Context of Global Public Goods." In *Development Evaluation in Times of Turbulence: Dealing with Crises That Endanger Our Future,* edited by Marie-Helene Boily, Frederic R. Martin, and Ray C. Rist. Washington, DC: World Bank.

Vázquez Lobo, Ricardo Alejandro. 2011. "Educación, Salud y Nutrición Bono 10 Mil—Honduras." In *Informe de diagnostico del Sistema de Monitoreo y Evaluación del Programa Presidencial.* Tegucigalpa, Honduras: Secretaria de la Integración Social Centroamericana.

———. 2012. "Educación, Salud y Nutrición de Honduras (Bono 10 Mil)." In *Plan de Acción para el Mejoramiento del Sistema de Monitoreo y Evaluación del Programa Presidencial.* Tegucigalpa, Honduras: Secretaria de la Integración Social Centroamericana.

CHAPTER 14

Conclusion

Marie-Helene Boily and Frederic R. Martin

This book has focused on the implications of turbulent times, especially the food, fuel, and financial (3F) crisis, for the evaluation world. Signs of turbulent times are everywhere: let us name only the financial crisis affecting mainly Europe and the United States, the food crisis in the Sahel and Southern Africa, the fuel crisis with yo-yoing oil and mineral prices and the Fukoshima nuclear disaster, the growing number and magnitude of natural disasters everywhere in the world, the rapidly changing political order with revolutions in the Maghreb and the Middle East, and the growing redistribution of power toward Asia; and, some would add, the values crises that shake a number of rapidly changing societies through the breakdown of traditional beliefs and institutions, as well as mounting racism, ethnic conflicts, and religious obscurantism as correlates.

However, turbulence is nothing new. Many previous crises have occurred in human history: during the 20th century alone, we witnessed numerous famines (mainly in Asia and Africa, but also in other regions such as the "bread" revolts in the Middle East), financial and economic system crashes (North America and Europe in 1929, Asia in the 1990s), fuel crises (two oil shocks), environmental disasters (tsunamis, hurricanes, and typhoons as well as nuclear catastrophes at Chernobyl and Fukoshima), and too many wars and revolutions to count. Beyond these transitory crises, there is the much less media-covered chronic crisis of the poor, both poor individuals and poor countries, who are living in a permanent state of crisis. United Nations and World Bank reports regularly remind us that 2.7 billion people live on less than US$2 a day and 1.1 billion live on less than US$1 a day. So why has the idea of turbulent times come to the fore today?

Many factors contribute to this complex situation, and their importance varies depending on the type of crisis, the concerned sector, and the affected region. However, several factors contribute more than others to the perception of greater turbulent times. First, all countries and citizens, rich and poor alike, are affected. Second, the number and speed of interconnections among systems have increased as a result of the liberalization of world trade and financial markets and the progress and generalization of information technology and media coverage. Third, financial market deregulation has led to the development of new financial products and decision-making models that have increased markets' instability. Fourth, many governments have not been able to control market failures because of failures within government itself, such as unsustainable indebtedness, corruption, inefficiencies, and petty political games.

Beyond those obvious factors hides a more global factor, that is, the perception by a growing number of intellectuals and practitioners, including evaluators, that the past schemes and policies are no longer working. Ibrahim (chapter 1) tells us that we need to revisit our economic and social policies, which are too short-sighted. Furubo (chapter 2) questions the traditional approach of evaluation based on the assumption that the situation is changing incrementally and that future impacts of policies can be predicted by analyzing past realities. Honesty commands us to admit that we are good at explaining the past and why our ex-ante evaluations were wrong.

The human evaluation software needs to be upgraded. Social and management sciences provide the bulk of analytical underpinnings and methods behind many program evaluations. However, the silo mentality of many disciplines does not help provide a 360-degree understanding of a particular public program and its results. Among the social sciences, economics has contributed to a structured analytical framework of the effects of economic and social policies through economic theory and analytical methods. However, the core analytical approach in neoclassical economics, that is, marginal economic analysis, looks at incremental movements around the equilibrium or moving from one equilibrium point to another equilibrium point.

This approach is insufficient to assess the impact of public policies and programs. Comparative statistics often involve a leap of faith about the dynamics of change, which are what evaluation of public programs is largely about. The term *ceteris paribus* (all other things being equal) is too often invoked to justify our ignorance of "noneconomic" factors. Economists are not the only ones to be blamed, though they are easy culprits. For example, management sciences have also contributed to a better understanding of the decision-making process of business and public institutions. However, program management specialists still rely heavily on tools adapted to simple situations that are rarely encountered in the real world. A good example is the common requirement by many governments, international organizations, and donor agencies to include in the ex-ante evaluation of a project a "logical framework," which is a simplistic appreciation of how change is implemented through linear causality and how the environment and the project interact. Other social scientists have often rightly complained about the simplistic and incomplete analytical framework used by economists and management specialists and argued for the inclusion of other relevant key issues in the evaluation of policies and programs. However, a number of them have themselves remained prisoners of a reductionist prism of analysis—be it social class, ethnic group, gender, race, or power games—that prevents them from providing a convincing explanation of what is really happening and why.

To counter those limitations, systemic analysis has been proposed to model the evolution of complex systems over time, incorporating feedback loops and turning points. It has been used for modeling natural systems and some social systems, but the mere complexity of differential equations models and their requirements in time, data, and skills make them of limited practical value for the time-short and resource-scarce evaluator of public programs.

A good example of our limited capacity to properly assess and then influence decision making is provided by the issue of climate change. First came the challenge of scientific measurement: finding statistically significant evidence of change. Scientists argued for the past 20 years about the correlation of climate change with carbon emissions due to human activity and only recently have the majority of them assessed that this hypothesis "cannot be rejected." Second, the potential losers, vested interests like oil companies, have strongly lobbied against policy change, arguing that moving away from oil would hurt economic growth and employment. Third, a majority of citizens in rich countries find it easier to retain their cosy lifestyles, looking away from evidence that does not fit their beliefs, and staying in their mental comfort zone. A number of their counterparts in emerging countries are so eager to enjoy and show off their new material wealth that "long-term" concerns about climate change are the least of their priorities. Many politicians are not ready to argue for or implement policies that will result in long-term sustainable development. They prefer quick wins and populist measures that will keep them in power for the duration of their political horizon. All of them are guilty of human shortsightedness and ego-centricity: they lack the realization that what is slow change on the human clock is actually extremely rapid change on the Earth clock.

Implications for Evaluation

What are the implications for the young profession of evaluation? The chapters in this book offer several lines of thought and action.

Several papers make proposals about how we conceive of evaluation. First, they suggest enlarging the scope of evaluation. Menon (chapter 3) proposes considering other criteria such as equity, innovation, human rights, and gender equality. Van den Berg (chapter 4) alerts us about the urgency of taking into account in our evaluations the rising global public costs stemming from climate change, mass extinction of biodiversity, and spread of poisonous chemicals. Agrawal (chapter 6) argues that a comprehensive monitoring system should not only consider inputs and outputs, but also outcomes and even impacts to better feed into evaluation.

Several papers argue for fundamental shifts of approach in evaluation. Furubo suggests that in a turbulent environment, evaluation questions should be addressed more ex ante in the sense of "identifying the best possible knowledge that can be of use in discussing alternative solutions" rather than relying on past evidence. Van den Berg suggests analyzing relevance not only in terms of consistency with government's strategic priorities, but also in terms of whether the problem addressed was solved. He also suggests going beyond counterfactual analysis of short-term impact to consider long-term impact.

Not only should we modify our approach to evaluation, but also we should change the way we conduct evaluation.

- First, several chapters argue for more integrated and combined approaches. Ahmar and Kolbe (chapter 5) demonstrate the benefit of a holistic, multidisciplinary, and coordinated approach to evaluation in a difficult evaluation terrain. Along the same lines, Lohani, Gurung, and Bashyal (chapter 7) show the potential of an evaluation approach combining household, school, and community monitoring. Lage de Sousa (chapter 9) demonstrates how a variety of models can be used to test the impact of a government loan program.
- Second, participation of key stakeholders is perceived not as a loss of time, but rather as a condition for ownership, involvement, and sustainability of the M&E system. Qudisat (chapter 11) outlines the importance

of information sharing and setting targets in a participatory way to reverse the mentality of public civil servants from representing obstacles to evaluation to becoming co-owners of an M&E system. Menon underlines that national M&E systems must involve not only government, but require the participation of other stakeholders as well. Gildemyn (chapter 10) points out the contribution that a central statistics office can make in leading M&E efforts toward improving the accountability of public officials and service providers.

- Third, evaluation is advocated more as a learning process than as a product. Agrawal outlines the need for capacity building and knowledge dissemination among all stakeholders. Al-Zoubi (chapter 8) stresses capacity building to increase the quality and relevance of evaluations and to develop a culture of evaluation, progressively convincing stakeholders that the benefits of evaluation outweigh its costs.

- Fourth, in a context of constant change and high risk, building national M&E systems that can inform decision makers of developing situations and provide empirical evidence to guide their decisions becomes of paramount importance. Implementing the emerging new paradigm of national M&E systems involves addressing a number of institutional and technical issues. Lahey (Chapter 12) identifies four building blocks: a vision of the leaders; an enabling environment; a capacity to supply credible, timely M&E information; and a capacity by key users to demand and use M&E information. Abreu and others (Chapter 13) propose an operational process and related information system tool to progressively improve the capacity of M&E systems, whether at the national/subnational, sectoral, or program/project level, through capacity-building cycles. Each cycle starts with a participatory, structured diagnostic of the M&E system and design of an action plan to improve this system, then continues with the implementation of the plan and follow up by the stakeholders—until the next diagnostic.

In conclusion, this book has demonstrated that turbulent times force us to rethink our evaluation approaches and our ways of conducting evaluations. Beyond the individual contributions made by each chapter, this book is both a lesson in modesty and a message of hope. It evokes the modesty we should all feel as evaluators before the challenge of providing evaluations that capture the essentials of complex and rapidly evolving situations. And it gives us hope because contributors from around the world offer glimpses of how to approach those challenges both theoretically and operationally. This book is a testimony to the contribution of the International Development Evaluation Association (IDEAS) to our profession.

Index

Boxes, figures, notes, and tables are indicated by b, f, n, and t following the page number.

Alkin, Marvin C., 7
ANDS (Afghan National Development Strategy), 57
Annual Industrial Research (Brazil), 119
Annual Social Information Report (Brazil), 119
ANP (Afghan National Police), 61–62
answerability, 149, 160
Arab Spring (2011), xiii, xiv, 2, 229
Asian Development Bank, 36
Assessing Aid: What Works, What Doesn't and Why (World Bank), 42
Automatic BNDES, 118–20, 123, 130, 135
available data (secondary data), 71–76
  case studies, 73–75
  lessons learned, 75–76
  project-monitoring data, 72
  quality of, 72–73, 73t
  socioeconomic data, 72
  types of, 71–72
average productivity cut-off, 122, 122f

B
Bahrain, Arab Spring protests in, xiii
Bamberger, M. J., 71
Banco Nacional de Desenvolvimento Economico e Social (BNDES, Brazil)
  financing schemes of, 118–19. *See also specific financing schemes*
  productivity assessment of programs, 115–42. *See also* productivity assessment of BNDES programs
Banerjee, A. V., 115
Barloworld, 203b
Bashyal, Laxman, 81, 232
bats, 39
Baumgartner, F. R., 10, 13
beneficiaries' index, 179–82, 179–82f
Bennet, C. J., 13
biodiversity, 34, 38–41
Bisphenol A (BPA), 40
Blasio, G. d., 129
BNDES. *See* Banco Nacional de Desenvolvimento Economico e Social
Boily, Marie-Helene, xv, 213, 229
Bolsa Familia (Brazil), 214
Bono 10000, Programa de Asignacion (Honduras), 214, 221
Boswell, C., 16, 19
Botswana
  enabling environment in, 193–94
  key result areas (KRAs) in, 192, 196–97, 197b, 200, 202, 203b

  national M&E development in, xv, 192–205
    lessons learned, 204–5, 205–6b
  national performance report. *See Botswana's Performance Report (2009)*
  political will in, 193–94
  technical capacity in, 194–95
  Vision 2016 in, 192–93, 197b
Botswana's Performance Report (2009), 195–204
  data collection for, 196–202, 198f, 199–201b
  distribution of, 202–4
  performance measurement and reporting, 195–96
  "Status at a Glance," 204, 207–11
BPA (Bisphenol A), 40
Brahmins, 90, 102n14
Brazil. *See also* Banco Nacional de Desenvolvimento Economico e Social (BNDES); productivity assessment of BNDES programs
  social protection programs in, xiv, 214
Brazilian Central Bank, 119
Brazilian Development Bank. *See* Banco Nacional de Desenvolvimento Economico e Social (BNDES)
Brazilian Institute of Geography and Statistics, 119
Brett, E. A., 149
Bronzini, R., 129
budgets
  evaluations of, 4, 7
  for national M&E systems, 216, 217t
Busan Partnership Agreement (2011), 146

C
Cameron, David, 51
Canada, agricultural sector in, 39
capacity building
  for civil society organizations, 145
  for evaluation, 26–27, 76
  in Jordan, 107, 111, 174
  for national M&E development, 195–204, 215
capital goods acquisition, 132–33
Capoccia, G., 10
Carleton University, 196
Cato the Elder, 47–48
Central Statistics Office (CSO, Botswana), 196, 198, 204

Gulf Consultative Council (GCC), 2
Gurung, Purnima, 81, 232

H

head of household (HOH) surveys, 59, 60, 61
health care as economic development
        factor, 2
Heckman, J. J., 115
Helmand Monitoring and Evaluation
        Programme (HMEP), 57–66
    analytical approach, 62–64
    background and overview, 57
    data collection, 58–61
    GIS mapping, 65–66
    information use, 66
    online database, 65
    presentational features, 64–66
    quantitative and qualitative approach,
        61–62
    sampling strategy, 58–61, 60t
    theory of change and, 62–64, 63f
    time-series analysis, 61
Helmand Province, Afghanistan, 51–68. *See
        also* Helmand Monitoring and
        Evaluation Programme (HMEP)
    challenges to evaluation in, 53–56
    cultural challenges in, 56
    institutional challenges in, 54–55
    logistical challenges in, 55–56
    monitoring and evaluation in, 57–66
    political challenges in, 54–55
Henry, G. T., 155, 155f
HMEP. *See* Helmand Monitoring and
        Evaluation Programme
HOH. *See* head of household surveys
Honduras, pilot program for national M&E
        in, 221
Hood, C., 13
horizontal accountability, 150
household workload, 87, 88, 91, 92
Howlett, M., 13
Human Development Observatory of
        Morocco, 29
human rights, 2, 30
hunger, 87, 89, 100
Hyasat, Amer, 185
hybrid accountability, 150

I

IAU (Impact Assessment Unit, Jordan),
        106, 109
IBGE (Instituto Brasíleiro de Geografia e
        Estatística), 119, 140n7

IBRD (International Bank for
        Reconstruction and Development),
        36–37
IDEA-AIM4R (Assessing and Improving
        M&E for Results) tool, 220, 221,
        225n4
IDEAS. *See* International Development
        Evaluation Association
IDRC (International Development
        Research Centre), 157
    evaluation framework, 159–60, 159f
IMF. *See* International Monetary Fund
impact assessment evaluations, xiv,
        105–13
    challenges for, 112
    information sharing, 111, 111f
    mechanism for, 108–9
    methodology, 109–11, 110b, 110f
    status quo review, 107–8
Impact Assessment Unit (IAU, Jordan),
        106, 109
implementation phase of impact
        assessments, 109
imported capital goods, 133
incremental change, 5–22
    costs of, 9
    crises and, 12–13
    evaluation's role in, 15–16
    future of, 11–12
    nonincremental change vs., 8–15
    turbulence and, 13–15
    turning points for, 9–11
Independent Commission for Aid Impact
        (UK), 52
India
    evaluation case studies, 69–77
    evaluation in, 30
    labor migration to, 96
industrial sector, 84
infant mortality, 168
inflation, 3, 83
information use
    CSO evaluation use and influence,
        154–57, 155f, 156t
    diffusion of ideas, 12
    dissemination of M&E data, 76, 178–79
    in fragile and conflict-affected states, 66
    impact assessment data sharing, 111, 111f
    knowledge/research-policy interface in
        developing countries, 157
institutional framework
    in fragile and conflict-affected states,
        54–55

M

Machines and Equipment (FINAME, Brazil), 118
Malaysia, labor migration to, 84
Malena, C., 151
malnutrition, 3
M&E. *See* monitoring and evaluation
Mark, M. M., 155, 155*f*
market failures, 35, 38
Market Watch Nepal, 83
Martin, Frederic, xv, 213, 229
Martin, R., 115, 134, 135
Marx, K., xiv, 9
Massachusetts Institute of Technology (MIT), 42
maternal mortality, 168
McGee, R., 151
media freedom, 158
Melitz, M., 120
Menon, Saraswathi, xiv, 25, 232, 233
Merton, R. K., 6
Mexico, social protection programs in, 214
migration for employment, 84, 84*f*, 87, 95–96, 101*n*6
Millennium Challenge Account, 226*n*7
Millennium Development Goals (MDGs), 54, 158, 168, 187, 198
Mind the Gap: Perspective on Policy Evaluation and the Social Sciences (Vaessen & Leeuw), 18
Ministry of Industrial Development and Foreign Trade (Brazil), 119
Ministry of Interior (Afghanistan), 59
Ministry of Interior Affairs (MoI, Jordan), 173
Ministry of Planning and International Cooperation (MoPIC, Jordan), 105–7
Ministry of Social Development (MoSD, Jordan)
  beneficiaries' index, 179–82, 179–82*f*
  desk reviews, 176–77
  dissemination of data, 178–79
  Dynamic Index, 180–81, 181*f*
  early warning system role of M&E, 182–84, 183–84*f*
  establishment of, 173–74
  Fixed Index, 181–82, 182*f*
  goals of, 173*b*
  M&E in, 175–84, 175*f*
  testing of M&E system by, 177–78, 177*b*
MIT (Massachusetts Institute of Technology), 42

Mitchell, Andrew, 51
Moen, J., 115
MoI (Ministry of Interior Affairs, Jordan), 173
monitoring and evaluation (M&E). *See also* evaluation; national M&E development
  analytical framework to diagnose M&E systems, 215–16, 217–18*t*
  CSOs role in, 146–47, 147*t*, 160–62, 161*f*
  as decision support system, 176, 176*b*
  as demand-driven response, 176, 176*b*
  as early warning system, 176, 176*b*, 182–84, 183–84*f*
  feedback/learning function of, 153–60
  in Jordan, 167–86
  in Latin America, 213–27
  operational approach to evaluation of M&E systems, 218–24
  results-based, 52
  testing of system, 177–78, 177*b*
  as tool for change, 176, 176*b*
  uses of, 176*b*
Monteiro Filha, D. C., 116
Montreal Protocol, 40
MoPIC (Ministry of Planning and International Cooperation, Jordan), 105–7
Morocco, economic shocks in, 2
Morra Imas, L., 70
MoSD. *See* Ministry of Social Development
Motor Centre Group, 203*b*
Myrdal, Gunnar, 6

N

national M&E development, 187–212
  in Botswana, 192–204
  building blocks for, 189–90, 189*f*, 190–91*b*, 216
  defined, 211*n*1
  enabling environment for, 190*b*, 193–94
  framework for, 188–92
  functions of, 146–47
  in Latin America, 213–27
  lessons learned, 204–5, 205–6*b*
  national performance report, 195–204
    data collection for, 196–202, 198*f*, 199–201*b*
    performance measurement and reporting, 195–96
    "Status at a Glance," 204, 207–11
  performance measurement and reporting, 195–96

pilot application of operational approach, 220–24, 222–23*f*
political will for, 193–94
success factors for, 190–92
technical capacity for, 191*b*, 194–95
National Research Council (U.S.), 18
National Sample Survey Organization, 74
Negri, F., 119
Negri, J. A., 119
Nepal
  child labor in, 92–93
  dropout rate in, 94–98, 95–97*f*
  education impact of 3 F's in, 85–99, 86*f*, 99*f*
  food, fuel, and financial crisis in, xiv, 82–85, 84–85*f*
  learning achievement in, 90–92, 90*t*
  student attendance rates in, 86–90, 87*f*, 88*t*, 89*f*
Nepal Association of Foreign Employment Agencies, 84
Nepal Rastra Bank, 83
Newars, 90, 102*n*14
nongovernmental organizations (NGOs), 150, 192. *See also* civil society organizations (CSOs)
nonincremental change, 8–15
nutrition programs, 100

O

O'Donnell, G., 150
OECD. *See* Organisation for Economic Co-operation and Development
oil. *See* fuel prices
Oportunidades (Mexico), 214
opportunity cost, 89, 102*n*20
organic pollutants. *See* persistent organic pollutants
Organisation for Economic Co-operation and Development (OECD), 7, 37, 45
Ottaviano, G., 116, 117, 119, 134, 135, 140*n*16
overage students, 94, 98, 102*n*20
Overman, H. G., 115, 134, 135
Overseas Development Institute (ODI), 157
Owen, J. M., 19
ozone depletion, 39–40

P

Panama
  pilot program for national M&E in, 221
  social protection programs in, 214
Paris Declaration (2005), 146, 158

path dependence, 9
PATI (Programa de Atención Temporal de Ingreso, El Salvador), 221, 222–23*f*
Patton, M. Q., 154
Pereira, R. O., 116
performance measurement and reporting, 195–96
persistent organic pollutants, 34, 39–41
Peruzzotti, E., 151
Pesquisa Industrial Anual (PIA, Brazil), 119
Petrobras, 125
Philippines, GEF-funded programs in, 43
PIA (Pesquisa Industrial Anual, Brazil), 119
"piecemeal engineering," 13
Pierson, P., 9
planning phase of impact assessments, 109
The Plundered Planet (Collier), 38
Polanyi, K., 10
policy self-destruction, 13
politics
  of evaluation, 30
  in fragile and conflict-affected states, 54–55
  incremental change in, 16
  in national M&E systems development, 205*b*
  political use of evaluation, 154, 158
  political will for evaluation, 189–90, 189*f*, 193–94
  social sciences and, 8
pollution. *See* persistent organic pollutants
poverty
  BNDES loans and, 126
  chronic crisis of, 230
  food security and, 3
  in Jordan, 168, 173*b*
  in Latin America, 213
poverty lab (MIT), 42
Poverty Reduction Strategy Papers (PRSPs), 146, 147, 148, 187
private sector
  in Botswana, 95, 192, 198, 202
  in Jordan, 171
  in national M&E systems development, 225
  productivity, 115–42
process use of evaluations, 154
production costs, 135

Vision Council (Botswana), 192–93, 194, 195, 198, 200, 211*n*2
Vision Secretariat (Botswana), 192, 193, 198, 200
vulnerability assessment and monitoring (VAM), 82

W

Weiss, C. H., 7, 8, 19
West Bank, economic shocks in, 2
WFP (World Food Programme), 82
white-nose syndrome, 39
white rhinoceros, 42
Wikileaks, 29
Wildavsky, A., 11, 13
women. *See also* gender differences
    in fragile and conflict-affected countries, 56
    qualitative research for opinions of, 61
World Bank
    on aid's contribution to development, 42
    capacity building and, 196

"end-of-project" evaluations, 42
evaluation development role of, 7, 221
on food prices, 3
global governance and, 36
local budgets evaluated by, 4
on media freedom, 158
on national M&E systems development, 193, 226*n*7
on poverty, 230
on social accountability, 151
World Development Report 2004 (World Bank), 148
World Food Programme (WFP), 82

Y

Yemen
    Arab Spring protests in, xiii
    economic shocks in, 2

Z

zero cut-off profit (ZCP), 121–22
Al-Zoubi, Lamia, 105, 233